GW00715381

CONTENTS

Editorial: Shifting Territories: Feminisms and Europe   **1**
Helen Crowley, Barbara Einhorn, Catherine Hall, Maxine Molyneux, Lynne Segal

Between Hope and Helplessness: Women in the GDR after the 'Turning Point'   **3**
Irene Dölling

Where Have All the Women Gone? Women and the Women's Movement in East Central Europe   **16**
Barbara Einhorn

The End of Socialism in Europe: A New Challenge for Socialist Feminism?   **37**
Frigga Haug

The Second 'No': Women in Hungary   **49**
Yudit Kiss

The Citizenship Debate: Women, Ethnic Processes and the State   **58**
Nira Yuval-Davis

Fortress Europe and Migrant Women   **69**
Mirjana Morokvasic

Racial Equality and '1992'   **85**
Ann Dummett

Questioning *Perestroika*: A Socialist–feminist Interrogation   **91**
Ruth Pearson

Postmodernism and its Discontents   **97**
Kate Soper

FEMINISTS AND SOCIALISM

After the Cold War　　109
Mary Kaldor

Socialism Out of the Common Pots　　115
Swasti Mitter

1989 and All That　　119
Beatrix Campbell

In Listening Mode　　124
Cynthia Cockburn

WOMEN IN ACTION: COUNTRY BY COUNTRY

The Soviet Union:

**Feminist Manifesto – 'Democracy Without Women is No
Democracy': A Founding Document**　　127

Interview with Anastasya Posadskaya　　133
Maxine Molyneux

**Soviet Women Hold Their First Autonomous National Con-
ference: Conference Report and Concluding Document from
the First Independent Women's Forum of the Soviet Union**　　141
introduced by Cynthia Cockburn

Yugoslavia:

**Democracy Between Tyranny and Liberty: Women in Post-
'Socialist' Slovenia**　　149
Milica G. Antić

**A Women's Political Party for Yugoslavia: Introduction to the
Serbian Feminist Manifesto**　　155
Cynthia Cockburn

Czechoslovakia:

Interview with Alena Valterova　　161
by Mita Castle-Kanerová

Hungary:

Hungary: A Loss of Rights?　　166
Maria Adamik

Declaration of Intent　　171
Feminist Network of Hungary

Poland:

Abortion, Church and Politics in Poland　　174
Hanna Jankowska

Women in Poland: Choices to be Made　　182
Małgorzata Tarasiewicz

REPORTS

Lisa Power on the International Lesbian and Gay Association   **187**

Elizabeth Szondi on Black Women and Europe 1992   **189**

REVIEWS

Amrit Wilson and Julia Bard on *Against the Grain: A Celebration of Survival and Struggle*   **193**

Chris Corrin on *Promissory Notes: Women in the Transition to Socialism*   **198**

Alison Light on *Mad Forest*   **204**

Letter   **210**

Noticeboard   **212**

Feminist Review is published three times a year by a collective based in London, with help from women and groups all over the UK.

The Collective: Alison Light, Alison Read, Annie Whitehead, Catherine Hall, Clara Connolly, Dot Griffiths, Erica Carter, Helen Crowley, Inge Blackman, Loretta Loach, Lynne Segal, Mary McIntosh, Mica Nava, Naila Kabeer, Sue O'Sullivan.

Guest editors this issue: Barbara Einhorn and Maxine Molyneux.

Correspondence and advertising
For contributions and all other correspondence please write to:
Feminist Review, 11 Carleton Gardens, Brecknock Road, London N19 5AQ.
For advertising please write to:
David Polley, Routledge, 11 New Fetter Lane, London EC4P 4EE

Subscriptions
Please write to: Subscriptions Department, Routledge Journals, Cheriton House, North Way, Andover, Hants SP10 5BE.

Contributions
Feminist Review is happy to discuss proposed work with intending authors at an early stage. We need copy to come to us in our house style with references complete and in the right form. We can supply you with a style sheet. Please send in 4 copies plus the original (5 copies in all). In cases of hardship 2 copies will do.

Bookshop distribution in the USA
Inland Book Company Inc., 22 Hemingway Avenue, East Haven, CT 06512, USA.

Typeset by Type Study, Scarborough
Printed in Great Britain
at the University Press, Cambridge

ISSN 0141-7789

EDITORIAL

SHIFTING TERRITORIES: Feminisms and Europe

In March 1990 the *Feminist Review* collective met for our annual weekend at which we plan our special issue for the year ahead. Immensely moved by the events of 1989 and uncertain of the meanings and potential of a socialist-feminist project in the 1990s, we decided to construct a special issue round the theme of 'shifting territories' – linking the shifts that had occurred within Europe to the changes that are to come with 1992 and to the five-hundred-year anniversary of Columbus's 'discovery' of America and the emergence of the new empires of the West. As we began to develop a sense of the potential scope of the issue we realized that we had been too ambitious and decided to focus on the impact of 1989 on Europe and the formation of a new Europe – while insisting on the centrality of maintaining a global perspective on those changes and the consequent shifts in the relations between First and Third Worlds.

Our title *Shifting Territories* refers then to the changes in the political boundaries – the disintegration of the old East/West dichotomy, the collapse of Eastern European socialism, the revival of nationalism and the re-mapping of Europe. How should we make sense of these major transformations? How should we respond to them? What new political, intellectual and creative changes do they offer? How have these changes been represented? What part have women played in them and what are their implications for women?

Feminists have long been critics of the old order. What part can and should they play in the new? How new is the new for women? The collapse of state socialism clearly has profound implications for women who have identified themselves as socialists and feminists and we have tried in this issue to begin to address the theoretical and political questions which this has raised.

One of the problems we have faced in producing this issue has been witnessing a seemingly steady shift in the aspirations of progressive women in East Central Europe from new levels of confidence as political agents to growing fears of marginalization. Continuing upheaval in all these societies means that we can only capture a fragmentary and partial picture of the implications of the last two years. Our coverage is limited by the particular networks with which we have been able to make contact; for example, the selection of documents in our dossier 'Women in Action: Country by Country' represents only a selection from women's groups and movements in East Central Europe.

It has also been hard to keep a grip on possible ways forward for women at a time when we are facing new world crises of terrifying dimensions. From the devastations of communities caused by the Gulf War, to global economic recession – hunger, poverty and immiseration seem to be reaching unprecedented levels. We are also witnessing a rise in conflicts around racial, ethnic and national identities both in contemporary Europe and elsewhere. So new and complex are these problems that it has been hard to find articles which deal with these issues while maintaining perspectives on women. In these times, steering a course between hope and helplessness, as Irene Dölling points out, remains a precondition for any new forms of socialism and feminism.

Helen Crowley, Barbara Einhorn, Catherine Hall, Maxine Molyneux, Lynne Segal

The addition of two guest editors to our editorial collective for this issue has been vital, and is an already established practice with special issues that we hope to continue and extend. Barbara Einhorn's and Maxine Molyneux's knowledge of East Central Europe and their many contacts with women, women's organizations and feminist groups have been invaluable. They have been most generous with their time. We also owe a debt to many others who have contributed contacts, ideas and suggestions and we would particularly like to thank Cynthia Cockburn.

BETWEEN HOPE AND HELPLESSNESS:
Women in the GDR after the 'Turning Point'

Irene Dölling

I

Women were well represented at the demonstrations in the German Democratic Republic in October and November 1989, but they soon realized that their presence in the public political sphere was hardly recognized and was not assessed as a factor calling for a new political culture. One of the popular slogans of the time was: 'The country needs new men!' Women optimistically entered the public sphere with demands of their own.

In early November, several Women's Studies researchers registered their criticism of the marginalization of women under the headline 'Is the revolution passing women by?' They self-confidently projected the path to a society in which the previous disadvantaging of women would be the object of public criticism and its abolition an important goal of practical politics. Other women took up these demands and publicized them at a demonstration. The active engagement of large numbers of women in grass-roots democratic initiatives, self-help, consciousness-raising and discussion groups made us optimistic. A broad range of topics, from a critique of the social order to the issue of marital violence, was addressed. Their practical dimensions reached from the formulation of political programmes to plans for setting up women's centres and houses for battered women and rape victims.

At the beginning of December, the hope that women would henceforth become so vast a force that they could no longer be overlooked, was strengthened when over a thousand women from throughout the GDR met in a large Berlin theatre and voted to found an independent women's union. A few days later, representatives of the Independent Women's Union took their places as members of the Central Round Table. They also participated in the Modrow government, delegating a Minister without Portfolio. Representatives of the

Independent Women's Union played a not insignificant role in composing the Social Charter (guarantee of the social rights of GDR citizens in the process of unifying the two German states) and drafting a plan for a women's ministry or ministry for questions of equality. In none of the other socialist countries now involved in the process of change have women organized themselves into a comparable political force.

The Independent Women's Union participated in a joint election campaign with the Green Party and received 2.7 per cent of the vote, unfortunately receiving no seats in the parliament, due to their placement on the election lists. It must be noted that this result was less than the expected 4–5 per cent of the vote. The German Democratic Women's Union (the official women's organization for the past forty years until now guaranteed representation in the parliament) only received 0.03 per cent of the vote, despite a membership of 1.5 million. Over 46 per cent of all registered women voters chose the conservative CDU led Alliance for Germany.[1] These results were both disappointing and sobering. This voting behaviour, however, provides us with unexpectedly clear evidence for a number of conclusions regarding the situation of women in the GDR after the 'turning point'.

Firstly, it makes distinctly clear that the vast majority of women in the GDR do not associate themselves with emancipatory or feminist ideas and practices and, in fact, reject them. Although the Independent Women's Union entered the elections with a programme directly addressed to the need to preserve social institutions such as kindergartens, the school lunch programme and the right to work, it appealed to only a small number of women voters. I think that the irreverent speech and slightly odd appearance of its representatives, who do not attempt to conform to general standards of dress or behaviour, as well as their insistence upon women's autonomy and independence, was perceived as alienating and provoked a fearful and aggressive response. So-called 'normal' women probably selectively registered only those characteristics which were foreign to them. The needs and behavioural structures of most women are obviously not what the Independent Women thought they were.

Secondly, the abrupt opening of the border on 9 November 1989, and the subsequent tide of visitors from the GDR into West Germany, triggered a shock reaction in many individuals whose only previous experience of the 'West' had been through the media: most of them had, in all likelihood, never imagined that the difference in the standard of living and levels of consumption could be so great. Based on this experience, many women – aware of the needs of their children and well acquainted with the difficulties of assuring daily existence in a shortage economy additionally hampered by a full working day – saw a clear advantage in a rapid assimilation of the West German standard of living. According to their campaign promises, the parties of the Alliance for Germany were the best guarantee of that.

Thirdly, the threat of unemployment, the unclear status of legal and property rights, the vacillation on the question of a currency union and its already visible effects (high prices for foodstuffs, inflation), etc., have led to a deep insecurity on the part of almost all GDR citizens. Although women are affected specifically as women – for example, at this point feminized job categories are especially threatened (women now make up more than 50 per cent of the unemployed and less than 25 per cent of those retired)[2] – they have hardly offered resistance. Helpless outrage at what is happening to them and their families, or resigned acceptance of the brutal forms of discrimination and exclusion with which primarily men are now beginning to practice competition, are 'normal' responses; organized forms of resistance are unfortunately the great exception. Even in those cases where women or parents have protested in front of their places of employment against the closing of employer-run day-care centres, they have directed their appeals to the management or the authorities to prevent the closings. At this point in time, individual initiatives which go beyond outraged protest have hardly developed.

In their growing insecurity, women look hopefully, as well as helplessly, to parties that are ready to take on the responsibility of making decisions in their interests. A slogan in circulation in Saxony during the election campaign, 'Helmut take us by the hand, lead us into economic wonderland', clearly addressed, for many women, certain longings which themselves are a manifestation of the dependence created by the specific form of patriarchy within state socialism.

My thesis is as follows: under state socialism women developed subjective structures which provide fertile soil for 'conservative' solutions to the conflicts arising in the process of radical change on the path to a 'different modernism' (Ulrich Beck). (One could probably identify a similar constellation among men. They, however, are not the object of my reflections.) The social 'achievements' of socialism must be examined critically from this perspective in order to understand the situation in which women of the GDR find themselves today. I will therefore devote the second part of this paper to a backward look and a discussion of the question: how really emancipatory or 'woman-friendly' were the conditions and social supports created for women under state socialism?

II

Formal legal equality, state measures and supports to allow women to combine career and motherhood, state programmes to raise women's level of education and qualification to equal that of men, etc., were – until now – internationally recognized advantages and 'achievements' of socialism in the GDR. In December 1989, Jane Fonda, the American actress, assured the GDR women to whom she spoke on the Alexanderplatz in Berlin that they enjoyed excellent conditions which would be the envy of many women in the USA. And at first glance, the facts and numbers reveal a very impressive balance. I list here a few of the social-policy measures which, until recently, were taken for granted

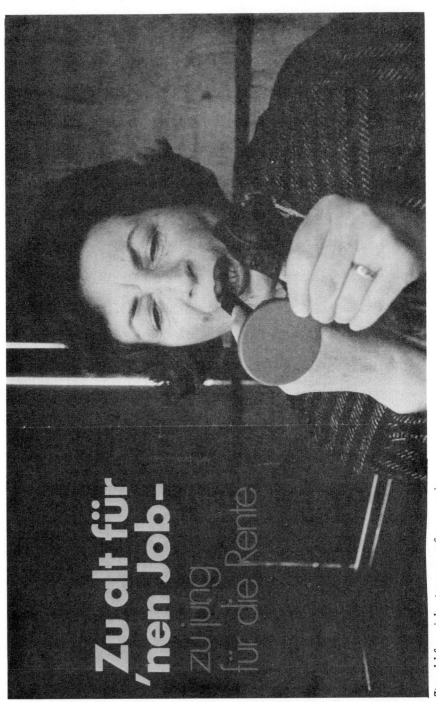

Too old for a job – too young for a pension

by women in the GDR. These measures, which must by all means be seen as a form of positive discrimination for women, that is, as measures which created *unequal rights*, were primarily directed towards *working women with children*. Among them are, for example:

- A 40-hour working week at full pay for all mothers with two or more children under sixteen years of age (in comparison: the normal working week in the GDR is 43¾ hours, or 40 to 42 hours per week for shift-workers). This ceased after unification.
- A monthly paid housework day for all married women, mothers of children under sixteen years of age and for all women over forty. This has also been cancelled as of 1 January 1991.
- 26 weeks of pregnancy or maternity leave (since 1976; in comparison: 1950: 11 weeks, 1963: 14 weeks, 1972: 18 weeks).
- A state birth premium of 1,000M, that is, about an average month's pay.
- Paid leave (between 70 and 90 per cent of the mother's average income) for one year after the birth of a first or second child, and eighteen months for each further child. Return to the original workplace was guaranteed. Since 1986, the 'baby year' could be taken by either the mother or the father or could be divided between them.

    As of 1 January 1991 this was reduced to only 8 weeks of maternity leave instead of the 26 weeks previously available in the former GDR followed by 1½ years of paid leave. The two extensions in the absence of day-care space (as has been usual until now) are cancelled. The childcare allowance is 600DM per month until the child is six months old – irrespective of income – and is subject thereafter to income-related deductions if the parents' net monthly income exceeds 2,800DM.
- A financial support payment to unmarried mothers (at the moment, over 30 per cent of all first births are to unmarried mothers) at the level of sick pay (that is 70–90 per cent of average income) until the child is three years of age, if the child is unable to attend day care for health reasons or if no day care is available.
- Free contraception, and the choice for every woman to decide during the first twelve weeks of pregnancy whether she wants an abortion (also free of cost). Contraceptives will in future have to be purchased, as they are in the Federal Republic. Freedom of choice is currently under discussion. Since the elections for the Bundestag on 2 December 1990, a new debate is emerging around the terms governing abortion which had already been laid down in the unification treaty. These provided for a two-track regulation of abortion in the former *Länder* of the Federal Republic and the GDR during a transitional period. At present those laws stipulate that abortion is fundamentally a punishable offence in the former Federal Republic, although it may be permitted on social grounds after counselling, a ruling which is handled differently by the different *Länder*. Meanwhile, the still-current GDR law makes abortion

absolutely legal, decided by the woman alone, without any compulsion to undergo counselling. This is currently increasingly under
pressure from the churches and the Christian political parties. There
were many more women and men present at a demonstration 'to
protect unborn life' in East Berlin in the middle of November 1990
than there had been at a demonstration in the middle of May
opposing Paragraph 218 (the West German constitutional clause
making abortion illegal) and its extension to the territory of the
(former) GDR. A demonstration held in East and West Berlin on the
eve of unification, on 29 September, called on people to protest
'against the swallowing up of the GDR'. It was significant that this
demonstration, called by the UFV, the Independent Women's Union,
evoked a mass response. But perhaps this mass turnout resulted
from the wider political aims of the demonstration, which included
but was not exclusively focused on resistance to Paragraph 218.

● A broad network of state- and factory-supported childcare services
(crèches, nursery schools, after-school childcare, school-dinner programmes). As of 1988, 81 per cent of children under three were in
crèches and sufficient nursery-school places were available so that
any parent of a child between three and six years old who wished to
could place their child in kindergarten. The spaces in these centres
were free of cost, parents paying only a very modest fee (approximately 30 M per month) as a contribution to the cost of meals or milk.
The cost of day care rose sharply after 1 July to approximately
250–300DM per child per month. Many employers are closing their
day-care centres. Due to lack of funds, local authorities are in many
cases unable to take them over.

● A monthly state child-support payment for each child; and the same
financial support as received by apprentices for youngsters in the
11th and 12th grades.

In addition, all health-care services have until now been free of
charge and the prices of foodstuffs, rents, electricity, public transport,
and children's clothing, among other things, were heavily subsidized.
This comprehensive social-welfare policy, the financing of which con-
sumed an ever greater portion of the state budget, to a significant degree
relieved the individual of responsibility for his or her own living
conditions. This also to some extent compensated for the lack of goods,
services, and time, and resulted in an – at least partial – support of the
state by its citizens. For women however, this social-welfare policy also
meant the reinforcement of their traditional roles as mothers and the
unbroken reproduction of the traditional assignment of gender functions.

Equally contradictory is the situation in regard to skilled trades
and professional work, the level of qualification and the position of
women in leadership roles and in the public sphere. Here too, first
appearances are thoroughly positive: over 91% of working-age women
were until now either employed or in training programmes, the starting

level of skill or professional qualification in age cohorts up to forty years of age equal to that of men. In 1988, 87% of women had completed trade or professional training. Approximately 50% of college and university students are female and their representation at trade schools is over 70%. In a number of previously completely male-dominated professions, such as law and medicine, women are now represented by over 50%. Until now, nearly a third of all mayors were women and their representation in community, local and district councils lay between 30 and 40%.[3] None the less, women were hardly to be found in top positions in politics or the economy, and they comprised only about 7% of associate and full professors.

In 1988, nearly half of the working population (48.9%) was female; at the same time however, the vast majority of women are employed in non-productive branches of the economy. A broad overview reveals a pronounced gender-specific division of labour, amounting in some cases to a classification of entire trades and professions according to gender. In general, women perform the less qualified and accordingly less well-paid tasks. They are frequently assigned less well-paid tasks despite equal qualifications and training. In practice, this means that women in industry and construction earn on average 12% less than their male colleagues. More than half of all women production workers are in the two lowest wage categories (56.7%), but only 21.7% of male production workers. In contrast, 43.0% of male, but only 13.8% of female production workers are to be found in the middle-level wage categories.[4]

In addition, the 'typically female' professions in health care, social welfare and the service sector are very poorly paid, resulting in a significant income differential between men and women.[5] Finally, channelling, justified by women's reproductive tasks, limits female workers to specific areas and professions. Thus, in 1987, for example, 60% of female 10th grade graduates were distributed within 16 out of a total of 289 skilled trades training programmes open to 10th grade graduates.[6] In other words, the formal right to work and education, to equal pay for equal work turns out, in fact, to be extremely unequal for men and women. The majority of women are to this day less econ- omically independent than men, a fact which has until now been compensated for – to a certain degree – as well as hidden by, social-policy measures but is now being clearly revealed by social cut-backs. Nevertheless, many of the conditions affecting working women (with and without children), were until now more favourable in the GDR than for women in many 'Western' countries, who are also affected by the phenomenon of a gender-specific division of labour and the continued existence of traditional assignment of gender-role func- tions in childcare, childraising and housework. The fact is that the continuing labour shortage and the labour movement's traditional belief in the emancipatory power of paid labour, together with the ideological conviction that equality would be achieved 'in socialism' led to women being drawn into the labour force and the supportive social-policy measures being put into place in this process.

This wasn't necessarily 'woman-friendly' or emancipatory – women were regarded primarily functionally – as workers and as mothers – in these measures and not as subjects with a claim to self-determination and the responsibility for their own lives. Nevertheless, the mere statement of these facts and the contradictory effects of the social-policy measures affecting working women with children is not sufficient to explain women's current wavering between hope and helplessness, their lack of power to resist the beginning social cut-backs on the one hand, and the attractiveness of such traditional values as family, the roles of mother and housewife, etc., to a not insignificant number of women, on the other.

To approach a clearer understanding of the underlying causes, it is necessary first to examine the general role of patriarchy in state socialism and its influence on women's behavioural structures. I propose to do this in a series of theses – with accordingly brief analyses – in the final section.

III

1 State socialism is a form of modern society characterized by the dominance of political policy over all other systemic structures. That is, the political system provides the representation of all other systems. Like the *pater familias* in pre-bourgeois family-centred production, 'the Party', with its centralist-hierarchical structure led by its General Secretary as the 'Father of the Nation', takes over the function of speaking in the interest of the whole, of knowing what is good for everyone, as well as taking upon itself the responsibility for the welfare of all.

This patriarchal-paternalist principle combines with the political idea of a society of social equality and justice in the sense that the 'fatherly' Party, or State, assures justice and equality. This principle finds its expression, extension and stabilization in the practical and symbolic gender order, which orders the daily life of the individual. This means that patriarchal structures can *never* become the object of critical reflection or practical change: under these conditions, the criticism of patriarchal gender relations is direct criticism of the political system. Applied locally, individual efforts to depart from traditional gender roles and stereotypes becomes at best a 'purely personal', 'private' matter which cannot take on the quality of a public, institutionalized confrontation with patriarchal structures.

2 Representation means the disqualification of those who are represented, the repression of forms of a public political discourse and of 'civil society' in which the independent, differentiated interests of those represented could be presented, articulated and developed. The lack of a women's movement in the GDR (in all of the socialist countries) is thus in no way accidental. If women in the modern period have been at a general disadvantage because, since the nineteenth century, the constitution of the public political sphere has been a process primarily

MELANIE FRIEND/FORMAT

Symbols of Socialist Patriarchy

'of a man's affair among men',[7] a reinforcement of this trend was established with state socialism. This can be seen as a significant cause for the fact that, since October 1989, relatively few women have participated in the process of constructing a public political sphere in the GDR, or have been rapidly marginalized or have themselves withdrawn in resignation. Many of the women who became active in grass-roots organizations or in the old or new parties, were forced to recognize that after an 'open', 'euphoric' phase in the Fall of 1989, women's emancipatory claims did not carry a very high value in the developing struggle for the consolidation of political power. The distribution of positions is primarily a matter for men. The issue of quotas for women has not been mentioned in parliament since the March 1990 election.

3 Representation, however, also means relieving the individual of responsibility. The patriarchal-paternalistic principle generalizes a cultural pattern taken from daily life: the father or man takes responsibility for the children or wife – which also gives him the right and power to make decisions concerning them. Women in the GDR were until now integrated into full-time paid labour as well as carrying the responsibility for children and housework. This double and triple burden hardly left them room to escape the snares of a tutelary ideology, which was delivered to them free of charge – along with social-welfare measures to increase the compatibility of work and motherhood. The grateful acceptance of dependence is inscribed into this ideology. It may be that women in the GDR have – to a certain degree – overcome their dependence on their husbands through their paid labour. But they are caught at the same time in a dependence upon 'Father State' of which they are in most cases just as unaware as they would be of their dependence on a husband, and to which they even consent.

I therefore suspect that behind the demands of many so-called 'normal', that is nonfeminist women, for the guarantee of social-policy 'achievements', there *also* lies a massive fear of the loss of a social-welfare network which took care of them and their children or families according to a traditional cultural pattern. This is also a massive emotional fear of a situation in which individual lack of responsibility will no longer be rewarded, but more responsibility for oneself will be demanded. In the current context of radical change, this behaviour pattern, created and spread by a patriarchal state socialism, makes women susceptible to parties which are ready to relieve them of their responsibility once again. And the expectation that women and their children or families will be taken care of can, by all means, be used to support strategies for the social adjustment to unemployment, devaluation of qualifications and degrees, the cutting of social support, etc.

4 The lack of goods and services, as well as the previous absence of an 'elbow society' led to the striking stability of traditional living groups under state socialism. The family (in the broadest sense), circles of friends and acquaintances, group solidarity, etc., have acted in a form and with bonding power which, in West Germany for example, had begun to disappear in the 1950s.

One consequence of this is the conservation of traditional structures, especially gender roles and stereotypes. Despite their employment, most women experienced their traditional role within the family as something they did not want to lose and regarded it as their sphere of influence, not least because their paid work was frequently unskilled, monotonous, poorly paid and socially not as highly regarded as male work. This was also further reinforced by a 'Father State policy' which manifested itself in direct improvements in the quality of life as well as egalitarian social guarantees which an individual could definitely experience and evaluate positively. In this situation, women's dependence was increased in a manner specific to them: it meant that in line with their traditional 'vocation' to provide for their families and be responsible for their well-being, they were able to interpret the effects of the 'Father State policy' as being geared to fulfilling their *own* needs. This tutelary policy which in fact affected *everyone* and which was bound up with the (increasingly ideological) aspiration to achieve social equality, at one and the same time masked gender-specific differences and reinforced everyday cultural perceptions about gender-specific divisions of labour, capabilities, etc., which form the norms of life in the family, the peer group, and so on. The more 'society' was experienced as compulsion and oppression and the 'private sphere' correspondingly appeared as niche, refuge, 'antithesis', the less space remained here too for articulating and working through conflicts within gender relations.

All of this led to the fact that the majority of women in the GDR did not question their customary role in the family and regarded their employment primarily as a 'double burden' and not as a precondition for emancipation. This is also revealed in sociological studies which show that women in the GDR perform half to two-thirds of all housework and that, at the same time, despite the burden of full-time paid employment, almost 60 per cent of those interviewed were satisfied to very satisfied with the household division of labour.[8]

5 The subordination of the individual to a general concept has a further patriarchal dimension: certain aspects of common human interests are excluded *ex post facto*; 'human' interests, when looked at more closely, reveal themselves to be male. The 'builders of socialism' are of course male; women may take part in the process of socialist construction by 'working like a man'. Provided with an honorarium as a mother (preferably of three children), women play no role in public or publicized consciousness as the ones who perform the vastly greater part of unpaid household labour. As housewives, they do not exist within the general concept of 'the socialist individual'. This in no way contradicts the gender-specific division of labour practiced in daily family life, but is a generalized expression of it: here as well, a housewife's skills are valued less than the abilities and skills contributed by men.

Over several generations, women in the GDR have lived with and within a contradiction which demands of them all of the behaviours and qualities belonging to the traditional women's role while at the same time either ignoring significant aspects of the skills and abilities which belong to this role or disqualifying them as socially unimportant. Women were supposed to behave in a traditionally 'female' manner while neither 'femininity' in the customary sense, nor the insistence on gender difference was recognized or honoured – women were supposed to work, think, develop their abilities 'like men'. This multiple devaluation may have nourished among many women the furtive wish to live out this discriminated dimension of 'contextual female existence'. Now these longings can be openly articulated, and at the moment they conjoin with an emotional rejection of everything that was 'socialism'. The sudden attractiveness to many women of 'femininity' and 'motherliness' or even the vision of an existence without paid work which has also manifested itself in women's acceptance of 'Miss' contests, sexist portrayals of women and so forth, must be seen in relationship to the above-named symptomatic and affective methods of patriarchal state socialism.

Although I have been able to illustrate this problem only in a very shortened form, I hope that I have succeeded in establishing the beginnings of an explanation of the fact that the majority of women in the GDR, despite so many favourable conditions, have no – previously repressed – emancipatory demands which can now burst forth. At the moment, it is very difficult to predict what forms of resistance or 'rationalization' men and women will develop in response to the introduction of a market economy and profit-oriented performance criteria.

The question of how long-term effects of a 'heritage' of forty years of state socialism and patriarchal-paternalistic policies will express themselves remains open. We will have to wait to see how former GDR citizens use their newly gained freedoms within a bourgeois democracy as well as what role their previous experience and former rights – for example, to economic security – will play. For now, it is certainly realistic to assume that the specific manifestation of patriarchy within state socialism encouraged and stabilized, in the majority of individuals, behaviour and value structures which now provide a favourable basis for the transition to a modern society of the bourgeois-capitalist type. This transition is characterized by 'conservative' omens: for the reasons I have given, traditional projections of 'femininity' and women's role exert an attraction for women; male dominance, never questioned within state socialism, provides men with a good launching pad into the 'elbow society' and for a first robust and unselfconscious application of their elbow to women. The majority of men and women want to achieve the West German standard of living as quickly as possible and are therefore deaf to references to limitations or delays along this path required in the interests of an equality between the sexes, a healthy environment or people in the Third World.

It is in no way out of the question that these 'conservative' preconditions may, in fact, be favourable to a rapid transition to a different modern society and to the mitigation of the social conflicts arising from it. The price is, however, high: much of what has been accomplished in the past decades in the interest of dismantling patriarchal gender relations and the emancipation of women, laborious and inadequate as it has been, is now endangered in the East *and* the West. Achievements, already practically in hand, will probably be partially or totally lost, the utopia of an equality within difference between the sexes will survive only in a small minority, and it will be primarily women who pay this price. To be sure, improvements in the situation of women will in future be less a 'gift from above', than the result of women's own demands and struggles. Thus women will place a higher value on the fruits of their own efforts than on gifts, which generate dependence and for which gratitude is expected.

Notes

Irene Dölling is a professor of cultural theory at the Humboldt University in Berlin. She is co-founder and first director of ZiF, the Centre for Interdisciplinary Women's Studies at the Humboldt University.

1 The local elections (6 May 1990) and the county elections (for the governments of the recreated *Länder*) in the five new Federal *Länder* (14 October 1990) on the whole substantiated these trends. There are no data available as yet differentiating male from female votes for the various parties and political organizations, but it may be safely assumed that women's votes again accounted for a substantial proportion of the 43.6 per cent votes gained by the CDU in the *Länder* elections. Unfortunately, it isn't possible to say anything about how far women's votes accounted for the gains made by the grass-roots movements and the Greens in the elections for the parliaments of the *Länder*.

2 The unemployment figures have risen steeply since 2 July 1990 (the day when currency and economic union was introduced) and are still continuing to rise. The number of unemployed people and people working short hours in the *Länder* of the former Federal Republic is falling, whereas in the *Länder* of the former GDR, the rate of unemployment has risen by more than one percentage point per month and had reached 6.1 per cent by the beginning of November 1990. This figure does not include the people on short time, many of whom are actually working zero hours, nor the large number of people who have been forced to take early retirement (the number of whom rose from 130,000 to 300,000 between October and November 1990). In general, it is women and young people under twenty who are the worst affected by unemployment.

3 The parliamentary elections confirmed a trend already visible in the other socialist countries (e.g., Poland and Hungary): the radical changes have pushed women back out of the public political sphere. While women held 38 per cent of the seats in the last Parliament and district councils, since 18 March 1990 only 20.2 per cent of the members of Parliament are female.

In addition, while the CDU formally demonstrated their openness toward women's active participation in politics by nominating a woman as President, they simultaneously quietly swept the issue of quotas under the table – all of the important Ministries are held by men.

4 All statistics are taken from *Sozialreport 1990. Daten und Fakten zur sozialen Lage* edited by Gunnar Winkler. Berlin: Verlag Die Wirtschaft 1990, p. 122 ff.

5 In 1988, the proportion of women in those wage and income brackets earning 400–500M was 63.1%, and 77.7% of the bracket earning 600–700M, whereas only 17% of those earning 1,500–1,700M were women. (see *Frauenreport*, Berlin: Verlag Die Wirtschaft, 1990, p. 88). In concrete terms, that means that a large proportion of unemployed women is receiving unemployment benefit of less than 495DM (the sum which is regarded as the minimum for existence in the new *Länder*). It also implies that many single women and lone mothers with low incomes will be forced to apply for social-welfare support from the beginning of 1991 so as to be able to cover the rising costs of rent, electricity and so on.

6 See 'Studie zur beruflichen Orientierung der Mädchen und Frauen' Zentralinstitut für Berufsbildung, Berlin 1989, unpublished.

7 Karin Hausen, 'Thoughts on the gender-specific structural change of the public sphere'. Lecture at the congress 'Human rights have no/a gender', Frankfurt/Main 1989. (forthcoming 1990).

8 75% of the men answered accordingly in a 1988 study, while 31% of the women and 23% of the men gave 'more or less' as their degree of satisfaction (*Sozialreport, 1990*: 271).

WHERE HAVE ALL THE WOMEN GONE?
Women and the Women's Movement in East Central Europe

Barbara Einhorn

Where have all the women gone? This may seem a frivolous question: they haven't evaporated after all. But what has evaporated, it seems, along with the euphoria and the optimism, the hopes and dreams of a year ago, is the energy and potential for change on the part of women themselves. Gone too are both the much-vaunted economic indepen- dence and the resultant self-confidence of forty years of official commit- ment to a policy of 'emancipation' for women. Certainly, the notion that women going out to work is the norm – as it was in the state-socialist countries of East Central Europe for the past forty years – is up for reconsideration in the process of economic restructuring.

Will the need to shed labour push women out of the labour force and back into primary responsibility for the family? There are some signs that women themselves may accept this relegation with a sigh of relief. What does this imply for our own views on what it means to be liberated? Women's role is very much in question in the current transition period in East Central Europe. Hence the question in the title about women speaking for themselves, defending or demanding equal rights and equality of opportunity. For women in Western Europe these shifts demand a fundamental rethinking of our preconceptions. Bringing together voices from East and West in this volume can be regarded as a first step in a mutual process of rethinking feminism within – and helping to define – the parameters of a new Europe.

In terms of political representation, women were active at all levels in pre-1989 peace, human rights and other opposition or dissident movements in East Central Europe. Examples were Bärbel Bohley and Ulrike Poppe of Women for Peace in the GDR who went on to become leading figures amongst the founders of New Forum and Democracy Now, two of the movements responsible for the 'turning point' in autumn 1989. In Charter 77, 18 per cent of the signatories and 31 per cent of spokespersons were women (Siklova, 1990a). Yet in all those cases where past dissidents formed or were important in the first democratically elected governments – in pre-unification GDR, in Slovenia, in Czechoslovakia, in Poland – it is men, with very few exceptions (one in Czechoslovakia, and in Poland) who became government ministers. Women have almost zero visibility in terms of the prominent figures of the transition period. Women averaged 9–10 per cent of deputies in the first democratically elected parliaments of East Central Europe, compared with around 33⅓ per cent in the old state-socialist parliamentary structures. This has led to the characterization of the new political structures as 'male democracies' (Siklova, 1990a).

The high level of female political representation under the *ancien régimes* ensured that there was a pressure group for implementing women's equality, however narrowly conceived, within the political structures of government. This may have been tokenism, in the sense that it resulted from a system of fixed quotas for the official women's organizations as well as for women on other union and party candidate lists. In many senses, too, parliament was not the real political decision-making body under state socialism. And women were conspicuous by their absence from the politburos of all these countries.

Nevertheless, in face of high levels of female unemployment, closure of childcare facilities and the almost universal current attacks on women's reproductive rights, especially on abortion rights, in the countries of East Central Europe, the considerably less than 10 per cent female representation in the new democratically elected parliaments looks problematic. It is ironic that one of the central demands of the newly formed Independent Women's Association (UFV) in the GDR was the demand for quotas, rejecting tokenism, but seeing parity of numbers as the only way to defend and promote issues of women's rights in the new social and economic system (UFV Programme, 1990).

Writing a bare fifteen months after the 'velvet revolution' of Czechoslovakia or the 'turning point' in the former GDR is by no means easy. Indeed, it is as painful as it is difficult to extract coherence from the chaotic situation of material insecurity and psychic anxiety prevailing in most of the countries of East Central Europe at this juncture.

The past has been so utterly rejected that many East Germans, for example, speak of the 'scorched-earth policy' of the conquering, asset-stripping West Germans. But if the past was all bad, what does that leave to build on? Whether one supported or opposed the regimes of state socialism, the loss of all known economic, political and social parameters makes for huge social dislocations and personal disorientation.

For women, the repercussions of this total overturning of the old are fundamental. On the one hand, the process of economic restructuring means that, in the short term at least, women form the majority of the unemployed in most of East Central Europe (Einhorn and Mitter, 1991). The shedding of 'uneconomic' female labour is occurring mainly in industrial branches which have lost their competitive edge such as textiles which use antiquated technology, or from the top-heavy state administrative sector.[1] As yet it is unclear whether this could represent an opportunity for the future. Will women being re-employed in industrial branches using new micro-technology or in the much-needed expanded service sector, or, when new technology requires skill rather than mere dexterity, will men tend to displace women?[2]

The trend in high female unemployment is accompanied by an explicit rebirth of the ideology of women's primary role as wife and mother, tender of the domestic hearth. This new/old ideology is itself reinforced by the withdrawal of the state from welfare provision. This is perceived by some as representing a positive opportunity, in the sense of women and men having to become self-reliant, becoming responsible for their own lives. On the other hand, it is likely to create, as it has done in Britain, new structures of dependency, with women providing informal 'care in the community' for elderly and disabled people as well as childcare and the reproduction of the labour force.

As men have moved from former dissident organizations into the public political domain, what is left of the much-vaunted realm of civil society are the family and informal female networks. In the past, these networks had a crucial function as sources of solidarity and procurement in a shortage economy and repressive political environment. Hence women's role in them was correspondingly important.

It is a bitter irony that at the very moment when women are being driven out of labour-force participation in the formal economy and relegated to primary responsibility for the production as well as the consumption of welfare within the family, this institution is losing the significance it held in those informal social and economic networks under the old order. Put another way, whilst men become public political actors and in that sense political subjects, the laws of the market are tending to turn women into dependents or sexual objects. Violence against women and prostitution are sharply on the increase and the pornography industry is booming throughout East Central Europe, greeted by respected male journalists as a sign of liberation from the prudishness and oppressive censorship of state socialism.

In order to examine the assertion that women stand to lose more than they gain, at least in the short term, from the current transformation of East Central European societies, it is important to understand what rights they enjoyed before the clock struck midnight, in autumn 1989, and turned them into pumpkins.

How it was in the past: the reality of state-socialist policies for the 'emancipation' of women

Definitional problems and the dual/triple burden
It would be misleading to suggest, as is common in media accounts of the 'fall' of state socialism, that everything about it was bad as far as women

are concerned. Much of the legislation and some of the policy and practice in social welfare and reproductive rights were progressive in terms of women's rights, indeed were the objects of envy in some respects for Western feminists. The former GDR, for example, boasted some of the earliest legislation on behalf of women, with the Soviet Military Administration's Decree on Equal Pay for Equal Work in 1946, and the 1950 legislation on Mother and Child providing, among other things, for childcare facilities to facilitate women's labour-force participation, predating by several years the relevant UN Conventions (Einhorn, 1989; Heinen, 1990). Several East European countries had abortion laws which provided terminations free and virtually on demand within the first three months of pregnancy.

Many demands of the Western women's movement during the 1970s, for equal educational opportunities, for the right to work, for equal pay, for childcare facilities, for extended maternity/parental leave, for positive discrimination in terms of training and qualification, were taken for granted by women and men in Poland, the GDR, Hungary and Czechoslovakia.

The motivation for official commitment to women's labour-force participation has sometimes been questioned. Some critics have suggested that it was prompted by the shortage of labour post-World War II rather than by ideological commitment. In Poland, for example, government support was weak in terms of the creation of an infrastructure of childcare facilities, and appeared to fluctuate over the post-WWII period, alternating between measures designed to encourage women's labour-force participation and pro-natalist policies (Heinen, 1990). This gave rise to speculation that it was purely economically driven, varying with the economy's demand for labour. In Hungary and Czechoslovakia many people felt that the dominant reason women went to work was economic necessity, since one income was clearly not enough to support the family. Yet the GDR's official rhetoric defined women's labour-force participation as the precondition for emancipation not only in terms of economic independence from men, but also as a means to personal autonomy and fulfilment (Einhorn, 1989). Thus there were substantial variations in policies for women in the countries of East Central Europe under state socialism, just as there are culturally and historically conditioned differences emerging in the current transition period.

It was universally evident, however, that major contradictions existed between state-socialist regimes' official commitment to women's 'emancipation' and everyday reality as experienced by East Central European women themselves. The fundamental contradiction inherent in the paradigm adopted by state-socialist countries lay in a definition of women as workers *and* mothers without any parallel conceptualization of men's role. In addition, it maintained the notion that economic independence from men and hence female labour-force participation was the single necessary and, in their terms, sufficient condition for emancipation. This led to a focus on issues around women and work, education for work, and on the family as the supplier and servicer of labour.

The exclusion from the theoretical parameters of questions such as the gendered division of domestic labour meant that women continued to be responsible for the greater part of domestic tasks and childcare. Other issues which were considered too individualistic to feature in public discourse committed to social progress were sexuality, individual autonomy, and violence against women.

The legislatively enshrined double burden for women as workers *and* mothers was often extended to a triple burden by pressure on women to perform some public social or political role. The result was that women in state-socialist countries felt thoroughly overstretched and overstressed. The exigencies of this double and often triple burden meant that many East Central European women perceived their right to work rather more as an obligation. This view is understandable, given that access to many social benefits was tied to employment.

The great majority of women worked full time in addition to sustaining the overwhelming majority of childcare and domestic work. Surveys in Hungary, Poland and the former GDR have shown that women were responsible for 75 per cent of domestic labour (Koncz, 1987; Gysi, 1990; Nickel, 1990; Einhorn and Mitter, 1991: table 3). This meant, for example, that fully employed women in the former GDR spent an additional 2–3 hours daily on household chores. This time was increased by the necessity, in a shortage economy, of standing in the queue to acquire food for the family meal or access to scarce services. It is estimated that women in Czechoslovakia spent a total 9.5–10 hours away from home each day with work, commuting and shopping time (Kroupova, 1990).

Discrimination at work
Leaving aside state socialism's exclusion of gender issues, and the problem of the dual/triple role, huge inequalities remained. Even within the terms of women's emancipation defined as dependent on their labour force participation, contradictions meant that women experienced high levels of discrimination at work. What is especially disillusioning in retrospect is the extent to which this mirrored the level and types of discrimination experienced by Western women. Despite very early legislation on equal pay, what emerges at the end of the state-socialist period is that women earned only between 66 per cent and 75 per cent of men's wages, a proportion not dissimilar to that in Western Europe (Einhorn and Mitter, 1991: table 6).

In addition, women were concentrated in 'typically female-dominated' occupations and sectors of the economy, in light industry, especially textiles, in the retail and service sectors, in secretarial, cleaning and office jobs. Statistics show a persistent and, in the 1980s, even increasing trend for girls to choose traditionally 'feminine' occupations, thereby contradicting both past officially proclaimed equality of educational opportunity, and the widely held notion that education will overcome discrimination on the basis of gender (Einhorn and Mitter, 1991: tables 7, 8). In the former GDR, for example, in 1987, 60 per cent of female school leavers entered training for a mere 16 of a possible 259 occupations. In 1989, 95.5 per cent of trainee nurses and 99.8 per cent of trainee secretaries were women (Nickel, 1990; Winkler, 1990a).

Even in female-dominated sectors of industry, the number of women in managerial positions was very low. In professions like teaching and medicine where women made up the majority of the workforce, women were under-represented towards the top of career hierarchies – head teachers and consultant doctors tended to be male (Einhorn and Mitter, 1991: 13,14, table 9). As these professions became feminized, there was a tendency for them to become devalued in terms of status and remuneration. It also resulted in the rather dubious use of quotas to restrict female entry, without any equivalent quotas being applied to encourage men to enter, for example, nursing or childcare (Heinen, 1990).

Facilitating choice

Despite the problems of the dual burden, compounded by discrimination in the labour market, it should not be forgotten that women in many East Central European countries were not forced to choose between a career and children. Rather, generous maternity-leave provisions and the availability of childcare facilities gave them a degree of choice about whether and when to have children, whether and when to return to their jobs – which had to be kept open for them – after giving birth.

Differential implementation of the legislation with regard to childcare, however, meant substantial variations in availability, paralleling the variations, for example, between Britain and Belgium or France. Thus, whereas in Poland only 5 per cent of children under 3 were cared for in crèches and about 50 per cent of 3–6-year-olds had places in nursery schools as of 1989, the former GDR could claim that demand had been met, with 80 per cent and 95 per cent of the relevant age groups in crèches and nursery schools respectively, the rest being cared for by mothers on extended maternity leave (Einhorn and Mitter, 1991: table 1). The increased availability of GDR facilities from the 9 per cent who could get crèche places in 1955 and the 20 per cent who could get nursery-school places in 1950, also suggests an ongoing and real commitment in terms of financial resources, to real choice for women.

Criticisms of these benefits include the view that financial support for the extended period of maternity leave in Hungary or Poland was inadequate or non-existent, or that children spent too long each day away from home, in childcare facilities with unfavourable child/carer ratios, hence in care which tended to be impersonal and overly regimented. Nevertheless, it remains true that while there was considerable room for improvement in the past, many of these benefits are currently absolutely under threat from the supremacy of market-driven criteria in the transition period.

This means that the choice for women of whether to work or stay at home, oft repeated by spokespersons for the new politics as representing progress on the former situation where women felt they *had* to go out to work, is in effect nonexistent in a situation where childcare facilities are either being closed or priced out of range. Rather, choice about whether to go out to work with small children, and the possibility of combining motherhood with minimal career disruptions, are precisely what women in East Central Europe seem to be about to lose.

As Maria Lado (1991) puts it in a recent paper on Hungary:

> The basic question for women will not be the traditional one: how to combine paid employment with family chores, how to meet the double expectations. They will face a more dramatic dilemma: to choose between paid work and family, between a career and children. It will be, obviously, a step back concerning women's equal opportunities.

The current situation

Given the previously unknown opportunities for the free expression of opinion, and for political activism, why is there such lack of optimism, even loss of hope, in the countries of East Central Europe? Many news reports highlight a sense of disillusionment and the feeling of being cheated as the dominant mood in the former state socialist countries. In part this can be seen as the inevitable result of illusions about the West and the joys of capitalism, specifically the illusion that embracing a scarcely defined 'market economy' would be synonymous with becoming party to West European standards of living. Partly therefore, it is the disillusionment spawned by the realities of economic hardship, spiralling inflation, massive price increases, rising unemployment and the resulting material insecurity. It also reflects, however, the growing realization that a political democracy or democratic rights as such are by no means synonymous with political representation or with having a voice. This is an especially bitter realization, given that one of the main issues behind the final collapse of the state-socialist regimes was people's resentment at not being taken seriously or given the space to operate as autonomous political subjects. There is thus a growing feeling of *plus ça change*.

The problem is that the citizens of East Central Europe, invested for the first time with this right to become active political subjects, unconsciously followed a tradition familiar to Western democracies. That is, they voted *against* the *ancien régime*, rather than *for* a clearly conceived alternative. They were, understandably, motivated by the urge to reject wholesale all that had gone before. Yet women's rights are undoubtedly not the only candidate, as some East Central European writers feel, for productive nostalgia. Eva Schäfer (1990) has speculated that women may be in a position to mourn the past, while Curt Stauss (1990) has suggested that the inability to take leave from the past, to mourn it with all its faults and blemishes, leaves one unable to move forward positively into the future. The total annihilation of both the reality and the memory that was state socialism is equivalent to a complete loss of identity, a complete devaluation of one's own past life, a negation which robs it of any authenticity. The loss of past certainties and the inability to mourn what has gone create a paralysis of inertia, self-doubt and anxiety. This leads to potentially dangerous political passivity.

For women, this comes on top of the disillusioning realization that their past situation was much less 'emancipated' than they had imagined. Rage and disgust at the revelations after the demise of the old regimes were enhanced as time went on with the realization that women stand to lose at least initially in the new situation. Unfortunately, the new women's movements are discovering that the new experience of unemployment and material insecurity do not mobilize women; on the contrary, at least in the short term, they engender a state of shock which perpetuates the stance of political inactivity or inertia (Schindler, 1991). Not only are female redundancies very high in unprofitable industries using antiquated technology like textiles, and in the old administrative sector, especially in the old government ministries, but many of these 'feminized' occupations are set to be eliminated altogether in the process of economic restructuring.

Nor is it clear that industrial modernization and the introduction of new technology will benefit women. On the contrary, a recent Hungarian study suggests that previously male-dominated occupations now involving the relatively unskilled operation of robots tend to become feminized while, as new technology is introduced, men may move over to operating machinery requiring new skills (Lado and Toth, 1989). This trend is exacerbated by recent apprenticeship figures which show women being displaced by men in occupations requiring, for example, computer skills or electronics (Winkler, 1990a): table 2.9).

Simultaneously, the closure of childcare facilities or huge increases in their costs mean that women who become unemployed have extreme difficulty finding new employment. Job advertisements in the former GDR require applicants to be 'available' at short notice, something it is difficult for women with small children to do if they have lost their childcare place on first becoming unemployed. The fact that extended maternity-leave provisions in the past stipulated that their job be held open for them until their return means that women who choose to take a year or two off to be with the children have no experience which would prepare them for the fact that they stand thereby to become long-term unemployed.

There is a shortage, at the present time, with the exception of the ubiquitous computer courses, of retraining schemes specifically designed for women. Fears are being expressed that the much-needed and much-vaunted expansion of the service sector will tend to produce unskilled, badly paid jobs without union protection, or, that where the pay is enhanced, the jobs will be taken by men (Lipovskaya, 1991).

In addition to these probable effects of economic restructuring for women, there are social and political implications of the transition period which directly affect their position in society. The closure of and/or price rises for childcare facilities have already been mentioned. Price rises, the removal of subsidies (significantly, the first subsidy to be removed in many East Central European countries was that on children's clothes), and inflation are further pressures felt most acutely by women in their role of carrying prime responsibility for feeding and clothing the family.

Issues of reproductive choice are also emerging in all of these countries. Specifically, abortion rights seem to be almost universally under attack in campaigns by the Catholic Church and male politicians to assert new/old spiritual and moral values centred on the family. This is reinforced by re-emerging nationalist currents which tend to instrumentalize women, exhorting them to produce babies 'for the nation' (Korac, 1991).

All of these trends in the labour market, as well as the diminution of social (welfare) and political rights, suggest that there are issues aplenty crying out for women to speak and act on their own behalf, form pressure groups, mount protest actions, participate in the political process.

The women's movement, past and present

The official women's unions or women's leagues of the past were, just like the official peace committees, bureaucracies which represented the extended arm of the state, despite their protestations of independence and mass membership. At their inception, this may not have been entirely the case, since they were formed in several of the state-socialist countries in the face of a Communist Party view that a women's organization independent of the Party was superfluous. This view held that women's exploitation, like men's, would be automatically eradicated with the overthrow of capitalist property relations.

The Democratic Women's Association of Germany (DFD) in the GDR always saw its role not only as encouraging women to enter the labour force in the post-war period with its dire shortage of labour, but also as an independent pressure group whose function it was to initiate legislation on behalf of women's equality. Later, too, they used their faction in the Volkskammer, the GDR parliament, in order to ensure implementation of the legislation, particularly at the workplace. Their other main function was as an educational body, with a network of local groups and paid employees who ran courses for women. These were initially designed to broaden women's horizon, to encompass the political, as well as to provide training possibilities. In later years, as a result of the very high labour-force participation of women, the activities of the DFD became geared to a tiny minority of full-time housewives. Their courses tended to focus on preparation for marriage and household management, to the point where they were derided by educated women as 'knitting and crochet circles' (Einhorn, 1989).

Even before the events of autumn 1989 it was clear from their membership figures as well as their activities that these organizations did not have the support of the majority of young adult women, nor were they addressing their main concerns. Regardless of the 1989 'revolutions' therefore, they had become bureaucratized and discredited organizations, not least because, in some cases at least, their mode of resource allocation in retrospect appeared corrupt. The Czechoslovak Women's League for example occupied and restored to its former glory a former Renaissance palace with the profits from their publishing house, while ordinary women felt bitterly that they did nothing to improve the status or living conditions of the mass of Czech and Slovak women. Their remoteness from ordinary women's needs and aspirations is aptly conveyed by the avowal of Isabela Nowacka (1990), young new acting president of the Polish Women's League that her organization had 'no experience of defending or fighting for women's rights' and hence wished to learn from the experience of the Western women's movement.

This raises the whole issue of rights under the tutelage of a paternalistic or even patriarchal socialist state as having been 'given', as opposed to won. Those rights women did enjoy were taken for granted, which goes a long way towards explaining why there is no explicitly feminist consciousness in these countries. 'The most terrible legacy of patriarchy is that its structures are present within us, within women. So women are also partly responsible [for the perpetuation of such structures]' (Fischer and Lux, 1990). In addition, as Irene Dölling so eloquently elaborates in this issue, 'Father State' brooked no disobedience from his subjects, so that there was no space for oppositional political activity. Both factors have combined to leave women facing present uncertainties with no tradition of public involvement or grass-roots struggle to win or defend rights.

Beyond this, it is striking that despite women's involvement in the 'dissident' human rights, peace, and environmental groups which were active in all of these countries during the 1980s, very few specifically women's groups emerged during that period. Traditions of patriarchy, the role of the socialist state as a patriarchal *pater familias*, women's dual or triple burden and the struggle to reproduce daily life, plus the lack of space for grass-roots political activity, all go some way towards explaining this. Nevertheless, it remains a paradox for which none of the many East Central European academics and activists to whom I have put the question can offer an adequate explanation.

In the present transition period, given high female unemployment, the attacks on abortion rights and the re-emergence of an ideology suggesting that women should play a subordinate role in society with primary responsibility for the family but not career independence, it is even more astonishing that the new women's groups in East Central Europe should have remained until now tiny minority groups.

An apparent exception to the trend in the early 1980s was Women for Peace, one of the first independent political groups to emerge in the GDR. However, it is noteworthy that their initial clustering together was in the name of support for their men, for the families of those men

Bärbel Bohley of Women for Peace and New Forum/Alliance 90

imprisoned for total conscientious objection (the GDR was one of the only state-socialist countries to offer the alternative, not of civilian service, but of non-weapon-carrying military service). Only in the second instance did they speak out on their own behalf following the promulgation in March 1982 of the revised Law on Conscription. Several hundred women signed a petition opposing a new clause which provided for the conscription of women in times of emergency. Nevertheless, initially they were opposed to the idea of 'women only' groups as in the Western women's or peace movement.

A year later, they had changed their views, not least because of their treatment by the male-dominated state security (Stasi). In response to their petition, many of them had been repeatedly held for questioning and asked which men had 'put them up to it'. They had received no substantive response from the authorities and felt they were not being taken seriously.

In December 1983 two of their members, Bärbel Bohley and Ulrike Poppe, were imprisoned for six weeks on charges of treason following an 'organized' refusal to appear at call-up medicals (thirty of them, dressed in black, had jointly posted their letters of refusal from the Alexanderplatz, the central square of East Berlin). During their subsequent imprisonment, the factor which seemed most to baffle and infuriate the Stasi was that, like the Greenham women and the Western women's movement and peace movements, whose example had by now greatly influenced them, and in defiance of the difficulties of networking without photocopying facilities or in many cases even phones, these women organized in a spontaneous and non hierarchical fashion. Hence the Stasi's efforts to isolate 'the ringleaders' were doomed to failure.

Despite its successes, Women for Peace subsequently dissolved itself, becoming in 1984 part of a mixed group known as the Initiative for Peace and Human Rights, with several of its members going on to become initiators of the other new political groupings of autumn 1989 and thereafter.

It was therefore a new departure when, in December 1989, a group of over a thousand women met in a theatre in East Berlin with the express purpose of forming the Independent Women's Association (UFV) as an umbrella organization for mushrooming women's groups throughout the GDR. Some of them, women's peace groups and lesbian groups in particular, had existed since the early 1980s under the umbrella of the Protestant Church, or as discussion groups of women academics. Others were new, seizing the moment when it seemed possible to expand and push forward a feminist agenda. The spectrum was broad, ranging from Christian and radical feminist to explicitly socialist-feminist groups.

The UFV was the largest explicitly feminist group in the formerly state-socialist countries; in addition, it differed from the very small groupings of feminists in Budapest or Warsaw in that it represented a country-wide network of groups. Its programme was based on a rejection of what its members perceived as the *Muttipolitik* ('Mummy' policies) of the years since the mid-seventies and on demands for genuine equality of opportunity, for equal pay for work of equal value, for equal representation in political structures, and for freedom from exploitation as sex objects. The preamble sounds remarkably similar to that of Western feminist documents, stating that:

> Women's disadvantaging, discrimination and oppression has continued over the centuries. Caught in the bind of a gendered division of labour which allocates to women the main burden in the family and the household and which makes them economically subservient to men, women are reduced to a mother-centred role expectation, are marketed as sex objects, and are largely excluded from the economic and political decision-making bodies . . . Socialism as we know it has also failed to transcend male-dominated structures, patriarchal gender relations (UFV Programme, 1990).

Considerable success was achieved in that almost every local council was persuaded to let women's groups take over former Stasi buildings with a view to establishing women's centres, some of them doubling up as women's refuges (e.g., Dresden, Erfurt, Stendal (*Die Zeit*, 1 February 1991) and providing crèches, cafés, counselling for unemployed women and a wide variety of courses. In Erfurt, there were splits between the more intellectual approach of the local UFV women and the practical

Alle Frauen sind schön!

'All women are beautiful!' Poster of the Independent Women's Association (UFV)

Alle Frauen sind
stark!

*'All women are strong!' Poster of the Independent Women's Association
(UFV)*

approach of the employees at the women's centre, many of them with a
background in administrative, practical trades or union work. Their
house was an enormous villa, previously the regional centre of the
Stasi's phone-tapping activities. It contained piles of abandoned ring-
binders from rooms previously filled with secret files, with a sauna and –
somewhat bizarrely – a foot-treatment centre in the basement. When I
visited there in September 1990, the women workers had invested huge
numbers of person hours in renovating and preparing the house to
provide a café-restaurant, accommodation for women and children
needing refuge, and in setting up a programme of courses and
counselling. Yet their future was still insecure financially, both from the
point of view of the city council subsidy and due to the fact that a
previous owner had appeared from the West. The women were not

Alle Frauen sind
mutig!

'All women are brave!' Poster of the Independent Women's Association (UFV)

convinced by his assurances that he would not dream of throwing them out.

Another success story was the appointment by the interim GDR government of a national spokesperson, Dr Marina Beyer, who proceeded to put together *Frauenreport 90*, the first ever collection of statistics pertaining specifically to women. In addition, every locality of more than 10,000 inhabitants in the former GDR was obliged to appoint a spokesperson for women.

Despite these successes and its apparently broadly based and widespread support, the UFV's progress has faltered very quickly. This is due to a combination of external and internal political factors. The rapid acceleration of, and the terms of, the process of unification meant that funding for the posts of spokesperson for women as well as women's refuges, women's centres, and retraining courses for women, are threatened. Disagreements and lack of political co-operation both within the UFV, and between the UFV and the Greens, for example, have doomed attempts at political representation. More recently, the UFV has decided against a coalition with Alliance 90 for this purpose in favour of continuing as a grass-roots pressure group outside the formal political structures.

In the former GDR as in all of the countries of East Central Europe, there is also resistance to co-operating with the re-formed but still discredited former official women's organizations. While this is understandable, it means forfeiting their existing networks, especially important in rural areas, since the new women's movements tend to be urban and based on groups of university-educated women.

The March 1991 National Congress of the UFV threw up considerable disagreements on strategy, with some groups like the Stinging Nettles from Erfurt wanting to focus more on lifestyle issues and others like SOFI (socialist feminists) being more concerned to protect women's rights in relation to employment, to preserve the network of childcare facilities, to establish retraining courses for unemployed women, or to struggle for an all-German law on abortion which maintains abortion as a legal right but rejects compulsory counselling, a compromise formula suggested by the West German Liberal (FDP) and Social Democrat (SPD) women.

There are problems inherent in the situation of the UFV in the former GDR, bordering and now incorporated into West Germany with its established women's movement. Nevertheless, they do not have to deal with the level of explicit and hostile resistance to feminism facing the new independent women's movements in the other East Central European countries and in the Soviet Union.

It is curious that in Czechoslovakia – ostensibly the most Western European in orientation as well as perhaps the most secular of those countries, with the longest tradition of civil society/dissident political activity represented by Charter 77 – there seems to be the strongest resistance to the idea of an explicitly feminist grouping. Civic Forum, all but one of whose spokespersons are male, their busy schedules mediated by glamorous female secretaries, explicitly reject the need for a policy for women in their programme. The new draft constitution does not even stipulate equal pay for women. A prominent surgeon and woman MP said that, although she could see it was perhaps mistaken in the long term, she felt 'allergic' to Western feminism (Moserova, 1990). This view is confirmed by Czechoslovak sociologist Hana Navarova, who has established that this allergy is widespread, albeit based on an almost total lack of knowledge of Western feminism (Navarova, 1990). As of early 1991 there was a plethora of thirty-seven registered small, often single-issue groups, of whom virtually none are feminist. One of the most active, Prague Mothers, is dedicated to campaigning against pollution and for women's right to choose motherhood rather than the dual burden. The first group to begin overcoming the resistance to feminism is Alena Valterova's Political Party of Women and Mothers (profiled in this issue).

The longest standing independent women's groups in Poland are the Warsaw-based Feminist Association and the Women's Club in Poznań, both of which began in the early 1980s. The announcement of the draft anti-abortion law in the early summer of 1989 led to the creation of at least twelve new groups, most of them, like Pro Femina, single-issue pro-choice in their approach (Jankowska, 1991). Despite this explicit attack on women's rights, public-opinion survey data from 1989 demonstrated that only 42.6 per cent of respondents strongly approved of the women's movement, as opposed to over 70 per cent who supported ecology, peace and human rights movements, with 9.3 per cent maintaining that there should not be a women's movement at all (Siemieńska, 1991). It appears likely that the law criminalizing abortion and even some forms of contraception will be passed in the near future.

In Hungary too, the Catholic Church, through Christian Democrat control of the Ministry of Health, has been influential in bringing abortion rights into question. Prejudice against feminism amongst women themselves as well as the public at large meant that choosing a name for the newly formed independent women's movement in 1990 proved a difficult process. After much deliberation the name Feminist Network was chosen for the somewhat negative reason that the word 'feminist' was one of the few terms as yet unused, hence untainted by association with state socialism's approach to women's 'emancipation'. Many Hungarian women express the view that there is something psychologically unhealthy about women who meet together without men. It is paradoxical that this atmosphere exists alongside a situation where there are many prominent women academics who have produced a more comprehensive body of research into the situation of Hungarian women than exists in most of the other East Central European countries.

Aside from internal disagreements there are also problems about gaining a hearing for new independent women's movements. A concrete illustration of the difficulty in finding a voice in the context of what many women experience as an opaque, as opposed to a blatant, form of manipulation, dictatorship of the market instead of the Party (Fischer and Lux, 1990: 99) can be seen in the fate of the East German women's journal *Für Dich*. Originally close to the DFD, the official women's association, it became after the 'turning point' of autumn 1989 a mouthpiece for demands to maintain and extend the agenda of women's rights, supporting the newly emerging women's movement, and instituting a women's helpline, giving information on how to deal with unemployment, on rights, women's refuges and women's centres.

When Berliner Verlag, the large publishing house formerly belonging to the SED and incorporating *Für Dich* was taken over by Robert Maxwell together with the West German firm Gruner & Jahr, the journal's editorial collective was presented with a totally new format along the lines of traditional Western women's magazines. As of April 1991, it seemed that staff suspicion that this was merely a veiled way of closing them down as an independent voice for women, as opposed to the direct interventionist censorship of the past regime, was about to become reality with the redundancy of 400 Berliner Verlag workers. Closure of *Für Dich* occurred in June 1991.

Feminisms and the misunderstandings East-West

The end of the Cold War has not brought automatic ease of communication across the former East-West divide. On the contrary, just as ignorance of women's lives under state socialism led to many oversimplifications in the past, lack of sensitivity, and a lacking awareness of how different the life experiences of women in those countries are from ours in Western Europe and from each other's, leads to misunderstandings in the present. Not only is supposed systemic congruence a myth: people's imaginings, hopes and fears about the current transformation process are very much conditioned by their experience of the changes as well as their differing history and cultural backgrounds.

In addition, women in the East are being forced by the total upheaval of their societies to rethink their preconceptions from scratch, whereas, as Christiane Schindler, spokesperson for UFV put it, West German feminists have an unbroken consciousness, hence do not feel the need to reconsider their views. There is a quite understandable ambivalence on the part of East Central European researchers and activists towards West European feminists. On the one hand they feel they have a lot of catching up to do – on Western feminist literature and political experience of the past twenty years. On the other, they feel sensitive about being patronized by Western feminists who, although ignorant of Eastern European women's lives, assume that their experience can be equated with their own, and that they are therefore in a position to 'help' their Eastern sisters.

Before Maxwell . . . 'Emancipated Woman or Mother?'

After Maxwell . . . 'As Beautiful as Springtime'

An illustration of the paradoxes engendered by the current situation is the envy of many West German feminists, who feel that whereas they had to make the choice between career and children, their East German sisters 'had it all'. Hence they are bemused at East German women's complaints about the double burden as workers *and* mothers.

The different value ascribed to the shifting boundaries between public and private spheres provides another example of profound East-West divergence. Women in the West have sought on the one hand to focus attention on the sphere of interpersonal relationships and the validity of subjective, lived experience. They have also attempted to make the private public under the slogan 'the personal is political', forcing into the public domain responsibility for the violence against women which occurs behind closed doors. For women in East Central Europe, the family was the only haven from the interfering long arm of the state. Hence they were prepared to pay the price for maintaining a space for individuality, and were even blind to the fact that the only autonomy thus rescued might be male. Many studies focus on the smaller leisure time at the disposal of women, be it for further education or for hobbies, that is for self-fulfilment and the development of individual potential.

Actions and interactions

For the moment at least it seems that women in East Central Europe are not mobilizing in support of those rights they stand to lose in the transition process. However, it is true to say that the feminist movement is at a low ebb in Western Europe too. It is also important for us as Western feminists not to impose our preconceptions on East Central European women. Many of the new movements in East Central Europe support the idea of a return to motherhood as woman's primary sphere of responsibility. They view this as an opportunity, a breathing space for a generation of women prematurely exhausted by the double burden. Young women, especially, frequently feel they do not wish their children to spend long days in childcare as they themselves did. They also feel they cannot regard their own overstretched mothers as role models, since all their hard work has not brought them material or career status rewards.

Some women in the former GDR and other East Central European countries feel this is a temporary phenomenon, and there are studies showing that women maintain they would still want to go to work, even if their husbands brought home a 'family wage'. The situation in East Central Europe is in flux. This should be regarded as an opportunity to reassess previously held convictions about what kind of conditions could best provide women with the space for development of their creative potential.

It will be somewhat bitter if the abortion issue, which seems to be under attack in all of East Central Europe, including Yugoslavia and most recently even in the traditionally culturally liberal, non-Catholic dominated Czechoslovakia, is to be welcomed as a rallying point for women, that is as the one issue which will galvanize women into speaking on their own behalf.

Taking a more positive view, it is clear that there is a great need for and also exciting creative potential inherent in a mutual process of listening and learning, of rethinking the concepts and the language of feminism.

Notes

Barbara Einhorn is currently researching women and women's movements in Czechoslovakia, Hungary, Poland and the former GDR. This work is funded by the John D. and Catherine T. MacArthur Foundation in Chicago.

1 Textiles were previously among the most profitable of exports from Czecho-slovakia, but the loss of the traditional 'transferable rouble' market in the Soviet Union due to the imposition of hard-currency trading, and the inability to compete with Third World textile industries using modernized machinery and employing even cheaper female labour, has rendered East Central European textiles uncompetitive.
2 Figures for the number of women in training for certain specific occupations involving new technology in the former GDR show that there is a declining number of women entering those occupations in the 1980s (see Einhorn and Mitter, 1991); this appears to confirm the prognosis of Lado and Toth (1989) on the introduction of new technology, suggesting that as occupations require skill as opposed to mere manual dexterity, women tend to be displaced by men.

References

DÖLLING, I (1991) 'Between Hope and Helplessness . . .', *Feminist Review*, 39.
EINHORN, B. (1989) 'Socialist emancipation: the women's movement in the GDR' in KRUKS, RAPP, and YOUNG (1989).
EINHORN, B. and MITTER, S. (1991) 'A comparative analysis of women's industrial participation during the transition from centrally planned to market economies in East Central Europe'. Paper prepared for UN Division for the Advancement of Women Regional Seminar on the Impact of Political and Economic Reform on the Status of Women in Eastern Europe and the USSR. Vienna, April 8–12.
FISCHER, E. and LUX, P. (1990) *Ohne uns ist kein Staat zu machen: DDR-Frauen nach der Wende* (No State Without Us: GDR Women after the Turning Point) Cologne: Kiepenheuer & Witsch, 85–100.
GYSI, J. (1990) 'Frauen in Partnerschaft und Familie: Sozialistisches Leitbild oder patriarchalisches Relikt?' ('Women in relationships and the family: socialist model or patriarchal relic?') in SCHWARZ and ZENNER (1990), 73–90.
HEINEN, J. (1990) 'The impact of social policy on the behaviour of women workers in Poland and East Germany' *Critical Social Policy* Issue 29, Vol. 10, No. 2, 79–91.

JANKOWSKA, H. (1991) 'Abortion, Church and Politics in Poland' *Feminist Review* 39.

KONCZ, K. (1987) 'Results and Tensions in Female Employment in Hungary' (mimeo).

KORAC, M. (1991) 'The state of gender research in Yugoslavia'. Paper prepared for ESRC/University of Sussex Workshop on Gender Relations in East Central Europe, Brighton, 12–13 April.

KROUPOVA, A. (1990) 'Women, employment and earnings in Central and East European countries'. Paper to Tripartite Symposium on Equality of Opportunity and Treatment for Men and Women in Employment in Industrialized Countries, Prague, May (mimeo).

KRUKS, S., RAPP, R. and YOUNG, M. (1989) editors, *Promissory Notes: Women in the Transition to Socialism* New York: Monthly Review Press.

LADO, M. (1991) 'Women in the transition to a market economy: the case of Hungary'. Paper prepared for UN Division for the Advancement of Women Regional Seminar on the Impact of Political and Economic Reform on the Status of Women in Eastern Europe and the USSR, Vienna, 8–12 April.

LADO, M. and TOTH, F. (1989) 'Zwei verschiedene Welten: Die neuen Technologien und Frauenarbeit' ('Two Separate Worlds: New Technologies and Women's Work').

LIPOVSKAYA, O. (1991) Interview with Jonathan Steele, *Guardian* 4 April.

MOSEROVA, J. (1990) Interview with B. Einhorn, Prague, September.

NAVAROVA, H. (1990) 'What did socialism give to women?' (mimeo).

NICKEL, H-M. (1990) 'Ein perfektes Drehbuch: Geschlechtertrennung durch Arbeit und Sozialisation' in AICHHOLZER, G. and G. SCHIENSTOCK (eds), *Arbeitsbeziehungen im technischen Wandel* Berlin: Edition Sigma, 201–14. ('A perfect script: gender divisions at work and through socialisation' in SCHWARZ and ZENNER, (1990), 90–120.

NOWACKA, I. (1990) Interview for Swiss feminist radio programme, Helsinki Citizens' Assembly Founding Congress, Prague, 19–21 October.

SCHÄFER, E. (1990) 'Die fröhliche Revolution der Frauen: Frauenbewegung in Ost und West' ('Women's merry revolution: the women's movement in East and West') in SCHWARZ and ZENNER (1990), 17–35.

SCHINDLER, C. (1991) Interview with B. Einhorn, Berlin, 11 March.

SCHWARZ, G. and C. ZENNER (1990) editors, *Wir wollen mehr als ein 'Vaterland'* (We Want More than a 'Fatherland') Reinbek bei Hamburg: Rowohlt.

SIEMIENSKA, R. (1991) 'Women's issues in the transitional period in Poland' (mimeo).

SIKLOVA, J. (1990a) 'Feminism, post-feminism, sexism and women's studies in Czechoslovakia' *Maxima* (Prague), 4/1990.

SIKLOVA, J. (1990b) 'Women and democracy in Czechoslovakia'. Interview with Ruth Rosen, *Peace and Democracy News*, Fall.

STAUSS, C. (1990) 'The little red province' *New Internationalist*, No. 213, November, 14–16.

UFV PROGRAMME (1990) Programme and Statute of the Independent Women's Association, translated by B. Einhorn, *East European Reporter*, Vol. 4, No. 2, Spring/Summer 1990, 53–54; see also U. Kretschmar, 'Gleichstellung statt Gleichberechtigung: Frauenpolitik nach der "Wende"' ('Equal status instead of equal rights: policies on women after the "turning point"' in SCHWARZ and ZENNER (1990), 56–73.

WINKLER, G. (1990a) editor, *Frauenreport 90* Berlin: Verlag Die Wirtschaft.

WINKLER, G. (1990b) editor, *Sozialreport 90* Berlin: Verlag Die Wirtschaft.

THE END OF SOCIALISM IN EUROPE: A New Challenge for Socialist Feminism?

Frigga Haug

Women's issues as paradoxes

Rethinking the breakdown of the socialist countries and especially the unification of the two Germanies as a socialist feminist from the West, I am first of all confronted with the experience that a number of the Left's convictions have become problematic. Concepts such as market, plan and property have to be rethought by all branches of the Left. Are there also new uncertainties for socialist feminists? Thinking about women's issues in these times of rapid historical change, in which one entire world system is in collapse and the other winning a surprising victory, the first thing I notice is a series of paradoxes.

The political paradox
The former socialist model did not eliminate women's oppression; in fact, the situation of women was not even relevant to the dominant theory, which saw feminism as a *petit-bourgeois* deviation. Nevertheless, it is above all women in movements in the former socialist countries who appear to be ready to think about an improved model of socialism. The Independent Women's Union founded in December 1989 in East Germany was one of the groups which fought for a different socialism, rather than for incorporation by capitalism.

A paradox in theory
Socialist feminists all over the world have long sought to work out the correlation between capitalism and patriarchy (e.g., Hartmann, 1981). The question was not whether it was only capitalism which oppressed women or whether women's oppression would altogether disappear with the elimination of the capitalist mode of production. Rather, it was

necessary to understand the specific usefulness or even the fundamental role that women's oppression plays in the capitalist mode of
production. I have tried to outline this correlation as follows: the
production of use values in accordance with the profit motive is only
possible given the precondition that a whole series of use values – as well
as the production of life itself and its direct nurture and preservation –
operate beyond the laws of profit. Women provide this necessary pillar
in capitalist relations of production, owing to their ability to give life to
children, and as the outcome of struggles lasting throughout a long
period of history. The rest is the work of culture and ideology. This
system we understand as 'capitalist patriarchy'. But this confronts us
with a theoretical paradox: as much as this analysis might satisfy those
of us who live under capitalism, there remains the amazing discovery
that women's emancipation made hardly any progress in those countries which did not function according to the profit motive. Indeed, in the
various conferences of East and West German women in Berlin and
elsewhere after the opening of the Wall, the one point of dispute was
whether Western women were more liberated than those in the East,
who needed to be taught feminism by their *apparently* more advanced
Western sisters. Hope for a strengthening of the women's movement by
uniting forces with Eastern 'feminism' was soon overthrown by a sort of
Western despair that the unification would not only fail to strengthen
the movement but indeed weaken it, because of a gap in feminist
consciousness in the East.[1]

The cultural paradox
When we study the attitudes and behaviour of women in East and West,
we find other paradoxical results. After forty years of socialism, many
women from the East are much more self-confident than most women in
the West. Their stride seems more extended, they habitually walk erect,
and above all they lack what I will provisionally term a passive sexism.
By this I mean that they do not act as if they were constantly balancing
the effort to please men in a provocative or even exciting way while at
the same time maintaining the necessary distance and inaccessibility.
The recent victory of Beate Uhse in East Germany (who owns the
biggest chain of sex shops in the West), the invasion of Western
peepshows by Eastern men, and the new 'freedom' to obtain pornography all indicate that my impression of East German women is valid, and
that East German men 'suffered' from the freedom of their women. This
relative absence of pornography, while the oppression of women
continued, also serves to contradict recent feminist ideas about pornography being the original source and the basis of women's oppression.
This desexualization of the bodies of East German women coexists with
a lack of awareness, even an indifference, concerning quite obvious
instances of discrimination against the female sex. Among other things,
there has been no feminist revolution in language. Without any
hesitation, women in the East refer to themselves in the masculine form
(e.g., as businessmen or craftsmen). This is a particular problem in

Emancipation under Socialism[3]

German, for many occupational labels, including doctor, economist or historian, assume maleness; to refer to a woman the ending '-in' must be added. It was one of the victories of feminism in the West to bring this into public consciousness, but this has not taken place in East Germany. To speak a male language prevents any clear perception of existing masculinist culture, which among other things determines access to specific jobs.

I summarize these different observations as a paradox, because they point to a great self-confidence on the part of women in the former GDR combined with female support for a traditional division of labour. The self-confidence stemming from their being needed in society went along obviously with an acceptance of the very structures which we are accustomed to think of as especially oppressive for women.

The paradox of reproduction

We come to a further paradox – or more precisely to two – in regard to the intense struggle over the abortion law that has accompanied the new union of the two Germanies. On the one hand, a fight over reproduction technologies is taking place in the West which poses the question of whether experiments with human embryos should be allowed. On the other hand there is renewed strength in the effort to tighten the abortion law based upon a 'right to life'. This struggle is given new impetus by the East German demand to keep abortion legal. We hear male members of parliament in the West, whose bodies are affected neither by the law nor by the experience, showing endless bigotry as they debate which principle should govern abortion avail- ability, place of residence or site of operation, and whether the more liberal East German law should remain in force for another two years as a compromise.

But at the same time, this battle is fought with the female population in East Germany in the background, for they have obviously viewed having children as an essential dimension of their lives. Almost all East German women are employed, and almost all of them have children when relatively young (in their early twenties), regardless of their occupational and/or marital status. One lesson from East Ger- many might be that the more liberal the abortion law, the more children women have. The abortion law is therefore not so much a means of regulating birth-rates, but serves rather as another means of disciplin- ing women. (I should add that the abortion rate as well as the birth-rate was high in East Germany, indicating a rather casual attitude toward questions of contraception and conception.)

The paradox of labour

But the most difficult lesson arises from the paradox of female employment. The right to work is one of the cultural givens in socialist countries, and determines the identities of women – this has been so for more than forty years in East Germany and for more than seventy in the Soviet Union. That female employment is a precondition for their emancipation has been a staple item of progressive politics in the workers' movement (though not in its entirety) since Marx and Engels, Lenin and Rosa Luxemburg. In all socialist countries the right to work was a given (now denounced in the Western media as an effort to hide unemployment), and there was a correspondingly high rate of female employment (over 90 per cent). And yet nowhere did women achieve decision-making positions in numbers that could sway masculinist cultures; socialisms too, besides being authoritarian administrative structures, were above all patriarchies. And where women must return to the home, as Gorbachev recommended in the Soviet Union and as was urged in East Germany in the face of growing unemployment, rumour has it that the women prefer to go back into the privacy of their homes, to escape the stress of overwork and to catch up on unfinished housework. This is probably not true for the majority; the right to work is still one of the privileges that gave East Germany the advantage over the West. (While the politicians already accept and speak about an unemployment rate of 50 per cent for the so-called 'new countries' for the summer of 1991 the latest polls suggest that while 25 per cent of the women from the West agree that being a housewife is the job they really want, there are only 3 per cent from the former GDR who think so.)

Some theoretical and practical questions remain open: did the widespread employment of women in the former socialist countries hasten their emancipation, or are the structures indeed as hermetically patriarchal as the workings of political institutions suggest? And further: in rejecting the former model of socialism, are we dismissing a model of women's emancipation whose fruits we have yet to harvest? Has that model up to now been a burden to socialist feminists rather than wings on their heels only because of its specific form in East Germany? And above all there is the important question: was it correct to link women's emancipation to labour?

The concept of labour and the emancipation of humankind

'Our women are the miracle!' This was the title of a propaganda brochure from East Germany in the late seventies. This was at a time when the disadvantages and problems, the bureaucracies and inertias, were already so obvious that to juxtapose women and miracle with regard to the reality of the East communicated the same feeling of derision that Mother's Day does. At the same time it offered that unwelcome glorification of heroines that always turns up when something is going wrong. Then too, this particular adoration can be read as the translation of what we simply, but not very precisely, call the double burden. The term 'double burden', however, is problematic, for it focuses on time, as if someone simply has to carry out two jobs instead of one, which together add up to more than the usual working day in that society – say eight hours. But in reality it means that women are located in two areas with contradictory logics, one of which does not count because it does not bring any money. Is the main problem of women's oppression that they have to work both in the factory and at home, so that their working days are too long?

Although I did not agree with the forms of socialism that have existed to date, I think it is strange to posit the same answer to the question of women's oppression in the two quite different systems. Or, to put it in other words: has the situation of women nothing to do with

Women's split identity

the relations of production? Here I presume that the two societies had different relations of production. This is the only explanation for the energy with which West Germany eradicates root and branch any inkling of forms of production other than the capitalist mode, and this at every level, including its literature.[2]

Critique of the economy of time

Pondering further on this problem of work or, more exactly, on the notion that the project of women's liberation is tied to 'work' brings me to the idea that difficulties already arise with the very discovery of the sexual division of labour. Here I believe we can find the solution for our paradoxes as well.

Although this is very unfashionable today, I will once again return to Marx. He offers a few hints about gender relations in his discussions of work and, above all, we find the sexual division of labour at the most strategic points in the sketches for his complete project. In the *German Ideology* Marx formulates the division of labour as a juncture of oppositions and contradictions. He distinguishes between those divisions of labour in the whole of society: town/country, male/female, head/hand, work and nonwork; and those divisions within the labour process. He always studies the forms of division of labour in relation to the total work of a society. In this context we find the following remarkable sentence on family production as opposed to commodity production:

> For the study of common, or directly associated labour, we do not have to go back to its natural form, which we find on the threshold of the history of all civilized races. A closer example is the rural patriarchal industry of a peasant's family, that produces grain, cattle, yarn, linen, and clothing etc. These different things confront the family as different products of their family-work, but they do not confront each other as commodities . . . the different kinds of labour are in their natural form direct social functions, because they are functions of the family, which possesses its own natural division of labour as well as does a society based on commodity production . . . But the spending of individual labour power, measured by the duration of time, seems to be the social determination of the different

works itself, because the individual labour forces only function as organs of the common labour force – the family. (Marx and Engels, 1975 : Vol. 23, 92f)

It is astonishing that Marx did not further examine this finding that the various products were not measured and estimated as more or less valuable by the time spent on them, even though it certainly had consequences not only for the sexual division of labour but for our whole model of civilization as well. After all, the calculation of time spent also turns value into a curse from which the products have to be protected. In the end the only things that can stand the social test in capitalism are those which devour as little time as possible – which is the model both of progress and of pauperization. At the same time we get a hint of that yearning which validates the family and guarantees its continued existence, for it is the one place where production is not calculated only in terms of costs and labour. (I am leaving aside the effects that this lack of calculation has for the woman in the household.)

Over all, Marx portrays the division of labour with the following strategic dimensions: the domination of nonworkers over workers; the development of labour as a whole at the expense of the stagnation of the individual worker; the development of a socialization of labour without any consciousness or appropriate political actions on the part of the labour force. The peculiar thing that happened as it were behind the scenes of this categorization is that the sexual division of labour only appeared at the outset as a division of labour. Later on the role of women has vanished, at least as labour. They are named at the same time that they become nameless. From that point on, the terms 'division of labour' and 'total social labour' refer only to the partial labour of industrial and agricultural production for the market. There is no analysis of the problem which arises from the subordination of all activities that do not fit the waged labour model, and therefore the logic of a cost-benefit analysis. This is a problem crucial both for the development of humankind and its needs and for the judgements humans make concerning social meaning and value, thereby determining both culture and identities.

However, the consistently blank spaces, occurring where the activities of women should have been analyzed, appear only after Marx has already made elementary statements concerning gender relations and labour. To begin with, a sentence occurs in the *German Ideology* in a discussion of the relationship between property and the division of labour: 'This latent slavery in the family, though still very crude, is the first property, but even at this early stage it corresponds perfectly to the definition of modern economists, who call it the power to dispose of the labour-power of others.' (Vol. 23, p. 44) Engels viewed gender relations as 'the cells of civilized society' and 'the first class oppression of the female sex by the male' (Marx and Engels, 1975 : Vol. 21, 68). Domination therefore is inscribed in the division of labour between the sexes.

In his extensive analyses of labour in capitalism, the sexual division of labour no longer appears. Here Marx more or less assumes that women, usually referred to together with children, should not be included in the capitalist labour process in its current state (although he is ambiguous at this point). He describes their appearance in the factory as a particular misery, and also takes it for granted that the male worker should work and be paid both for his own and for his family's reproduction. In this connexion he seems to see the sexual division of labour chiefly as natural, a division occurring on a 'mere physiological basis', which through exchange leads to areas based on mutual dependence (Vol. 23, 372). But he does not go so far as to analyze the constellation of these areas, which is central for the capitalist model of civilization.

After all, it is upon this basis that a social formation has developed, in which more or less only those things are produced that bring profit; so that all work which cannot follow this logic, which can neither be rationalized, nor automized, nor accelerated – like cherishing and nurturing both humankind and nature – are neglected or left to women's unpaid care. Today we can proceed on the assumption that the crises concerning both the unrestrained and uncontrollable development of the productive forces and the ruinous exhaustion of nature are related to the logic and domain of profit, which rests upon women's oppression. Current discussions regarding an extended concept of labour, which would include reproductive and learning activities, and provide a minimal income to guarantee the survival of those who are not 'normally' incorporated in the employment process, show the convulsions occurring in an area where the sexual division of labour was taken for granted.

Here I want to take a further step by looking back from today's standpoint to the development of humankind in relation to those activities and needs which could pass the test of the market and upon which it therefore seemed worthwhile to spend time. All those products and activities which demanded an extensive amount of time, without resulting in a sufficiently grand product, fell by the wayside. Most agricultural activities as well as the conservation of nature, and even the rearing of children, were incompatible with the logic of continuous reduction. (The efforts to industrialize agriculture have produced those horrible products which Brecht predicted in the brief statement: 'You will no longer recognize the fruits by their taste'.) Although the products attained are indispensable for the survival of humankind in the short term, this development has accelerated the division of humanity into one group which can pass the test of the market and another group of partial people who live and work on a lower level than is usual in the industrial world. Here we find the countries of the Third World, with their continuous immiseration.

In the countries of the First World developments are more complex. On the one hand, women are kept economically dependent; at least most of them cannot survive on their own even when employed in a low-paid female job. They are supported economically by a husband, the same breadwinner Marx and Engels discussed. Were it not for them, the majority of those time-consuming activities would simply remain undone. Here humankind has not developed. Thus, as the productive forces develop industrially, creating ever-new human needs in the Western capitalist countries, a monstrous brutalization of humankind appears. Crimes, drugs and alcohol are merely the visible signs of a model of civilization in which human development is subordinated to utter rationalization, and to the products and needs established under its rule. The progress of the material productive forces is far from setting people free to take into their own hands their development as human beings. On the contrary, such human development remains a by-product of general industrial development and of the work of women. In this context it is logical that Gorbachev hopes to cure the demoralization of the youth by sending women back into their families. We also get a hint of this problematic when we recognize our feelings of longing when we come into contact with simpler civilizations and can enjoy their unselfconscious hospitality and the many delights coming from labour-intensive domestic production. In this sense the statement that the degree of human liberation can be measured from the degree of women's liberation is completely realistic today. It affects humans' interactions with each other, as well as their needs and their relationship to sensuality, to surrounding nature, to the work of hands and heads, and to themselves as individuals.

Rethinking again the puzzle concerning the passion with which men in government regulate the production of the species by law, we can decipher it as an effort to use the law to enforce those activities which cannot be regulated by profit and which therefore appear worthless. If women started to think about their desire for children from the perspective of their standard of living or of the most economic way to get by – that is, according to the predominating sense of time – they would repudiate such activities as a waste of time and energy. Thus there are legal safeguards to prevent women from yielding to the temptation of the predominant social logic of time. With moral concepts like 'love' and 'right to life', they are forced into a logic of life-consuming time which contradicts the logic of profit and of speed which they experience as members of capitalist societies. We will probably find that wherever the predominant cost-benefit analysis is not sufficient for survival, the law creates some compensation, which is imposed on women through appeals to morality, such as caring for the elderly or disabled. At the same time it is less of a puzzle why politics, which is after all the codification of human relations and the business of regulating society, had to remain a male domain through all the decades of the women's movement and the fight for equality. Women could make themselves rulers in a social structure that makes them subordinate beings on the basis of sex only at the cost of their very identities.

The answer to the question posed above, concerning whether it was appropriate to link the liberation of both women and humanity to work, has to be 'no' as long as work is conceived of only as waged labour, which has been and still is the tradition of the workers' movement. Here it is necessary to base our analysis on a concept of *self-determined social activity* instead of work. Or we could on the contrary expand the usual concept of work to include those activities necessary for the development of humankind, and adhere to it. It is a pragmatic question.

Economy of time in the former GDR

With these considerations in mind let us return to developments in the former socialist countries. To begin with, there was little readiness to take up the task of overcoming the divisions of labour and their effects throughout society. Following Lenin, some effort was made to reduce the cultural gap between city and countryside, but the question of gender relations fell into oblivion. Or more correctly there was a general assumption that including women in the social labour process was sufficient to overcome their oppression. Our Western media never grow tired of pointing out to us that things have been the same in East and West, as in both societies women bore responsibility for household and childcare and were therefore totally overworked, carrying the entire burden of labour-force participation. However, their mocking contempt of the socialist economy and its management points to inroads into the logic of profit-making that at least deserve mention.

East Germany was obviously more advanced in those very areas now blamed for being nonproductive and described as industrial scrap-yards. The fringe benefits offered by Eastern companies included some which contributed to women's liberation. They involved a partial suspension of the profit motive as the general basis of production. This made the companies appear particularly unproductive from the standpoint of the logic of profit. Childcare centres, meals, portions of health insurance were paid for by the companies, as were holiday centres. In regions of exceptional beauty, by the seashore, where we would expect grand hotels for the moneyed élites, we still find a variety of holiday camps run by different companies (these camps by the way offer a somewhat vulgar obstacle to proper capitalization).

It is true that the more 'society' appropriates the work of women free of charge, the richer it gets, so long as only healthy male workers are considered to be temporarily used while they exert their labour power to the utmost solely for the advantage of the company. As one might expect, the numbers of women and youth among the East German unemployed were already remarkably higher than those for adult men just four months after the introduction of West German currency.

Although our conservative press does not report on the brutality of the West, but only on its freedom, wealth and so forth, we can decipher out of the very details it does give just how great the dehumanization exported by West Germany really is. I will give one small example: a few months ago there was a short report on the unparalleled lack of productivity at an East German chemical company. As a result, 700 employees would be dismissed who were well over 65 years old. Women as old as 84 regularly came to the factory and were paid, because they were lonely at home. The company will now switch its policy and dismiss all persons over 57. It will also get rid of eighty Vietnamese workers and send them back to Vietnam. The company had also had a polyclinic staffed by thirty doctors that cared for the health of adults and children in the entire region. These institutions are to be separated from the company and only after all these improvements will a Western chemical factory be so kind as to appropriate this factory.

Let us assume that women's oppression is grounded in the division of society into an area that is 'productive' and one that is 'nonproductive' and therefore superfluous in terms of the logic of profit. Their inter-relation in the realm of political administration, which necessarily remains a male domain, decrees that women are responsible for the unproductive segment and ensures their nondevelopment culturally and bureaucratically. In this respect we see in the former socialist countries a deliberate effort to establish a cost-benefit analysis that takes a segment of those unproductive tasks over into the productive account balance. On this basis female waged employment became matter-of-fact and was culturally and politically realized.

The question remains of why this shift and rearrangement did not lead to a greater liberation and inclusion of women in the regulative structures of society. At present it appears as a problem of patriarchal bureaucracy. A burden was lifted for women so that they could enter the 'productive' area; but the division between these two areas, and the fact that social progress only related to one of them, was not recognized as the problem. Those at the top decided which products, which free spaces, which activities were to be exempted from the general cost-benefit analysis. Freedom planned from above cannot be perceived as freedom. Agreement to a certain way of life can only be productive and creative if those concerned take the satisfaction and development of their needs into their own hands. But to carry out the planned economy and the subsidizing of particular areas in the East, the eternal patriarchy was once again required, emerging from past circumstances both morally and mentally (as Marx put it in his *Critique of the Gotha Programme*). And this patriarchy believed it knew how best to foster human development and enacted laws, duties and regulations to accomplish it.

What could the 'miracle-women' do but agree? A women's move-ment aiming at liberation could hardly grow under these circumstances. But, on the other hand, it becomes clearer why women from the former East German state are less inclined to turn their backs on a socialist project. The so-called return to a market economy definitely hits them the hardest.

The development of one area was not simply accomplished at the cost of the other, men did not develop solely at the cost of women, but by the centuries-old neglect of human development, except as a by-product of profit and utilitarianism. Time for human development would have required the direct subjective participation of all concerned in order to achieve liberation, rather than planning, commands and administration. Such a step would have also shown that time is not only a dimension that is measured as productive in the sense of growth and competition in the world market, or unproductive in the sense of giving more scope to humanity and generally improving the standard of living, but that time is also a dimension that permits the development of human lives, and that it is necessary if people are to participate in the political regulation of the community as a civil society. Thus the women's question is a question of democracy and, concommitantly, there will be no democracy and no socialism without a solution to the women's question.

As far as the new reunified Germany is concerned there is a social commitment to the currently existing freedom and democracy of the West. Any violation will be prosecuted. As long as this democracy and this freedom are understood in the old patriarchal way, women will remain outlaws and will be forced to fight for a new order.

Notes

Frigga Haug teaches sociology and social psychology at the Hochschule für Wirtschaft und Politik in Hamburg. She also teaches women's studies at Hamburg University and Marxism at the Free University of Berlin. She has been active as a socialist feminist for twenty years and an editor of *Das Argument* for almost thirty years. She has contributed to fifteen collectively written books; of these, *Female Sexualization* was published in English by Verso in 1987. Thanks to Carole Elizabeth Adams for help in translating this English version.

1 This supports the conclusions of a recent comparative study on gender inequality in socialist and capitalist countries, which found that a strong women's movement is necessary for any form of women's emancipation. Hence the absence of any women's movement; and the concommitant lack of any feminist consciousness explains the almost total absence of women in decision-making positions in socialist countries (see Vianello and Siemienska, 1990).
2 See the fight against socialist literature in the Western media, especially against Christa Wolf.
3 This photograph from Irene Dölling (1991) *Der Mensch und sein Weib*, Berlin: Dietz Berlin.

References

HARTMANN, Heidi (1981) 'The unhappy marriage of Marxism and feminism: towards a more progressive union' in SARGENT (1981).

MARX, Karl and ENGELS, Frederick (1975–) *Collected Works* London: Lawrence & Wishart.

SARGENT, Lydia (1981) editor, *Women and Revolution: The Unhappy Marriage of Marxism and Feminism* London: Pluto.

VIANELLO, Mino and SIEMIENSKA, Renata et al. (1990) editors, *Gender Inequality: A Comparative Study of Discrimination and Participation* London: Sage.

THE SECOND 'NO': Women in Hungary

Yudit Kiss

The word 'gender' has the same form as 'no' in Hungarian. I remember how puzzled I was, finding the Hungarian translation of de Beauvoir's book *The Second Sex*. What was the first 'no', I wondered? Later on I came to realize how meaningful this misunderstanding was. Women's condition, sadly enough, is inevitably associated with the need to learn to say 'no'.

It would be very difficult to translate womankind into Hungarian, because we do not have a similarly general expression; the closest one, 'nö', means rather 'female'. Apart from that we have a whole range of words, showing the social and marital status of the female, the nicest of which is *feleseg* for wife, meaning 'your other half'. But to be a real half in a relationship assumes being a whole on your own; a rather challenging task, and even more so, if one has to face such an uneasy heritage as the one Hungarian history bequeathed to women.

Before World War II Hungary was an underdeveloped agrarian country. It was a male-dominated society where women were hardly visible. The surviving elements of a rigid, austere peasant culture, mixed with a conservative, strongly Catholic ideology, did not give much chance to women. Their reputation is mirrored by the popular sayings 'money to be counted, women to be battered' or 'woman is called silence'.

Most women were housewives, those of the lower classes worked in underpaid and low-status jobs, as domestic servants, agricultural labourers or unskilled factory workers, for whom to become an office employee meant the highest ambition. Few women were educated and even fewer played public roles. The ones who did came from the middle and upper classes, so their excellence might be interpreted as only due to their social status, as in the case of Katinka Karolyi, the 'Red Countess', or the few outstanding female scientists and artists, like Anna Lesznai or Margit Kafka. Women were a bit more involved in left-wing politics, probably due to self-education and the promise of universal equality. The leader of the Social Democrat Party, Anna Kethly, for example, was a well-known politician. There were some wonderful women, whom we only know because their mates – writers and poets – made them immortal. We recall them by their nicknames, Csinszka or Fanny, but do not even know their faces.

The radical socialist turnover brought dramatic changes into this picture. The new system aspired to abolish all economic, social, cultural or ethnic differences – everybody became a comrade and was treated as 'you' (the familiar form of address). In the process of socialist modernization, masses of women were drawn into work, encouraged to take up even those jobs which were previously reserved for men. Talented girls from the working class and remote villages were sent free to schools and universities; female doctors, engineers, lawyers and even tractorists were trained. Lots of women appeared in the political structures as well, although this first spontaneous breakthrough later on became a clumsy formality, prescribed by calculated statistical ratios, to show how 'representative' they were.

These huge changes of values and life opportunities taught women to say the first 'no', rejecting the traditional pattern that embittered the lives of their mothers and grandmothers. A whole new generation of self-conscious and active women emerged on the social scene in the post-war years, for whom working, playing active social roles, enjoying the benefits of social welfare, 'shaking the whole world' as the popular song said, was taken for granted.

Nevertheless this first, radical change was not followed by other substantial steps. Women were declared equal, on the basis of their social equality with men. This was a big achievement, but at the same time loaded with a series of contradictions, which were bound to escalate later on. The proclaimed social equality did not consider the basic biological, emotional, cultural, psychological differences between men and women. They did not form part of equality, although precisely the recognition of the fundamental differences of any kind of minority should create the basis for their incorporation in a genuinely democratic society.

A wide range of objective conditions – from economic and legal regulation to providing childcare facilities – was created for women to enable them to function as equal to men. But at the same time the whole universe of the particularly female experience and practice, like the constraints of social and family roles, questions of love, sex, friendship, motherhood, abortion, rape, sexual abuse, were never dealt with. On top of that, the dominant ideology was rather puritan, if not prudish; it was considered extravagant, egotistic, *petit bourgeois* or even subversive to be too elegant, to fall madly in love or to acclaim the right to have good sex without considering children.

Both the theory and practice of post-war socialism was concerned with the masses, social forces and historic necessities. Individuals, personal problems, questions of the intimate sphere were put aside, to such an extreme that psychology became labelled a bourgeoise science whose representatives – many of them outstanding students and colleagues of Freud, Jung and Reich – were 'advised' to do 'something useful'. (Their lack is painfully felt now, in the rocky times of massive social transformations.)

This neglect created a fair amount of self-ignorance, passivity and frustration in women, which is so deeply rooted that even today it hinders the articulation and representation of specifically gender problems. This is one of the multiple problems the newly emerging feminist movements in Hungary have to cope with.

On the other hand, equality was declared – it was given, although well-deserved, but as a gift from above and not an achievement from below. As a result those subtle, gradual changes that occur both in society and in souls, thanks to conscious social action, did not take place. Everyday structures, the way women and men treat each other – and themselves – in public and in their homes, hardly changed. That is why it was so easy to push women gradually back to the traditional patterns, in which the two sexes are aliens to themselves and easily set against each other as enemies. (As usual, ignorance and lack of self-knowledge becomes the source of hatred.)

In the subsequent thirty years a never recognized but obvious division of labour took shape, which rewarded men with the best-paid, highest prestige professions, opened a gap between male and female salaries and converted the social and political participation of women more and more into a formality. From the late sixties the emergence of the second economy made it possible to take second or third jobs, and because they were better remunerated it was mostly men who took them. It led to a dramatic decline in their health and life expectancy, and put a growing burden on women as well. Now even more they were left alone to cope with household, childcare and the time- and nerve-consuming everyday survival.

Through this slow, hardly noticeable process women found themselves pushed back into the private sphere. It was an ambivalent development. On the one hand, privacy was the territory of relative personal autonomy, tolerated by the Hungarian soft-authoritarian system, partly as a security valve, partly as the pledge of a wide social consensus of silence. It was an island, a refuge, where words and deeds did not diverge tragically, where it was possible to experience genuine solidarity, community, love. On the other hand, due to the above-mentioned shortcomings of human relationships, it did not have that much to offer women either. They were primarily companions, friends, lovers, catering for, showing solidarity with men, who were struggling for higher living standards, to make ends meet, or against political oppression.

Paradoxically enough, the spectacular political changes of 1989–90 seemed to emphasize this negative trend for women. They were present at the big demonstrations, on the happy streets, but disappeared from the negotiating tables. In the heroic battle on behalf of democracy, the male fighters tended to forget about the biggest, oppressed majority, 'their other halves'.

The only hopeful detail of the rather depressing Hungarian

MELANIE FRIEND/FORMAT

Time- and nerve-consuming everyday survival

electoral rally in this respect was a poster of the Young Democrats, which offered the image of a happily kissing young couple, to replace the image of Brezhnev and Honecker doing the same. Sadly enough, the most exposed female politician, Anna Petrasovits in the colours of the Social Democratic Party, could only render a clumsy caricature of Mrs Thatcher and Anna Kethly, convincing lots of hesitant voters that women's place is definitely in the kitchen.

The results of the first free elections are rather disheartening from the women's point of view. Overnight the token women of the old system disappeared from the scene. In the new Hungarian parliament out of 386 MPs there are only 28 women, out of whom 22 got into the benches on their Party's lists, not thanks to the voters of their constituency. This shows society's opinion about us, but also the real lack of socially competent women, proving that formal equality is insufficient to create genuine self-esteem and independence. Fortunately, the overall social awakening pressed several of the new parties to articulate their opinion concerning women, and gave an opportunity to some new, grass-roots women's organizations as well. Probably now they will have much more chance to be heard, because the situation of women in Hungary is markedly worsening. As a simple negation of vulgarized socialist ideology, the good old 'God, patria and home' trinity threatens to come back, casting women in the role of devoted, full-time mothers and faithful housewives.

It is rather telling that one of the first big discussions of the newly elected parliament took place about a draft law to ban abortion. It is rather intriguing that in the middle of a deep economic crisis, political chaos and social insecurity, when the very foundations of society are to be reshaped, abortion has become a primary question in almost all post-socialist countries.

There is a clear economic reason for it: the neo-classical type of economic restructuring will create massive unemployment, and it is easier and more comfortable to get rid of the female workforce, which is considered unreliable anyway. (Not only out of prejudice; the multiple childcare allowances provided by the previous regime made it possible for women to spend a significant amount of their working time with their new-born or sick children.)

It also has an ideological message: the new conservative, right-of-centre government puts the emphasis on the family – not on the community as did the socialists, but neither on the individual, as do 'genuine' capitalists. And women are expected to be the pillars, the caryatids of a newly painted, but badly designed old building, namely the unequal and oppressive traditional family.

It is illustrative that the most important women's weekly, *Nök Lapja*, has a new motto on its cover, written in the 1930s by the charming male poet, Deszo Kosztolanyi: 'Compassion be the bright light of your eyes'. However nice it is, the ideal again is caring, enduring and understanding – by no means awakening or demanding.

The discussion about abortion was also a lesson in governing: this is the way the new power treats its biggest majority – with sweet words of conviction and strict, administrative aggression. In case the argument about 'women's real vocation' is not convincing enough, the objective conditions of a freely chosen womanhood-motherhood are taken away, with the limitation of abortion rights, shutting down of the 'economically unprofitable' crèches, day schools, play centres, the cut-back of subsidies on restaurants, ready-made food, children's clothes, laundries, cultural services, etc. All this is happening in the name of freedom, democracy and economic efficiency, while in the actual productive sphere hardly anything is changing.

The questions of children, abortion and sex are obviously political issues, and are more clearly so in the case of Eastern Europe, with the long historical tradition of the state's interference in the citizen's personal life. The whole post-war political history of Hungary is mirrored in the history of abortion. In the severest Stalinist period of the 1950s under a female Minister of Health, Margit Ratko, contraception was difficult and abortion was strictly forbidden, so that both women and doctors could be gaoled if caught. Hungarians had to produce children in order to recover quickly from the human losses of the war and also to provide the workforce for the gloriously advancing socialist industry which was to conquer decaying capitalism. The massive generation of the 'children of Ratko' created an abnormal demographic pattern, causing dramatic peaks and recessions in births every twenty years – and the consequent cycles of shortage and abundance in the labour force and human infrastructure, jobs, flats, hospitals, crèches, schools.

In the golden years of the 'gulash socialism' of the 1960s with political liberalization and growing personal consumption, the dilemma of '*kicsi* vs *kocsi*?' ('a small one or a car?') kept Hungarian heads and beds busy. The majority tended to go for the car, causing serious bottlenecks in public transport and severe ecological damage, as well as panic about the extinction of the nation. There were vehement discussions in which demographic questions were often used to express political dissent. The biggest political crisis of the 1970s, the persecution and expulsion of the dissident intellectual élite, erupted when some of them began to criticise the new draft of the government's demographic policy.

Before the drastic changes of 1989 the situation was a true mirror of the ambivalent nature of the pseudo-liberal Kadar system; there were plenty of contraceptives and humiliating administrative restrictions on abortion which were fairly easy to shirk; there was propaganda about the beauty of a family with three children, as well as encouragement for men to take paternity leave, or take jobs previously considered exclusively feminine, like primary-school teachers or crèche workers. And now we see the new democratic (male) parliament discussing whose right it is to decide about human lives.

The abortion history of Hungary provides a rather clear lesson about the political nature of the intimate sphere. There is a hidden sensual dimension beneath every social formation, which is extremely revealing about the inner nature of the system. The way they treat love and sex gives a telling insight about them. Love is an ultimate expression of freedom – freedom of choice, freedom of becoming, unrestricted pleasure of being. Love does not accept social boundaries – Shakespeare's Romeo and Juliet the same way as Orwell's Winston and Julia, break through, almost unconsciously, unacceptable, mutilating social restrictions. That is why repressive systems fear love. They try to oppress it or try to convert it into something more manageable, channel it into religion, sell it in Hollywood, degrade it in sex shops, pervert it into warfare, which is a peculiar expression of impotence: an inability to make contact. (The soldiers in the Gulf, who use condoms to protect their rifles, instead of making love to their lovers, in my confused head recall the song of Hungary of the 1950s, 'The Worker's Guard has only one concern, why he does not have three lives, one to dedicate to the Party, one to give to his beloved one, and the third one, the third one is his weapon's'.) Liberal democracies which convert love and sex into commodities, also reveal their deep fear of freedom. Faceless sex, offered for sale, is a shocking form of human slavery and misery, both on the part of the sellers and the buyers, and the mediators do not differ too much from the arms dealers, who become rich on the cost of human misery.

The often mentioned paternalistic character of the Stalinist dictatorships has a deeply incestuous feature: Stalin, Rakosi or Kim Il Sung are 'the nation's fathers', and the masses are their devoted children, as nuns are the Brides of Christ. And while posterity might maliciously discover sensual pleasure on Saint Teresa's face, sensuality took the form of a pseudo-familiarity in the times of state socialism. Politicians used to speak in an undefined plural sense and, if you misbehaved, you were told off by the police, before being persecuted. The state-father violated and cared for his children, and the children, in hatred or obedience, were unable to detach themselves from this omnipotent – and always male – figure. In the chaos of the dissolving system, an enormous opportunity to grow up emerged. In the summer of 1989, in the massive demonstrations on the streets of Budapest, for the first time in my life I felt that we were all grown-up citizens, able to express our feelings and opinions, without any need for outside instructions or protection. Compared to this, the latest discouraging developments seem to suggest that a new style of 'phallocratic dictator-ship' (Thomas Mastnak's expression) is taking the place of socialist paternalism – apparently in most of the Eastern European countries.

It is also worth pondering why the opposite of political and sexual repression is not freedom, but its imitation. As a consequence of political and economic liberalization Hungary has been flooded with pornogra-phy. One million 'erotic and pornographic' magazines are published a month in a country of ten million inhabitants. If nothing else, this fact shows the frightening poverty of human relationships and the lack of a sensual culture. As if the country were taking the worst of both systems; pornography and religious hypocrisy, oppressed sexual needs and open violence.

In the big liberation of Eastern Europe women have become primary targets, objects and beneficiaries of consumption. While bombarded on the one hand with images of the happy traditional family, on the other hand they get the big offer of the new consumerism. In an avalanche of advertisements, new shops and services, imported models of Western lifestyle, a new type of consumption culture is presented to them. The now available good cars, nice furniture, a whole range of household gadgets, sophisticated clothes, food items and so on, make life easier and more pleasant. Their impact in countries like the Soviet Union or Romania must be even more dramatic, because there the setting up of a tampon factory or the provision of automatic washing machines is a real qualitative revolution. In Hungary, where living standards were traditionally higher than those of its Eastern neighbours, the new opportunities for consumption will have different social effects. A growing sector of society will be unable to afford them, while for the smaller, enriched part they are becoming the norm. And because women play a crucial role in promoting and using the fruits of consumerism, the female society is bound to show and suffer more the effects of growing social differentiation.

The present situation of women in Hungary creates a huge need and space for independent women's movements. Apart from the difficulties already mentioned, they will have to face the same troubles as other feminist movements do everywhere in the world. Although they also have some important general issues, like the need for women's economic and political emancipation, equal rights, etc., their ultimate scenario is in the realm of everyday personal life: how one feels walking on a street, travelling alone, going to public places, how difficult it is to find a place in the productive system or to express interests through the media, how natural it feels to communicate with others, known or alien, men or women. Small-scale, personal-level everyday struggles, without spectacular breakthroughs and public acknowledgements, are very characteristic of grass-roots movements – this is one reason why it is so difficult to keep them alive. In this sense the others, peace activists or Greens, are better off: their issues can more easily appear as general concerns. They may have more 'public places of battle', dams, nuclear plants, tropical forests, which can serve as uniting, general symbols of confrontation, argument and hopefully victory. And even so, they become really efficient only when global survival is at stake: neutron bombs threatening the whole human race, ecological damage destroying the whole earth. Women's movements can hardly present anything like this, but they still can represent the other side of any current coin, on behalf of the threatened, oppressed and humiliated. They may also fight publicly, and might even win in certain cases, but at the end of the day they can only win behind the closed doors of their homes. And for that, the whole society has to change. That is the reason why women's movements have the potential to become the new universal movement for freedom and democracy.

And the Eastern European contribution to this might be enormous, because women there have a huge amount of active knowledge about open and subtle repression, mechanisms of deception, the importance of the intimate sphere. They also carry the energy of awakening, which Western women in their relatively comfortable position might already have forgotten. They are starting to build up from the scratches and will have an enormous open space to discover, in a society where feminism was presented as a threat or something utterly ridiculous both by the media and by public opinion. Hungarian history, for example, was never rethought from the women's point of view, even the – few – outstanding figures of political struggles or art were considered peripheral, parts of a less important, hidden history. It is rather telling that one of last year's bestsellers, a novel called *Seventeen Swans*, a shocking fictive insight into the life of a young, working-class gypsy woman, was written by a man, Peter Esterhazy. Now women might begin to live and write their own history. With the discovery of their womanhood, a whole new dimension of their life will emerge, rewarding lots of pleasures and pain, that may become a huge social energy.

But for the time being, I wish they could organize themselves and gather strength to say the second 'no' to the offers presented to them by the new socio-political situation. And perhaps the time will come to be able to say 'yes' as well.

Note

Yudit Kiss is an economist working on parallels in the economic development of Hungary and Mexico. She is currently based at the Institute of Development Studies (IDS), University of Sussex, and is a Research Fellow at the World Institute of Development Economics Research (WIDER) of the United Nations University in Helsinki.

THE CITIZENSHIP DEBATE: Women, Ethnic Processes and the State[1]

Nira Yuval-Davis

As 1992 is fast approaching, and with all the implications of the Single European Act, many questions arise as to the nature of the future European society, and how relationships between individuals, social groupings, states and the European institutions are going to be affected and shaped.

One of the central as well as general questions which arises in this context is what will be the fate, in this 'new Europe', of those social groupings that at present have secondary access to state powers, such as ethnic minorities and women. There is a real danger that the common denominator among the different European states would be the lowest common denominator and that, while some of Europe's inhabitants would get higher degrees of freedom and mobility, others would be doubly discriminated against (Gordon, 1990).

It is not surprising, therefore, that 'citizenship' has become a very popular subject of debate recently, appropriated by both Left and Right. Citizenship, not just in the narrow formalistic meaning of having the right to carry a specific passport, but citizenship as an overall concept which sums up the relationship between the individual and the state. As Melanie Philips (1990) has put it, 'There appears to be a great yearning for it, even though no one actually knows what it is'.

This paper examines some of the problems that the treatment of the subject of citizenship in the literature reveals. In particular, the paper looks at various attempts by the Left and feminists to resolve the question of citizenship and social difference, especially in regard to ethnic minorities and women. The basic position of this paper is that, for an adequate theory of citizenship, the examination of the differential access of different categories of citizens to the state and the implications this has on relations of domination, is of central importance. At the same time these categories cannot be analyzed as unitary categories in themselves nor can citizenships in different states be analyzed as equivalent.

The point of departure of most of the studies I have read about citizenship has been the work of T. H. Marshall (1950; 1975; 1981). Although most writers are critical of some of the aspects of his work, there is a general acceptance of his notion of citizenship as 'full membership in a community', which encompasses civil, political and social rights and responsibilities. This definition has been accepted by people with a variety of theoretical perspectives.[2]

Before examining some of the more specific issues concerning citizenship and difference, one needs to evaluate the notion of 'the community' on which this approach to citizenship is based.

Part of the reason that the notion of 'the community' is being used is the wish to avoid identifying citizenship in its wide social definition simply with the nation-state (Hall and Held, 1989). Citizenship originally emerged as an ideology in the Greek Polis, where it was confined to cities. These days as well, there is a need to be able to relate citizenship to local politics, especially around ventures such as the GLC and other radical local authorities in Britain during the eighties. On the other hand, as mentioned above, with the development of the Single European Act and with the processes of economic and communicative globalization which progressively limit the autonomy of nation-states, citizenship must also be analyzed in international if not actually global terms. The notion of 'the community' is so vague as to extend from a village into the 'global village'. However, it also encompasses inherent assumptions which are detrimental to a politics of difference (Cain and Yuval-Davis, 1990).

One assumption is that of an organic wholeness. The community is a 'natural' social unit. It is 'out there' and one can either belong to it or not. Any notion of internal difference within the 'community', therefore, is subsumed to this organic construction. It can be either a functional difference which contributes to the smooth and efficient working of 'the community', or it is an anomaly, a pathological deviation. Moreover, the 'naturalness' of the 'community' assumes given boundaries – it allows for internal growth and probably differentiation, but not for ideological reconstructions.

Furthermore, it assumes a given collectivity. It does not approach it as an ideological and material construction, whose boundaries, structures and norms are a result of constant processes of struggles and negotiations, or more general social developments. Any dynamic notion of 'citizenship' must start from the processes which construct the collectivity and not just assume it.

This is true even when we are discussing passive, rather than just active notions of citizenship – to use Bryan Turner's typology. Turner contrasted the development of citizenship in Germany, France, Holland and the United States (accepting Mann's critique of Marshall's history of citizenship as constructed virtually only around the historical example of the UK). On the basis of his comparative overview, Turner identified two major variables, out of which he developed four types of citizenship. The first variable concerns the passive or active nature of the citizenship – whether it was developed from above (via the state) or from below (via local and workplace struggles, such as trade unions), the second concerns the relationship of the public and private sectors within civil society. An example of citizenship which combines active citizenship with strong emphasis on the public domain would be, according to Turner, the French revolutionary tradition; for active, more private citizenship, American liberalism; passive and public is Turner's characterization of the English case; and passive and private, German Fascism.

Without entering into an empirical evaluation of each of Turner's classifications, his whole approach is somewhat problematic. Although Turner expands the comparative basis on which he examines constructions of citizenship, and recognizes that citizenship cannot be examined as an homogeneous notion across different states (as well as in different historical periods), he still limits it to Western societies. There might be an argument which would historically connect the emergence of ideologies of citizenship with Western traditions. However, even if this were true, which is debatable in itself, it is quite clear that nowadays some notion of citizenship exists in all states. Although it might be the case that, in most of them, citizenship has been imposed from above and its models imported from colonial powers, nevertheless the result is a far more heterogeneous picture than the one portrayed by Turner. For example, Egyptian citizenship, especially of people from the rural areas, would no doubt fall under the rubric of passive and private. Yet the difference between this mode of citizenship and that of German Fascism is surely at least as great as that between the French and the American. Turner's classifications assume basic similarities in the civil societies of all his examples.

Assumptions concerning the nature of civil society present another basic problem when thinking about the construction of citizenship. This can be found in Marshall's work and that of most of his followers and was already present in Hegel's and Marx's writings when they developed the notion of civil society. With all the differences between their approaches, there is a common assumption about the overlap of the boundaries of civil and political society. This is not to say, of course, that they assume that all those who are included in civil society enjoy also citizenship rights. Marx's discussion of civil society was developed in relation to his argument in favour of giving the Jews citizenship rights. Marshall's work constructs an evolutionary model in which gradually more and more people who are members of the civil society acquire citizenship rights. But the boundaries of the 'society' in all these models are virtually static – the differentiation between civil and political societies is a functional differentiation concerning the same national collectivity or 'community' and the people within it.

As Stuart Hall and David Held (1989) point out, however, in real politics, the main, if not the only arena in which questions of citizenship have remained alive until recently, at least in the West, has been in relation to questions of race and immigration.

Debates around issues of the citizenship of ethnic and racial minorities have concentrated on all levels of citizenship – civil, political and social. However, the primary concern of many relevant struggles and debates has been around an even more basic right – the right to enter, or, once having entered, the right to remain in a specific country. Constructing boundaries according to various inclusionary and exclusionary criteria, which relate to ethnic and racial divisions as well as class and gender divisions, is one of the main arenas of struggle concerning citizenship that remain completely outside the agenda of Marshallian theories of citizenship. The 'freedom of movement within the European community', the Israeli Law of Return and the Patriality clause in British immigration legislation, are all instances of ideological, often racist constructions of boundaries which allow unrestricted immigration to some and block it completely to others.

Even when questions of entry and settlement have been resolved, the concerns of people of ethnic minorities might be different from those of other members of the society. For example, their right to formal citizenship might depend upon the rules and regulations of their country of origin as well as those of the country where they live, as well as the relationship between the two. Thus, people from some Caribbean islands who have been settled in Britain for years were told that they could not have a British passport because their country does not recognize dual citizenship and because they had not declared on time their intent to renounce the citizenship of their country of origin after it received independence. Concern over relatives and fear of not being allowed to visit their country of origin prevent others (such as Iranians and Turks) from giving up their original citizenship. Thus, although they might spend the rest of their lives in another country, they would have, at best, limited political rights in it. Also, given specific combinations of nationality laws, children can be born stateless in countries like Israel and Britain. Such countries confer citizenship on those whose parents are citizens rather than on those born in the country.

Immigrants can also be deprived of social rights enjoyed by other members of the society. Often, the right of entry to a country is conditional on a commitment by the immigrant that neither s/he nor any other member of their family will claim any welfare benefits from the state. Proof of a sizeable fortune in the bank can be used to override national/racial quotas for the right to settle in a country.

The most problematic aspects of citizenship rights for racial and ethnic minorities relate to their social rights and to the notion of multiculturalism (see, for example, Bhaku Parekh, 1990; Laksiri Jayasuriya, 1990). The whole notion of social rights, as it has developed in the welfare state and been described by Marshall and others, assumes a notion of difference, as determined by social needs. In the words of Edwards (1988: 135):

> Those with similar needs ought to get similar resources and those with different needs, different resources, or – more succinctly – treatment as equals rather than equal treatment.

As originally envisaged by Beveridge and others, social-welfare rights were linked directly to class difference. Welfare rights were aimed at improving the quality of life of the working classes as well as the smooth working of capitalism. Marshall calls it 'the Hyphenated society' (1981), in which there are inevitable tensions between a capitalist economy, a welfare state and the requirements of the modern state.

The debate about multiculturalism and citizenship has concentrated on two critical issues:

> One is the centrality of needs in the collective provision of welfare and the other is the difficult question of boundaries of need in claiming for one's right. (Jayasuriya, 1990: 23)

The question of a collective provision of needs relates to policies of positive action aimed at group rather than individual rights. Multiculturalist policies construct the population, or – more correctly – the poor and working classes, in terms of ethnic and racial collectivities with collective needs, based on their different culture as well as their structural disadvantages. Resistance to these policies has been expressed by claims that constructing employment and welfare policies in terms of group rights can conflict with individual rights and are therefore discriminatory, but generally it has been widely accepted that in order to overcome the practical effects of racism rather than just its ideology, collective provisions and positive action based on group membership are the only effective measures to be taken (Burney, 1988; Cain and Yuval-Davis, 1990).

The question becomes more problematic when the provision relates not to differential treatment in terms of access to employment or welfare but to what has been defined as the different cultural needs of different ethnicities. These can vary from the provision of interpreters to the provision of funds to religious organizations. In the most extreme cases, as in the debates around Aborigines on the one hand and Muslim minorities around the Rushdie Affair on the other, there have been claims for enabling the minorities to operate according to their own customary and religious legal systems. While the counter arguments have ranged from the fact that this would imply a *de facto* apartheid system to arguments about social unity and political hegemony, those who support these claims have seen it as a natural extrapolation of the minorities' social and political rights. This raises the question of how one defines the boundaries of citizens' rights. Jayasuriya (1990), distinguishes between needs, which require satisfaction by the state, and wants, which fall outside the public sector and are to be satisfied within the private domain.

The differentiation between the public and private domain plays a central role in delineating boundaries of citizenship in the literature. Turner, as mentioned above, has anchored his typology of citizenship on the extent to which the state enters or abstains from entering the private domain. However, as the examples above show,[3] the dichotomous constructions of private/public spheres are culturally specific in themselves. The whole debate on multiculturalism stumbles on the fact that the boundaries of difference, as well as the boundaries of social rights, are determined by specific hegemonic, maybe universalistic, but definitely not universal, discourses.

However, the differentiation between the public and private domains on which so much of the citizenship discourse hinges is not just culture specific – it is also gender specific. Feminist critique has attacked and successfully demolished this differentiation already years ago (Wilson, 1978; Eisenstein, 1984). It is the state and the public arena which structures and determines the boundaries of the private domain – it is not pre-given. In the welfare state it is not only the civil sector – the economy, the production of culture and education, and the voluntary sector – which is largely structured by the state, but also, in what is considered to be the private domain, the family and the household. This does not mean that the state is unitary in its practices, its intentions or its effects – but unlike some other theorizations of the state, the position of this paper is that it is important to retain the concept of the state, in order to be able to retain an adequate political analysis of the power relations involved. As Floya Anthias and I argued (1989: 5):

> We can specify the state in terms of a body of institutions which are centrally organized around the intentionality of control with a given apparatus of enforcement at its command and basis.

The state, however, cannot be understood as a neutral universalistic institution. It has its own history and its own material and ideological origins and effects.

Feminist critiques have highlighted the sexist bias inherent in this construction. Carol Pateman (1988), for instance, has shown how the whole social philosophy which was at the base of the rise of the notion of state citizenship, far from being universalistic, was constructed in terms of the 'Rights of Man'. Ursula Vogel (1989) has shown that women were not simply latecomers to citizenship rights, as in Marshall's evolutionary model. Their exclusion was part and parcel of the construction of the entitlement of men to democratic participation which

> conferred citizen status not upon individuals as such, but upon men in their capacity as members and representatives of a family (i.e., a group of non-citizens). (Vogel, 1989: 2)

Unlike in Marshall's scheme where political rights followed civil rights, married women have still not been given full civil and legal rights. And, as Vogel points out, the image of the Thatcherite 'Active Citizen' which has emerged these days in Britain, is still portrayed in the image of the man as responsible head of his family. The construction by the state of relationships in the private domain, i.e., marriage and the family, is what has determined women's status as citizens within the public domain.

An interesting question in this respect is the possible effect of the participation of women in their own rights not only in the civil labour market, but also in the military (Yuval-Davis, 1985; and forthcoming). Some feminist organizations (NOW in the USA, ANMLAE in Nicaragua, and others) have fought for the inclusion of women on an equal footing to that of men in the military, arguing that once women share with men the ultimate citizen's duty – to die for one's country, they would be able to gain also equal citizenship rights to that of men. In the recent Gulf War women fought together with the men in the American army, in almost indistinguishable tasks as well as uniforms.[4] This experience raises several sobering thoughts in relation to this kind of argument.

Firstly, the experience of some of the women who had to leave small babies behind (mostly to the care of their own mothers, as often the husbands of these women serve in the army as well), show that feminist equal-opportunity slogans can be used to create further pressures on women, rather than promote their rights. Secondly, their experience shows that the differential relations of power between men and women continue also within the military domain, including sexual harassment, and therefore it cannot automatically be considered as empowering women. Thirdly, and probably most importantly, this argument ignores the general social and political context of the military and its use. Empowering women to play global policemen on equal footing with men, is not what feminists (at least not socialist, antiracist feminists) should be engaged in.

Given these arguments, one might sum up with the claim that the treatment of the category of women, as well as that of ethnic and racial minorities, challenges common notions about citizenship which have been constructed around the individual rights of men within a class-differentiated society.

However, although valid, the above statement nevertheless reflects a major flaw within the discourses of both antiracist and feminist critiques of citizenship. They have tended to treat both women and ethnic/racial minorities as homogeneous categories. Comparing the status of women to that of minorities in itself assumes women to be members of the dominant group and the minorities to be men. Women of majority and minority groups are affected differently by sexist limitations to their citizenship rights. This can concern their rights to enter the country or bring in their husbands, their rights to receive child benefits or their right to confer citizenship on their children – to mention just a few examples (see, the WING book (1985) on differential effects of the British New Nationality Law of 1981). Similarly, men and women of ethnic and racial minorities suffer from gender specific racisms – their rights to bring their families to the country can differ, their participation in political organizations, and a whole host of civil and social rights which differentiate between the sexes (see Bryan *et al.*, 1988; Anthias and Yuval-Davis, forthcoming).

Given the heterogeneity, not only among women and ethnic and racial minorities, but among all citizens – on the basis of class, gender, ethnicity and race, stage in the life cycle, sexuality, ability, and more – some writers on the question of citizenship have developed a postmodern critique of the notion:

> In this society citizenship is an archaic term . . . because social evolution
> has not only gone beyond the social context of its origin, but also beyond
> the welfare industrial society in which Marshall placed it in dialectical
> relation to equality. Society has changed so much that the social
> prerequisites for citizenship – rationality and solidarity – seem to have
> disappeared . . . Contemporary society killed the Enlightenment's modern
> individual, first by commodification, then by communication. (Wexler,
> 1990: 164–5)

According to Wexler, for the notion of citizenship to be meaningful again, it needs to adapt to the present semiotic society, in which exists 'the free play of signifiers without reference'. Culture, narrations of collective memories and identity politics are offered as the basis of this new mode of citizenship, although Wexler admits that:

> How much postmodern collective identity projects touch the structurally
> reproductive energies fed by class division is not clear to me. (1990: 173)

Feminist and antiracist critiques of traditional ideologies of citizenship have, in their limited way, expanded our understanding of the complexity of both the analytical and political issues which are involved. Postmodernist analyses, by abolishing the notions of grand narratives and universal signifiers, have abandoned not only any attempt at general comprehension of the issues involved but also any universal discourse which can be used as a criteria for evaluating specific narratives and specific collective endeavours (Zubaida, 1989; Moghadam, 1989; Yuval-Davis, forthcoming).

This, however, is not a necessary result of accounting for difference. For example, another perspective from which to look at the question of the multiplexity of difference and citizenship emerges in the work of Anne Showstack Sassoon:

> While criticizing the abstract, universal dimensions of the concept (of
> citizenship), what takes place is a complex redefinition of the individual
> . . . In a sense what we have in common is our separateness, our

uniqueness, the fact that we are different, our sense of being alone. Disarticulating and making concrete the abstract concept of the individual, helps us to recognize something else: viewed from one facet or another of our identity or our subjectivity, we each belong to a partial group, we are each an 'other', whatever our race, gender, nationality. (forthcoming: 14)

Anne Sassoon's perspective, while recognizing and cultivating multidimensional difference and differentiation in a similar way to the postmodern discourse, retains the reality of these differences and attaches references to the postmodern 'free play of signifiers'. However, in her anxiety to acknowledge all forms of difference and their unique combinations within different individuals, Sassoon portrays a society composed of minorities. In other words, she *de facto* excludes the crucial dimension of the power relations between the different categories to which people belong and the complex dynamics of exclusionary/inclusionary struggles which exist between them.

There is no space in this paper to enter into the complex debate around 'identity politics' and its relationship to antiracist and feminist struggles (Yuval-Davis, forthcoming). Nor can we develop here a coherent theory of citizenship which would take full account of the various critiques which I have mentioned in this paper. As a general guideline for such a theory, however, I would like to make the following points.

Firstly, such a theory should not take the state as a unitary given, but should retain the notion of the state as the focus of the intentionality of control. At the same time it should acknowledge that not all levels of the state, nor all states have the same degrees of control (or even its intentionality). The relative positioning of different states in the 'New World Order' is a case in point.

Secondly, such a theory should not assume 'society' or 'the community' as a given, but should see struggles over the construction of their boundaries as one of the major foci of struggles on the nature of citizenship within a specific society. This is one of the major conjunctures in which analysis of racism relates to the heart of theorizing state and society.

Thirdly, such a theory should not accept the boundaries between the public and private domains as a given but again as a focus for struggles which determine gender divisions of labour as well as ethnic patterns of cultural hegemony within the society. At the same time, such a theory should not automatically equate participation in the public domain with a higher degree of empowerment.

Furthermore, such a theory should not assume a Eurocentric perspective for developing the framework of its assertions. Citizenship today is a global phenomenon and less culturally specific tools are needed to analyze it.

And last but not least – such a theory should develop a notion of difference which would retain the multiplexity and multidimensionality of identities within contemporary society, but without losing sight of the differential power dimension of different collectivities and groupings within the society and the variety of relationships of domination/subordination between them.

As the saying goes: Equality (and difference) is not *only* in the eye of the beholder . . .

Notes

Nira Yuval-Davis is Reader in Ethnic and Gender Studies at Thames Polytechnic. She is the editor with Floya Anthias of *Woman-Nation-State* and has written extensively on gender, racism and nationalism. She is currently editing a collection with Gita Sahgal: *Refusing Holy Orders: Women and Fundamentalism in Britain*, which will be published shortly by Virago.

1 An early draft of this paper was presented at the Racism and Migration in Europe conference in Hamburg, Institut fur Sozialforschung, September 1990.
2 For example, such as those of Stuart Hall and David Held (1989), Sheila Allen and Mary Macey (1990) and the Speaker's Commission on Citizenship (1990).
3 And as Turner himself argues when he compares Christian and Muslim ideologies.
4 These uniforms have been designed for ABC (Atomic, biological and chemical) warfare which seem to be quite indifferent to the 'type' of human 'bodies' underneath them.

References

ALLEN, Sheila and MACEY, Mary (1990) 'At the cutting edge of citizenship: race & ethnicity in Europe 1992'. Paper presented at the conference New Issues in Black Politics, Warwick, May.

ANTHIAS, Floya and YUVAL-DAVIS, Nira (1989) 'Introduction' in YUVAL-DAVIS and ANTHIAS (editors), *Woman-Nation-State* London: Macmillan.

ANTHIAS, Floya and YUVAL-DAVIS, Nira (forthcoming) *Racialized Boundaries* London: Routledge.

BRESHEETH, Haim and YUVAL-DAVIS, Nira (forthcoming) *The Gulf War: Another Perspective* London: Zed Books.

BRYAN, B. *et al.* (1988) *The Heart of the Race* London: Virago.

BURNEY, Elizabeth (1988) *Steps to Social Equality: Positive Action in a Negative Climate* London: Runnymede Trust.

CAIN, Harriet and YUVAL-DAVIS, Nira (1990) ' "The Equal Opportunities Community" and the Anti-Racist Struggle' *Critical Social Policy* Autumn.

EISENSTEIN, Zilla (1984) *Feminism and Sexual Equality: A Crisis in Liberal America* New York: Monthly Review Press.

GORDON, Paul (1990) *Fortress Europe* London: Runnymede Trust.

HALL, Stuart and HELD, David (1989) 'Citizens and citizenship' in HALL and JACQUES (1989).

HALL, Stuart and JACQUES, Martin (1989) editors, *New Times* London: Lawrence & Wishart.

JAYASURIYA, L. (1990) 'Multiculturalism, citizenship and welfare: new directions for the 1990s'. Paper presented at the 50th Anniversary Lecture Series, Dept. of Social Work and Social Policy, University of Sydney.

MCLELLAN, David and SAYERS, Sean (forthcoming) editors, *Democracy & Socialism* London: Macmillan.

MARSHALL, T. H. (1950) *Citizenship and Social Class* Cambridge: Cambridge University Press.

MARSHALL, T. H. (1975) (original edition 1965) *Social Policy in the Twentieth Century* London: Hutchinson.

MARSHALL, T. H. (1981) *The Right To Welfare and Other Essays* London: Heinemann Educational Books.

MOGHADAM, Val (1989) 'Against Eurocentrism and nativism: a review essay on Samir Amin's *Eurocentrism* and other texts' *Socialism and Democracy* Fall/Winter.

MOGHADAM, Val (forthcoming) editor, *Women and Identity Politics* Oxford: Clarendon.

PAREKH, B. (1990) 'The Rushdie affair and the British press: some salutary lessons' in *Free Speech*, a report of a CRE seminar, London.

PHILIPS, Melanie (1990) 'Citizenship sham in our secret society' *Guardian* 14 September.

SHOWSTACK SASSOON, Anne (forthcoming) 'Equality and difference: the emergence of a new concept of citizenship' in MCLELLAN and SAYERS (forthcoming).

TURNER, Bryan (1990a) 'Outline of a theory of citizenship' *Sociology* Vol. 24, No. 2.

TURNER, Bryan (1990b) editor, *Theories of Modernity and Postmodernity* London: Sage.

VOGEL, Ursula (1989) 'Is citizenship gender specific?'. Paper presented at PSA Annual Conference, April.

WEXLER, Philip (1990) 'Citizenship in a semiotic society' in TURNER (1990b).

WILSON, Elizabeth (1977) *Women and the Welfare State* London: Tavistock.

WING (Women, Immigration and Nationality Group) (1985) *Worlds Apart: Women under Immigration and Nationality Laws* London: Pluto Press.

YUVAL-DAVIS, Nira (1985) 'Front and rear: the sexual division of labour in the Israeli army' *Feminist Studies* Vol. 11, No. 3.

YUVAL-DAVIS, Nira (forthcoming) 'Identity politics and women's ethnicity' in MOGHADAM (forthcoming).

YUVAL-DAVIS, Nira (forthcoming) 'The gendered Gulf War: women's citizenship and modern warfare' in BRESHEETH and YUVAL-DAVIS (forthcoming).

YUVAL-DAVIS, Nira (forthcoming) *Women, Ethnicity and Empowerment* London: Sage.

ZUBAIDA, Sami (1988) 'Islam, cultural nationalism and the Left' *Review of Middle East Studies* No. 4.

FORTRESS EUROPE AND MIGRANT WOMEN

Mirjana Morokvasic

One of the best-read German newspapers published an interview with Mr WB, owner of a marriage bureau, in which Mr WB praises the 'goods' he has on offer for his potential clients, German men: a Polish wife (to be) for only 390DM. The client is free to select four among some 1,500 photos. For each he gets to know as much as her WEIGHT and AGE, sometimes accompanied by attributes like 'super sexy' or 'extremely full bosom'. He can try them out, and even make another selection of four. If HE is not satisfied SHE goes back to Poland. WB's speciality was South East Asian women but he is now switching to Poles for whom there is a growing demand, especially among retired, divorced and not directly well-off men. No German woman would take them – but for Poles they are good enough. Besides, 'Poles are cheaper than Asians both in terms of capital investment and in maintenance: what is a cheap train ticket in comparison to a 5,000DM air ticket from Bangkok or Manila? And, whereas a Thai is unprepared for cold German winters – one has to buy her clothes – a Pole brings her own boots and a fur coat. And she is as good in bed and industrious in the kitchen'. (*Bild*, 9 January 1991)

Arranged marriages of this kind, and trade with women in different European states in which sex industries are flourishing are the most perverse facet of the European fortress and its treatment of *others*. Since the opening of East-West frontiers these agencies have been shifting their source of women from the Far East to nearby Poland, Hungary and soon, says WB, to Romania and Bulgaria. *Perestroika* and the collapse of communism are creating new opportunities for this sector which counts some 3,000 agencies in Germany. If each of them successfully arranges about 300–400 marriages a year, as WB claims he does, then the usual estimates about the number of women being brought into the country through the organized channels of trade into prostitution and dubious marriages are too low (several thousand from Asia). (*Tagesspiegel*, 3 February 1991; *Frankfurter Allgemeine Zeitung*, 25 June 1987)

Marriage bureau

Two trends characterize European migration phenomena on the eve of 1992. One is the settlement and stabilization of immigrant populations: about 15 million foreigners are residents of different West European states. Most of them have been there for over ten years. Almost half are women: in Germany 49 per cent (according to the latest Population Census of 1987), in France about 43 per cent (Population Census of 1982), to mention just the two most significant receiving countries.

The second trend is the increasing mobility of populations which had only slowed down for a while after the generalized migration stop of 1973/74. This present mobility is mostly due to traditional migratory flows from the South to the North and the newest East-West ones. The potential for new migrations is high due to political and economic pressures and ethnic conflicts. But possibilities for legal immigration to the industrialized developed European countries are extremely re-stricted: only people recognized as 'nationals' of one of the member states (basically ethnic Germans from ex-communist countries so far), those who can prove that they are politically persecuted or those who want to join family members or enter for marriage purposes are admitted; there is no admission to the labour market except for a very limited number of entries on a short-term contract basis for specific economic sectors in need of seasonal workforces. That is why un-documented flows are increasing, as are the various organized channels for getting people in, including specialized marriage bureaux.

The nation-states of Europe have followed the exclusion/inclusion strategies in their treatment of foreigners and immigrants, selectively integrating some (those who conform to the racial, ethnic lines present within the resident population) and keeping others out. At present, the opening to the East is followed by closing doors to the South. The combination of universalistic and nationalistic principles have produced insiders and outsiders with boundaries between them flexible enough to suit the needs of the labour market.

Among the immigrant/minority population and among migrants, women are those who suffer most from this treatment by the state, whether directly or indirectly, although the legislation is not directly more discriminatory *vis-à-vis* migrant women than migrant men (Tapinos, 1990), all other aspects being equal. But other aspects are not equal. Because, as Boyd (1991) says, some groups, including women, more than others, fall into certain classification categories used in policies. Thus migrant women end up having access to a very limited number of positions in society and in the labour market. The explanation for this situation has far too often adopted the 'blame the victim' paradigm: it has been assumed that migrant women's culture of origin, their lack of preparation for modern, urban societies and work are responsible for their situation and lack of choices. This strong focus on mostly socially constructed, cultural distance, masks other social forces and barriers, often state violence, which these women have to face and fight against.

I have been arguing that the position of migrant women in industrialized developed societies is determined by the articulation of different power relationships, the most important being gender, class relationships and migrant women's relation to the nation-state as immigrants, foreigners or members of ethnic minorities (Morokvasic, 1987a). Of course, migrant women have been in these relationships on the non-power side, and the accumulation of the situations of non-power is hardly likely, in itself, to lead to the improvement of their situation.

Migration and gender

Gender divisions crosscut other social relations in a society. It is a socially constructed category which produces asymmetries and inequalities which assign almost universally more value to men's characteristics, behaviour and beliefs than to women's.

Both societies of origin and societies of immigration are to a different extent and in different ways marked by sexist ideologies. In many societies of origin patriarchal structures prevail, inheritance laws discriminate against women and even when direct legal discrimination does not exist, women are, in practice, discriminated against. In the immigration countries women are incorporated into sexually segregated labour markets, usually at the lowest stratum of female-type jobs in modern technology industries or in those sectors which remained labour intensive and were obliged to turn to the cheapest workforce in order to remain competitive. In the society at large they encounter a new world which in a different way also discriminates against women.

Gender is an important factor in assessing decision-making processes prior to migrations and conducive to migrations, in assessing the role of men and women in family strategies of migration and in networking. Social constraints on mobility or on observance of specific social norms have more impact on the emigration of women than of men: marital discord and physical violence, the impossibility of divorce, or unhappy and broken marriages (Little, 1973), disadvantages in terms of property rights (Abadan-Unat, 1977), or the transgression of rigidly defined sex-role behaviour like having out-of-wedlock children (Morokvasic, 1987), have been mentioned as situations provoking the emigration of women, but not of men.

Gender-specific expectations combined with different economic opportunities at the place of origin and destination can effect the differing patterns of migratory movement of women and men. It has been observed since Ravenstein (1885 and 1889) that women are more likely than men to be in short-distance migrations. A number of studies have also pointed to the commuting aspect of the migration of women (Balan, 1988; Fernandez-Kelly, 1974). My ongoing research on East-West migrations points to the commuting feature of moves in particular among Polish traders and women going into domestic service: the latter have set up a system of rotation so that they can go home at regular intervals while their replacements takes up their cleaning jobs in the meantime. Undocumented female aliens cross the Mexican-US border in both directions more frequently than men. 'Men, socialized to act as providers, are expected to send money and/or presents to their families in Mexico and to visit occasionally. Women, on the other hand, are expected to take full responsibility for the daily care of their children and their homes. If they must migrate, they must also return to the homestead more frequently. Thus, the widespread ideological notion that "man was made to work, and woman to care for the house" impinges upon the likelihood of crossing the border.' (Fernandez-Kelly, 1974: 213) In rural-urban migrations young women are 'selected out' for migration because at home they do not have any viable alternatives and in the cities they can get employment as domestics (Young, 1982; Trager, 1984; Khoo, Smith and Fawcett, 1984).

Constraints on the spatial mobility of women in some societies may prevent the majority of women from moving but also, paradoxically, force women who have been socially marginalized to move (Pittin, 1984; Morokvasic, 1984).

Gender has also been important for assessing social changes resulting from or related to migration, although systematic comparison between pre- and post-migration experiences is lacking. Although, theoretically, one could expect that a new context could lead to the challenging of gender-specific roles and expectations, often one observes only a somewhat more satisfactory redefinition of those roles (Pessar,

1984), or adaptation to new circumstances (Morokvasic, 1987a). It could be argued that, since women and men have unequal access to resources, paid employment through migration does not lead straightforwardly to improving the position of women relative to men. (Morokvasic, 1984; Tienda and Booth, 1991).

Migrant women and the nation-state

Nation-states of Europe protect their nationals and maintain a system of exclusion of others according to a hierarchy: their own citizens first, EEC citizens second, non-EEC citizens last, and among the latter distinguish according to different residence permits, ethnic and racial origins, etc. Their restrictive policies have admitted migrants as guest workers, their residence status largely dependent on their status on the labour market. This has had implications not only directly for those who could no longer legitimize their stay by work but also for those who came as spouses and who, for up to four years, were not considered as residents in their own right. In both cases, women rather than men have been experiencing the consequences of this regulation: they are more likely to lose jobs in the process of restructuring and are therefore more likely to lose their status as workers and related residence status. In Germany a person receiving welfare aid is expellable. Women are also more likely to join husbands in the migratory chain than vice versa and therefore they are less likely to have a permit in their own right. As a result, during the years of institutional dependency on her husband's permit, a woman may not, for instance, be in a position to resolve a potential conflict in the couple by separation. She may have either to tacitly accept conflict, often violence or, if not, put herself in a situation where the risk of being deported is high and left to the arbitrary decision of the administration.

A guest-worker system looks at human beings only as instruments of the labour market. In that situation children are unwelcome. In the ex-GDR, where female guest workers were given the pill upon their arrival, one could witness a *déjà vu* situation, in a modernized version: Vietnamese women workers had a medical check and a pregnancy test at the selection stage, as were Yugoslav women workers heading for the FRG some twenty years ago. But twenty years ago tests were not as reliable as they are now, pills and abortions not available (Morokvasic, 1984) and, if pregnant, Yugoslavs undertook long trips by train to abort in Yugoslavia in order to keep their jobs. The socialist state of the GDR also *confronted* guest workers with the alternative: either an abortion (offering facilities on the spot), or return. Meanwhile, in the Western part of the country, memories are short and analogies hard to accept. But the law must be applied: an asylum-seeker whose demand was refused was in her sixth month of pregnancy when she was expelled! The state treats cases individually, separating families, husband and wife, if their cases are decided differently.

A large proportion of women who came to Germany as guest workers left their children at home. Several surveys have pointed to separation from children and dislocated families as one of the features of migrants' situations in the receiving country (Mehrländer, 1981; Morokvasic, 1987a; Nauck, 1987). Separation was, in the beginning, accepted by women as a temporary evil since it fitted into the temporary orientation that migrants in the beginning believed in. It paralleled a situation in which combining childrearing and full-time work in factories was impossible and expensive. A generation of youngsters has been brought up by grandparents or relatives. The state made sure to prevent late reunification of children with parents by limiting the age at which children could be reunited with their parents (in their own interests, of course).

The nation-state which protects the family and considers it as a basic institution of society applies other principles in the case of immigrants: a typical migrant family has had its members separated for a long period of time. Nauck (1987) shows that only about 10 per cent of families came to Germany together, at the same time, and that they were well off, urbanized middle class who could afford the move together.

The receiving state also uses its own definition of the family, which in some immigrant groups isolates women from important family networks. Or, if exceptions are made, this can happen only on a temporary basis: according to a decision of an administrative court in Mannheim, Germany (reg. no. 13 S 268/90) a Turkish grandmother is to be expelled from the country. She was admitted to take care of her grandchildren; they are now nine and eleven and 'old enough to be taken care of by another person'. It is argued 'that the public interest in limiting immigration is of more importance than the special relationship between the grandmother and the children that has developed over the years'.

Immigration of fiancés in some countries has been subjected to virginity controls (Wilson, 1978). The new legislation in Germany defines naturalization as a condition for a second-generation immigrant to bring a bride(groom) from the home country.

Depending on their ethnicity, women experience racism, xenophobia or various forms of paternalism differently. This indeed can be independent from their acquisition of the nationality of their country of residence. But whether they are nationals/citizens or not, they are mostly stigmatized as *others*. The relationship of women migrants to the nation-state and its institutions bears the mark of colonialist ideology. The colonial past in some countries or economic supremacy in others is the stigma that migrant and minority women have to cope with long before the emigration has taken place, let alone after. The degree to which and the way in which this has become a part of their own personal history and the treatment they receive upon immigration varies with their ethnicity and so will their reactions to the new environment.

Migrant women at work

Reliance on a migrant labour system can be seen as one of many capitalist strategies in search of an ever cheaper labour force. Even if migrants do not enter the country as labour but as asylum-seekers, or as families – which since the 1973/74 recruitment halt have been the major entry possibilities to Europe – they enter the labour market. Only, in this case, they are on an even lower rung of the wage, social-security and social-status ladder.

Migrant women can be found in jobs often below their qualifications and competence, characterized by insecurity, low wages, and high safety and health risks. They may have this in common with migrant men. The difference is that the work women do – very much like women in general – often does not fit in with the reigning ideology of work, and is poorly assessed by official data and not always recognized as an economic activity at all. They are employed in services, domestic service, petty trade, jobs with high seasonal variations like agro-industry and garments, assembling garments or electronic equipment in their own homes; they are employed as undocumented workers or have jobs for only a short period of their life. Women in these types of job may all be assessed as being outside the labour force – because they are outside the formal economy.

Official economic activity rates showing the number of migrant women active in the labour force (in 1982 it was 23.4 per cent in France and 36.8 per cent in Germany) largely underestimate their economic participation, in particular for some immigrant groups (North African in France, Turkish in Germany).

Even more than women in general, migrant women have been vulnerable to economic restructuring and were the first victims of redundancies in the garment and electronic industries. Their current unemployment rates are almost twice as high as those of native women (20 per cent in France). The shift to the service sector and general casualization of labour are tendencies that mark their situation in the labour market. The difference is that migrant women are again occupying the positions at the bottom whereas native women have greater access to white-collar jobs. This is partly due to their skills and educational level, but also to institutional discrimination which, in most European countries, prevents foreigners from entering the public-sector services.

Although the situation of some women may be socially constructed as 'outside of the labour force', it should be stressed that women have always worked. They are not 'in' and 'out' of economic activity, but they are either paid for their work or not paid, their work is either recognized as economic activity or not. The same work can be either paid activity in a formal or informal set-up, or unpaid activity at home. A woman can, for instance, sew clothes on a formal basis, in the factory, and be paid a woman's wage. Or, she can do the same work on a seasonal basis, be

Polish trader in Berlin, Winter 1990

declared a housewife and paid off the books. She can of course, do the same kind of work at home, sew clothes for her family, for no pay at all.

The fact that women's work is often seen either as an extension of women's domestic roles, or is accomplished on domestic premises, points to the crucial question of the interrelationship between women's position in the household and their position in the economic system. Migrant women's role in waged employment is not considered as their primary role, neither by them nor by their employers. Their role or role-to-be of housewife-mother legitimizes considering them as subsidiary workers and the level of their wages as complementary wages only. As Moser and Young put it, 'Women tend to be segregated into particular occupations which are carefully delimited by an ideology linking their activity to their gender, with the vast majority, therefore, working in occupations defined as having some structural resemblance to their family role' (1981: 57).

In Europe the migrant-labour system was, until 1973/74, sustained by policies which tended to limit immigration to single workers only, thereby avoiding the costs attached to maintenance of all other persons related to these workers if they were not themselves in waged employment. Women who joined these migration streams were faced with the dominant Western ideology where a breadwinner is a man and a woman a dependent, and were assigned the status of dependents, whether this dependency was genuine or not. This ideology of male support has not only shaped migrant women's social, legal and economic position in the immigration countries, but it has usually been assumed to apply even more so to their societies of origin. In Germany, for instance, where the ideal of woman as housewife has been particularly strong, Turkish women and, by means of abusive generalization, all migrant women whose labour participation has for a long time been higher than that of German women (given the demographic structure of the population), were often labelled as victims of *their* tradition, of Islam or of the male-chauvinist attitudes of their husbands. The poorly paid, insecure work these women did, appeared as nothing but a blessing of modern societies and as a means out of their oppressive traditions (Morokvasic, 1985). So the cause of restricted access to formal employment has been attributed to women's own cultural heritage and the oppression of their own societies. This, in turn, has often shaped the limited job supply for immigrant women (Saifullah-Khan, 1979; Parmar, 1982) and limited their access to occupations which were not disruptive of the supposedly cultural prescriptions of acceptable work. Their background is then used as a means of exploiting them both by native and by immigrant employers.

In these informal work situations, characteristic of much of migrant women's employment, the employer/employee relationships are regulated through social, kin, family *arrangements* and not through enforceable *work agreements*. These unwritten and unspoken contracts have strong implications for the outcome of women's work: even though they have access to work and income this may not challenge the existing power hierarchies; upward social mobility is limited and the patriarchal relations of the family are extended to work relations. These arrangements, rather than leading to independent status, increase women's dependency and thereby their vulnerability.

The extreme case is prostitution and the slave trade, the least-known aspect of migrant women's presence in Europe. According to a Dutch report on prostitution and trade in women (*Frankfurter Allgemeine Zeitung*, 25 June 1987; 'The trade routes of sex', *Guardian*, 5 April 1991), Amsterdam and Frankfurt are the European centres to which the modern slave traders bring women from Latin America, the Caribbean, South East Asia and Africa to be dispatched on to other European countries. It is estimated that about 40 per cent of women working under appalling conditions in the sex industry in Holland are 'imported'. Among an estimated 2,000 Thai women in the city of Berlin, 20–30 per cent are in prostitution (according to information from the Ban Ying German-Thai Women Association, *Tagesspiegel*, 3 March 1991). These women were attracted by false promises of a 'happy marriage' or a job as a 'waitress'. There are millions of women like them in their countries of origin. Peasants pauperized through the development of export-oriented agriculture sell their daughters into cities for work in sex centres. It is estimated that in Brazil 4.5 million women under twenty are in prostitution; in Manila 50 per cent of boys and girls are in child prostitution. In Thailand, where tourism is the prime source of hard currency, sex tourism is blooming: among several million tourists a year, 3 out of 4 are men. About half a million to a million prostitutes and entertainers are at their disposal – About 30,000 under the age of fifteen in Bangkok alone. (*Tagesspiegel*, 17 June 1990)

Most dream of going West, but the conditions there can be even worse. 'Marriage' can involve them in large debt (50,000DM) that women have to pay back by prostituting themselves. A minimum is set per week and if they do not make it the debt increases and they are brutally punished. Women who managed to escape from brothels tell of their 18-hour working day and a life in seclusion. (*Frankfurter Allgemeine Zeitung*, 25 June 1987)

Brothel owners rotate their personnel across European borders to prevent any establishment of longer connexions by these women with the outside world. Since the women are mostly illegal they can be expelled at any time. Therefore they cannot ask the police for protection even if they manage to escape. If they return to their countries of origin they are no longer accepted socially and prostitution is again the only option for them.

Articulation

These gender/class/ethnicity power relationships articulated in different ways determine to a large extent the position of migrant women, limiting their choices and freedom of movement in the extreme. As one of the women interviewed recently in Britain said: 'Being Asian, black and a woman you do not go very far in this society.' Barriers are erected when women try to get out of the professional and social space which is supposedly theirs: 'Who do you think you are?' was a bank manager's welcome to a black woman. She was enquiring about loans to start up an au-pair agency in a white-dominated, middle-class area of London.

Given their working experience, migrant women are far less likely than migrant men to benefit from legislation that might improve their status. For instance, regularizations and amnesties usually stipulate conditions which they cannot fulfil, such as continuity at work or long-term engagement: their work is marked by discontinuity and short-term, sporadic arrangements. The French legalization procedure of 1982 which benefited some 135,000 illegal immigrant workers, by-passed women: only 17 per cent of them were legalized, only slightly more in sectors where women were typically a majority (Morokvasic, 1987b). State regulatory tools and gender-specific discrimination at work combined, give a precarious condition a permanent touch.

My work on Yugoslav migrant women (Morokvasic, 1987a) suggests that it is the discrimination against them as migrants or foreigners that is the most sharply felt and tends to neutralize, to mask, the exploitation by a male (co-ethnic) employer or force a woman to stand by her husband whatever her relationship with him. Also, there is a strong interrelationship between working-class status and gender: paid work may enable women to assert their economic independence *vis-à-vis* men to an extent but this creates dependency on work and blocks possible reaction to oppressive working conditions. Besides, the unequal power distribution and decision-making in the household is seldom questioned because work experience outside the household is often unrewarding and does not represent a sufficiently attractive alternative to social recognition. Therefore, performance in household tasks may remain the only possible source for such recognition and women may accept the status quo in domestic relations. In a hostile environment they may also feel themselves to be in the same boat as their husband and look for compromises rather than change through conflict. These findings run counter to all those views in feminist research which put the central focus on the family as the primary and most significant site for women's oppression (see discussion by Stasiulis, 1987).

Migrant women have to cope with oppression and discrimination. Research on migrant women has often implied that they take their subordinate position for granted. The assumption that this subordinate position is a result of migrant women's own cultural heritage not only contributes to their victimization but also defines them as partly responsible for their situation. In practice this has led to a proliferation of helping agencies and institutionalized assistance. These used to be useful as transitory measures. Today they are often outdated in their objectives, and as services tend to control migrant women and jeopardize their own initiatives.

Polish trader in Berlin, Winter 1990

The evidence from a study on migrant women in self-employment (Morokvasic, 1988) suggests that the best help facilitates self-help. Access to self-employment can be a survival strategy when no other alternative is possible: this is the case with many immigrant women in Portugal, for instance, where the boundaries between the informal sector and self-employment are blurred. Access to waged employment in the formal sector is practically impossible. But although self-employment often masks a lack of real choices, it can also be a form of migrant women's resistance to gender-specific or minority-specific obstacles or even a way of circumventing rigid state rules. It also reflects a need for a new quality of relationships and a more independent status. The strategies they adopt or are obliged to adopt are extremely varied. Some put family needs in the forefront, setting up shops and opening restaurants in order to provide employment for family members who have no other option. Others give priority to entrepreneurial objectives while making considerable sacrifices in private life. One thing is certain: they are less able to rely on co-ethnic networks for financial support and labour than men and are therefore more bound to turn to extra-community, often women-specific, networks. Therefore, they look for new forms of solidarity, beyond the boundaries of their ethnic group – which is an important dimension of the quality of their integration into the society.

Migration, gender and change

There is some evidence in research that migrant women can find strength and power in the oppressive conditions that characterize their lives. The intensification of gender and racial subordination through wage labour may produce over time liberating potential (Wilson, 1978; Phizacklea, 1982). Parmar (1982) points to the active role of women in fighting their oppression: 'Asian women have a tradition of struggle where they have used and converted their so-called weakness into strengths and developed gender- and culturally specific forms of resistance' (1982: 264). Pittin (1984) argues that Hausa women, while projecting a self-image as victims of fate and circumstances, capitalize on male ideology in pursuit of their own objectives and priorities which may not be achievable within the confines of marriage and rural society. My own empirical investigations have shown that women, whether individually or collectively, resist rather than take their situation for granted (Morokvasic 1987a). It is resistance rather than the direct adoption of values and behaviour in the new society that is the basis for change.

People migrate in search of new opportunities to improve their situation. Does migration lead also to the redefinition of gender relations? This was the question implicitly raised in a number of studies. Theoretically, yes: previous values and behaviour, distribution of roles and the particular type of gender inequality may not be adequate to the new environment. But migration may only change the expression, the façade, not the the content of unequal relations. Behaviour may change, but the norms may still be unchanged and vice versa (Morokvasic, 1987a). In reality, one generalized answer is practically impossible, but it would be true to say that gender inequalities remain intact although some facets of gender relations may have been modified. The new environment certainly may increase women's awareness of possibilities, if not immediately then in the long run or for the generations to come (Morokvasic, 1986). But in order to speak about change one should be able to compare past and present experiences in a number of areas: participation in paid activity; income distribution and the possibility for control of earnings; distribution of household activities and decision-making. In each particular case the outcome is determined by the cultural context, by the social class of the migrants, by the interaction between gender relationships in the family and in the work situation outside the family. Most currently available evidence does not cover all these aspects. The lack of systematic pre- and post-migration evidence is the most serious gap. The pre-migration 'evidence' sometimes consists of little more than assumptions (for example, that societies of origin are 'traditional' and backward, and that gender relationships are less egalitarian than in the receiving societies) or by comparisons between migrant and native women on some out-of-context criteria (birth-rates, economic activity, etc.). A closer look at activity rates per group of origin, however, suggests that migrant women with high activity rates or those with lower birth-rates come from the countries where the activity rates are already high and birth-rates low.

Migration and access to paid employment is not an open door to improvement of women's status or to more egalitarian gender relations. It brings both gains and losses. Depending on prior experience it may strengthen the existing gender relations, increase inequalities or, on the contrary, contribute to more equal relationships. Different surveys suggest that women have been differently prepared to perceive and seize the opportunities in the new environment. It seems that women with prior experience of paid employment in an urban environment and with above-average educational levels have been better prepared to face the challenges of the new environment than other women.

On the other hand, the presence of migrants and minorities is both a chance and a challenge for European societies to develop new forms of solidarity and new forms of citizenship in multicultural Europe than those we have now as the legacy of nation-states.

Notes

Mirjana Morokvasic, Phd, is a sociologist. She holds her degrees from the Université René Descartes Paris V-Sorbonne and the Ecole Pratique des Hautes Etudes (now Ecole des Hautes Etudes en Sciences Sociales). She lectured in social psychology and the sociology of education at the Université Lille III from 1970–79 and has since been a research fellow at the Centre National de la Recherche Scientifique, Paris. Most of her work has been in the field of international migration. Her recent studies focused on female migration, and on undocumented labour, and her latest research is a comparative study of entrepreneurial strategies of self-employed immigrant and minority women in five European states. She has authored and edited a number of publications in the field of migration (among others, a special issue of *Current Sociology*, 1984, and of *International Migration Review* 1984, and a book on women in migration *Emigration und Danach*, Stroemfeld, Frankfurt 1987). She is currently conducting research on new migratory movements from Eastern Europe and transnationalization of networks at the Freie Universität Berlin. She is also co-ordinating a comparative research investigation on East-West/South-North migrations in Europe within the Migration Programme of the European Co-ordination Centre for Research and Documentation in Social Sciences, Vienna.

I would like to thank Barbara Einhorn for her encouragement, insightful comments and patience.

References

ABADAN-UNAT, Nermin (1977) 'Implications of migration on emancipation and pseudo emancipation of Turkish women' *International Migration Review*, Vol. 2, No. 1, pp. 31–57.

APPLEYARD, Reginald (1988) editor, *International Migration Today* Paris: Unesco.

BALAN, Jorge (1988) 'International migration in Latin America; trends and consequences' in APPLEYARD (1988) pp. 210–63.

BOYD, Monica (1991) 'Migrant women and integration policies'. Document prepared for the International Conference on Migration, Rome, Italy, 13–15 March.

CENTRE FOR CONTEMPORARY CULTURAL STUDIES (1982) *The Empire Strikes Back* London: Macmillan.

FERNANDEZ-KELLY, Maria Patrizia (1974) 'Mexican border industrialization, female labor force participation and migration' in NASH and FERNANDEZ-KELLY (1974). pp. 205–23.

KHOO, Siew-Ean, SMITH, Peter and FAWCETT, James (1984) 'Migration of women to cities: the Asian situation in comparative perspective' *International Migration Review*, Vol. 18, No., 4, pp. 1247–63.

LITTLE, Kenneth (1973) *African Women in Towns* London, Cambridge University Press.

MEHRLÄNDER, Ursula (1981) *Situation der ausländischen Arbeitnehmer und ihrer Familienangehörigen in der Bundesrepublik Deutschland. Repräsentativuntersuchung '80* Bonn: Der Bundesminister für Arbeit und Sozialordnung.

MOROKVASIC, Mirjana (1984) guest editor, 'Women in migration' *International Migration Review* Vol. 18, No. 4, winter.

MOROKVASIC, Mirjana (1986) 'Jeunes filles Yougoslaves: de l'ambiguité de la socialisation à une scolarisation réussie' *Studi Emigrazione* Vol. 23, No. 81, pp. 72–90.

MOROKVASIC, Mirjana (1987a) *Jugoslawische Frauen. Die Emigration und Danach* Frankfurt/Main: Stroemfeld Roter Stern.

MOROKVASIC, Mirjana (1987b) 'Immigrants in Parisian garment industry' *Work Employment and Society* Vol. 1, No. 4, pp. 441–62.

MOROKVASIC, Mirjana (1988) *Minority and Immigrant Women in Self-employment and Business in France, Great Britain, Italy, Portugal and Federal Republic of Germany* EEC, Paris-Brussels, V/1871/88/Engl.

MOSER, Caroline and YOUNG, Kate (1982) 'Women and the working poor' *IDS Bulletin* Vol. 12 No. 3, pp. 54–62.

NASH, June and FERNANDEZ-KELLY, Maria Patrizia (1974) *Women, Men and the International Division of Labor* Albany: State University of New York Press.

NAUCK, Bernhard and ÖZEL, Sule (1987) 'Kettenmigration in türkischen Familien' *Migration* No. 2, pp. 61–94.

PARMAR, P. (1982) 'Gender, race and class: Asian women in resistance' in CENTRE FOR CONTEMPORARY CULTURAL STUDIES (1982).

PESSAR, Patrizia (1984) 'The linkage between the household and the workplace in the experience of Dominican immigrant women in the United States' *International Migration Review* Vol. 18, No. 4, pp. 1188–211.

PHIZACKLEA, Annie (1982) 'Migrant women and wage labour: the case of the West Indian women in Britain', in WEST (1982).

PITTIN, Renée (1984) 'Migration of women in Nigeria: the Hausa case' *International Migration Review*, Vol. 18, No. 4, pp. 1293–314.

RAVENSTEIN, Ernest George (1885) 'The laws of migration' *Journal of Royal Statistical Society* Vol. XLVIII, pp. 167–227.

RAVENSTEIN, Ernest George (1889) 'The laws of migration' *Journal of Royal Statistical Society* Vol. LII, pp. 241–301.

SAIFULLAH-KHAN, Verity (1979) 'Work and network' in WALLMAN (1979).

STASIULIS, K. Daiva (1987) 'Rainbow feminism: perspectives on minority women in Canada' *Resources for Feminist Research* Vol. 16, No. 1, pp. 5–9.

TAPINOS, Georges Photios (1990) 'Immigration féminine et statut des femmes immigrées en France', United Nations Expert Group Meeting on International Migration Policies and the status of female migrations, San Miniato, Italy, 27–30 March, 1990.

TIENDA, Marta and BOOTH, Karen (1991) 'Migration, gender and social change' *International Sociology* Vol. 6, No. 1, pp. 51–72.

TRAGER, Lilian (1984) 'Family strategies and the migration of women: migrants to Dagupan City, Philippines' *International Migration Review* Vol. 18, No. 4, pp. 1264–77.

WALLMAN, Sandra (1979) editor, *Ethnicity at Work* London: Macmillan.

WEST, Jackie (1982) editor, *Work, Women and the Labour Market* London: Routledge & Kegan Paul.

WILSON, Amrit (1978) *Finding a Voice* London, Virago.

RACIAL EQUALITY AND '1992'

Ann Dummett

Underlying all British discussions of the European Community are two major difficulties. One is a near-universal British ignorance of the Community's character, structure and purposes. The other, which is particularly important in discussions of rights and opportunities, is the large difference between British constitutional law, legal habits of thought and political history and the political and constitutional norms of Continental countries. Of course the latter differ among themselves, but there is still a marked difference between British habits of thought on these matters and Continental thinking in general. Because Britain came late into it, the Community's laws and structures are entirely of Continental formation, and as a result there are continual misunderstandings between disputants from Britain and from other countries about the very bases of their discussions. Add to these difficulties a dash of British insularity, and a taste of conviction that British ways are best, and one has a potent recipe for getting nowhere.

It is only over the last two years, at most, that ethnic minorities in Britain have become concerned about the consequences for them of British membership of the Community. Like others in Britain, they took little notice of 'Europe', as the EC is frequently and misleadingly called, until government propaganda about the single market and 1992 became pervasive. The first reaction was alarm. In the seventies, there was already resentment that Britain had cut old Commonwealth ties for the sake of closer ties with the EC. Now, with talk of a single external border round the Community and a common visa policy, there were fears of a white man's Fortress Europe in which oppression of blacks would worsen and from which blacks might be forcibly expelled.

Another anxiety is that blacks in European countries have little or no protection against racial discrimination. There are legal bans on discrimination but, except in the Netherlands, the machinery for enforcing such bans is thoroughly unsatisfactory. Moreover, the British Race Relations Act which protects everyone in the jurisdiction is very different from constitutional and legal guarantees in certain other countries which apply only to citizens and not foreigners. The European Community's own constitution, the Treaty of Rome, nowhere mentions racial discrimination. It does, in Article 119, require each member state of the EC to ensure that men and women should receive equal pay for equal work, *without* specifying the nationality of the men and women concerned, and therefore the Community has clear legal competence to deal with matters of sex equality for everyone in the jurisdiction, citizen or alien (the basic principle about pay having been expanded upon somewhat since the Treaty was drawn up). Racial, or ethnic, minorities on the Continent therefore often lack the protection of either national law or Community law in matters where women and men may be able to have recourse to both.

This distinction between national laws and Community law, between the Community as such and the various countries which belong to it, is a crucial one. But because of the general British vagueness about the EC, a vagueness which ethnic minorities in Britain share, it is a distinction rarely drawn or understood. Every item of racist behaviour – and there are many – on the Continent is characterized as 'European' and so, presumably, something to do with the EC. The Community is seen as a threat because French racism and German racism are seen as threats.

There is often a confusion here, of just the same kind the white British majority makes, between 'Europe' in the sense of the European Community, 'Europe' as a collection of twelve separate states which belong to the EC but retain their own character and many distinct national policies, and 'Europe' as the Continent at large. A cloudy fog of foreignness and otherness envelops them all and blurs the distinctions. Racism exists in member countries of the EC: this does not mean the EC as such is racist. It is vitally important for the minorities to understand these distinctions if they are to fight successfully for their rights. The Community provides a machinery which can be used to obtain rights which national governments seek to deny: how this works will be described below. Further confusion arises from the use (now quite common among minority members) of the term '1992' as a code word for everything that is supposed to be threatening about 'Europe'. Nineteen ninety-two is simply a target date for the completion of the single European market, in which there is to be free movement within the Community of persons, services, goods and capital. This target for achieving free movement has implications, which may work one way or another, for ethnic minorities: in itself, it does not have to be threatening, and indeed the ideas emerging from several Community institutions lately about free movement, and the right to work, for all foreigners legally resident in any Community country, in all the other countries, could be positively beneficial to minorities.

Of course there are some justified anxieties: the problem is, how to separate these clearly from baseless ones and, as a next step, to work out how to tackle the real worries – whether by lobbying MEPs, or co-operating with ethnic minorities elsewhere in Europe, or by going exclusively through British political machinery. The justified anxieties arise from widespread racism in European countries and a fear that no adequate machinery exists to tackle it. The single market may increase the problems now faced by minorities in Britain in certain particulars. For example, one British trade union has recorded this incident: two British lorry-drivers, a white and a black, drove loads of perishable goods from Britain to the south of France. The white one experienced only cursory customs checks. The black one, who had locks and was wearing a tam, was stopped by police and other officials ninety-nine times during the journey. This did no good at all to the perishables. There is no Race Relations Act like ours in France: racial discrimination is forbidden under the criminal law, but it is very difficult for an individual to seek redress under this law and prosecutions are rare. Moreover, the European Community as such does not outlaw racial discrimination. The Treaty of Rome (the Community's constitution) does not mention race.

This lorry-driver could get no help from either French law or Community law. Naturally, there are anxieties that, as international traffic increases with the full implementation of the single market, British employers will try to avoid employing people from ethnic minorities who could encounter problems on the Continent: while there *is* some protection under our law from such discrimination by an employer, some problems are sure to arise unless and until Community law itself provides protection against racial discrimination throughout the member states.

It is striking that some black people in Britain who have been highly critical of the Race Relations Act are now praising it and (again like the white majority) taking the line that Britain is way ahead of the Continentals and British ways should be imitated abroad. Unfortunately, the British record in the Community has consistently been an irritation to other member countries because of just such superior manners, and the ethnic minorities are probably making a serious tactical mistake, against their own interest, if they take this line.

Where there is discussion between British people, black or white, and people on the Continent about antidiscrimination legislation, it rapidly gets bogged down in problems of terminology and assumptions based on all sorts of historical differences. The notion of racism is dominated by memories of Nazi anti-Semitism among older people in countries that were once Nazi-ruled. Sometimes they can see racism only in terms of the extreme political Right, and cannot come to terms with a picture of racism in which liberal and leftist groups can be guilty of it. Where an inferior status for foreign workers is regularized by law, it often seems natural and right to citizens that their own status is superior. Nothing racial about it if, say, Turks in Germany work for lower pay, in worse conditions and with less right to family life than German citizens. In France, the path to equality is by citizenship: whatever race you belong to you deserve equality if you become legally, culturally and politically French, but you cannot claim consideration on the basis of belonging to a minority group, for French political theory has room only for individual members of the French nation. Assumptions like these (admittedly very crudely put here) are baffling to the British. But on the British side there are blindnesses that are just as annoying to Continentals. Race relations have evolved in Britain in terms of black and white: 'black' has become an elastic political term that covers many shades of skin but the essential distinction is between white and nonwhite. Some black British people, used to this distinction, cannot take seriously the discrimination against Turks, Yugoslavs, south Italians and others found on the Continent, although its methods and results are so similar to antiblack discrimination here. Anti-Muslim hostility is frequently interpreted in Britain as racial hostility in religious guise: within Britain this interpretation is often true but on the Continent religious bigotry has a life of its own. It is noteworthy that the headmaster who started all the trouble about Muslim girls wearing headscarves to school, repeatedly forbidding them, was an assimilated black Frenchman.

Against this dispiriting background, it is hard to envisage rapid agreement among the European Community's ethnic minorities on a joint campaign platform to get a Community regulation, binding on all member states, outlawing racial discrimination effectively. Some attempts will perhaps be made shortly by the Migrants Forum which the European Commission has recently established. The Forum had a preliminary meeting in late 1990 and elected a committee of seventeen from the twelve member states: a full meeting, co-option of new members (including, one hopes, some women – there are none on the committee at present) and the development of a programme are expected during 1991. The Forum has a budget from the Commission but its functions will be advisory only, as with the already functioning Youth Forum. Even with this financial help and semi-official status, the Forum has to cope with many problems. Unofficial attempts at 'networking' face even more. There is a formidable language problem for all written and spoken communications between migrants from dozens of countries who have often learnt only one of the Community's languages. Money for fares and interpretation is hard to find for any effort spanning twelve countries, with numbers of people needing to meet.

But the power of a Community regulation is great. A major example is Regulation 1612/68, under which a national of any Community country who finds work in another Community country is entitled to be joined by a spouse of either sex, dependent children under twenty-one, dependent parents and grandparents and, under certain circumstances, other relatives who have lived habitually under the same roof. The point about a Community regulation is that, if it conflicts with a national law, it overrides that law. Thus a French citizen who comes to work in Britain and has an Indian spouse has a right to be joined by that spouse even though British immigration law would deny him or her entry. Similarly, a British citizen who emigrates to another Community country can be joined there by the relatives specified above, regardless of those relatives' nationality. For some time now, the Immigration Law Practitioners' Association has been advising nonwhite British citizens who have tried and failed for years to get their spouses here under British immigration law, to cross the Channel, get a job and then be joined promptly by their dependents.

The position is not yet clear whether someone who does this can then bring the dependents back to Britain on the ground that she or he is still moving between Community countries. A case went to the Immigration Appeals Tribunal, which found in favour of Mr Surinder Singh's right to do just this, but the Home Office appealed against the decision. The case went to the Divisional Court, and is still unresolved at the time of writing. It may go all the way to the European Court of Justice at Luxembourg, whose decision will be final.

A great disadvantage faced by ethnic minorities in the EC is that many of them have no votes. The Netherlands has given the vote in local elections to resident aliens. Britain gives it to Irish and Commonwealth citizens but not aliens. Germany and France are firmly opposed to any such policy, which would require amendment of the national constitutions. Although minority members who are citizens of EC countries (gypsies in Spain, some French citizens of Algerian descent, black British people) can vote, they are very small minorities within their respective nations of residence. It must be emphasized that women, as a group, have much more political clout simply because they constitute roughly half the electorate everywhere. Given that women are still a long way from achieving the parity they want in many fields, it is evident that the ethnic minorities, facing all the problems of hatred, racial violence, official and legalized discrimination and a sad lack of legal protection as well as disenfranchisement, have a long way to go.

Outside Britain, the term 'migrants' is often used for minorities who are targets of discrimination. Since, in many Continental countries, citizenship is not acquired by birth on the territory but by birth to a citizen parent, 'second-generation migrant' is a term with a real meaning, referring to children who have known no home outside Europe and yet who suffer the legal disadvantages of being alien residents on a par with new immigrants. These migrants are a relatively powerless group, whose chief day-to-day worries are insecurity of residence and uncertainty about future employment. On average, they are much poorer than the majority, worse housed and more vulnerable to police harassment. Because they are poor and powerless, the battle on their behalf is being conducted mainly by a few 'leaders' whose claim to be representative is difficult to verify and by a mixture of European Commission officials, Members of the European Parliament, people working with the Council of Europe, the International Labour Organization, etc., and some nationally based politicians – most of these, of course, being part of the white citizen majority (although there are notable exceptions, some MEPs being black women, like Dacia Valent, for example). The allies of migrants have come up with a number of positive ideas, including one for a 'European citizenship', to be held alongside one's own nationality and extended to all legal residents, whether they are EC nationals or not.

Such measures would require an enlarged competence for Community law, which the British government is unwilling to agree to. Competence itself, independently of the particular policies at issue, meets British resistance because of an obsession with retaining 'sovereignty'. When British politicians praise co-operation in the Community, they are calling for national policies harmonized with each other but enacted and administered by national rather than Community institutions. They are not agreeing to an extension of Community-made law. Yet it is Community-made law which minorities will increasingly need for their protection in the 1990s and beyond. A key question is the implementation of a common policy on the single external border round the EC, and abolition of internal border controls between nations, which the single market is supposed to require. All the negotiations on this so far have been ordinary inter-governmental negotiations conducted between the Schengen countries (of which Britain is not one), the Trevi group and the Ad Hoc Working Group on Immigration (to which Britain does belong) and several other committees. Neither national parliaments nor the European Parliament has had the chance to scrutinize their proceedings, nor of course have the resident migrants who will be particularly affected.

Under Community law, black British citizens may not, as British citizens, be treated less favourably than citizens of any other Community country in which they are present, in several important respects (e.g., when applying for employment). But this level of protection is not enough. Ethnic minorities need the protection of Community law on more specific grounds. The tragedy is that the minorities' suspicions of a racist Europe stand in the way of their using Community institutions for their own aims.

Note

Ann Dummett works part time as a consultant on European issues for the Commission for Racial Equality. She is one of the authors of *Subjects, Citizens Aliens and Others* published by Weidenfeld in 1990.

QUESTIONING *PERESTROIKA*:
A Socialist-feminist Interrogation

Ruth Pearson

At the end of 1989 when I was asked to write a background paper about trends in the world economy and the implications for women in Europe, the scenario seemed manageable. I was able – if somewhat tentatively – to identify five major trends and to speculate on their implications for women in Europe in the context of the changes in Eastern Europe and the USSR which were beginning to unfold.[1]

But, by post-Gulf War 1991, predictions are no longer feasible. All that is possible is to try and catch the questions which subsequent and continuing events have disclosed, and to map out some of the parameters which might constrain the answers.

The first task therefore is to grasp the implications of opening up the Eastern European states and the Soviet Union, not only to the global economy, but to the systems of trade and finance which govern international economic relations. The need to earn hard currency has been met in various Third World countries by export of manufactured goods which are competitive in Western markets because they are based on the exploitation of cheap female labour (Elson and Pearson, 1981). The enthusiasm of reforming East European governments and their advisers from the World Bank and the International Monetary Fund (IMF) for the privatization of industry and the elimination of obstacles to trading outside the protective barriers of COMECON have raised the possibility in many quarters of foreign investment in Eastern Europe and the USSR on a similar basis to the export platforms of South East Asia, Northern Mexico and elsewhere (*South*, 1990). Indeed during recent months the administrations of several Soviet cities and states, including Leningrad (CDSP, 1990a), and Sakhalin Island in the Soviet Far East (*The Economist*, 1990) have proposed establishing Free Economic Zones, where economic and legal restraints to private enterprise will be removed. These proposals echo the logic of Free Trade Zones and Export Processing Zones where much of Third World export processing is based, and of the Special Economic Zones which have provided the entry point for foreign capital to manufacture in the Republic of China.

This kind of speculation is based on an assumption that *perestroika* will open up the potential to exploit women's labour as the basis of a low-wage, export-led strategy oriented to Western markets. The raw-materials base of the extensive Eastern European land mass, the relatively well-developed industrial infrastructure, the increasing investment in land and telecommunications offer a dream scenario for the development of such a strategy, even on the basis of the high participation of local capital required in most European states in their revision of their laws on foreign investment which is part of the new economic policy packages to promote private investment.

Such a scenario, much vaunted in 1989, has so far failed to materialize. Foreign investment east of the Oder-Neisse line has been slow and hesitant, more so as the instability of the USSR and its constituent republics has reduced the ability of these economies to offer stable political and economic locations for investment by foreign capital. The hasty reunification of Germany has made the former state of East Germany an option mainly for West German capital, concentrated in heavy industry and vehicles rather than labour-intensive consumer goods which might compete with imports from South Korea, Mauritius and other Third World locations. Consequently, what foreign investment that has taken place has been in industries which primarily employ male not female labour. Eastern Europe offers an industrially skilled and trained labour force; it would appear more likely at this point in time that incorporation into the world economy will lead to the expansion, if deskilling, of a predominately male labour force, based on heavy industry and engineering rather than garment production and processing of electronic components. So instead of predicting another example of export-led growth based on cheap women's labour, the reality seems much more likely to be an economic *perestroika* which will marginalize women in terms of industrial employment.

One factor which might change this is the future role of the former East European states in the EEC. The establishment of the single European market in 1992 already poses a threat to the rapid industrial expansion of Third World states such as Mauritius which has based its recent rapid industrial development on exports of garments to the EEC under the preferential terms of the Lomé agreement (McQueen, 1990). While Lomé has been renegotiated to retain the bulk of EEC trade preferences for member countries till the end of the century, the incorporation behind protective tariff walls of an enlarged Europe stretching from the Urals to the Atlantic might make the logic of seeking pools of cheap female labour within the single market more rational. The peripheral 'new' European states of Turkey, Greece and Portugal are already competing to provide the cheap labour base within a grander Europe. Women's labour which is more productive, better disciplined, educated and working from a higher technological and training base might yet become the basis of Eastern Europe's strategy in the twenty-first century. All that is clear at the moment is that the predictions of T-shirts and trainers made in Crackow or Leningrad flooding Western markets no longer seem a feasible proposition within the foreseeable future.

Instability and political uncertainty are not the only reasons to draw back from automatically assuming that East European women will become the new cheap workforce in the international division of labour. In Third World states where export processing has become a major part of development strategy it is clear that it relies on a very specific cohort of the potential labour force. Generally young women who do not have domestic responsibilities and who do not necessarily expect long-term industrial employment are those who are recruited for employment in the manufacture and assembly of consumer goods for Western markets. In these situations capital is able to extract women's labour from its reproductive role by specifically targeting women before they take on marriage and childbearing. It is not clear, in the emerging geography of Eastern Europe, whether such a separation will be so straightforward. In former East Germany which had one of the highest rates of female labour-force participation in manufacturing as well as services, women's employment was premissed on the state facilitating the combining of women's paid employment with reproductive roles, however inadequate, paternalistic, if not downright oppressive such state provision became (Dölling, 1991). Withdrawal of state support in terms of childcare and maternity leave is more likely to deconstruct the identity of women as workers and reproducers combined and to replace them with an exclusive ideology of reproduction reminiscent of Britain in the 1950s and early 1960s. Given the rapid rise in unemployment caused both by the inability of East German enterprises to compete in the era of post-unification currency parity, plus the demolition of the former state with its bureaucracy and civil services, the likely outcome is a reduction of employment possibilities for women. Any development of labour-intensive industry will not compensate for the overall reduction in the demand for women's labour, and will assume a truncated labour-force participation for women workers, reinforcing the mutual exclusivity of reproduction and productive work in an ideological climate that foregrounds reproduction.

Similar predictions about reduced employment possibilities for women in the USSR have been expressed as enterprises adopt efficiency/productivity-based hiring and firing policies. Because of the reality of women's lives and the complexity of fulfilling the requirements of daily reproduction – shopping, cooking and housework as well as generational reproduction – social reality added to social prejudice is unlikely to define women as being the most productive labour as state enterprises and co-operatives adopt a capitalist enterprise form. Statements emanating from the official newspaper *Pravda* denouncing the high rate of abortion amongst women and urging 'pregnant girls' to feel chosen like the Virgin Mary and not to abort (CDSP, 1990b) are indicative of how far the current state is shifting its ideological construction of women from workers to reproducers.

One of the ways in which women's labour in modern manufacturing plants producing for the international market has been constructed and maintained as cheap labour in Third World countries has been to deny women workers social wage benefits such as health and unemployment insurance, pension entitlements and housing benefits. These entitlements were associated with industrial labour in the post-war boom in the West and with the male labour aristocracy in foreign-owned industries in the Third World. In Eastern Europe, until economic reform became politically inevitable, the major mechanism for entitlement, access and distribution of state benefits and services was the maintenance of near-universal employment opportunities (Fitzgerald, 1991). Economic reforms, directed by IMF- and World Bank-devised adjustment policies are able at the same time to promote the extension of women's productive activities, particularly in export sectors of agriculture and industry, while reducing or eliminating the already minimal state-funded services such as health, education and housing which might support women in combining reproduction with productive work. Such expenditures are conceptualized as unproductive, and the assumption is made that reproduction is compatible with market-oriented productive work without requiring expenditure and investment from the state. Thus the strategy of promoting women's employment in export sectors without giving them access to social benefits only reinforces the situation which existed in the pre-reform era. It does not require a fundamental reconstruction of women's role. It takes place in the context of an economic and political system where women factory workers, together with the majority of the population who seek their livelihoods in the informal sector (outside organized and regulated employment), have no access or entitlement to social benefits.[2]

The prospects for women in Eastern Europe are likely to be a diminution in employment opportunities, and in the social benefits previously offered by the state. This could well be accompanied by a reconstruction of reproduction not only as the appropriate role for women in opposition to productive work, but as an individual activity for which the household (women) have total responsibility. Thus economic reform, even if modelled along the lines of structural adjustment policies developed for Third World economies will have different consequences for women in Eastern Europe. Not only will they lose income and employment opportunities; at the same time they will forfeit their entitlement to state services which previously had contributed to their ability to carry out their reproductive roles. Given that the level of productivity, and the appropriate infrastructural context for efficient, cost-effective, high-quality, high-volume consumer-good production scarcely exists anywhere in Eastern Europe, women will not be offered the choice to combine productive work in the formal economy with reproduction. Reproduction will be clawed back to the individual and the household making it easier to dismantle expectations about state provision and delivery of services by diminishing the visible and actual presence of women in productive enterprises.

Relegating women to reproduction, or at least assuming that reproductive work can be carried out with no investment or 'non-productive' expenditure on the part of the state might appear economically rational or even politically desirable, given the absence of any feminist critique or mobilization which has been able effectively to integrate the 'Woman Question' with the discourses about economic reform in Eastern Europe and the Soviet Union.[3] However, at the level of real political and economic processes such integration is unavoidable. The debates and uncertainties surrounding Gorbachev's stop-start approach to economic liberalization and reform in the USSR are to a large part being played out over issues of consumption, and thus over issues concerning women's ability to fulfil their role as ensurers of the daily reproduction of their households. Shortages last year of cigarettes, a primarily male consumption good, resulted in strikes and shut-downs and a state commitment to resume supplies. The more recent problems over the availability of food produce in stores in urban centres is less tractable. Since the beginning of the year when international trade between COMECON has proceeded on the basis of world prices, set in hard currency, the interchange which formally took place between the individual republics of the USSR and the states of Eastern Europe has been severely disrupted. When the USSR stopped supplying petroleum and industrial raw materials to the Balkan States, they responded by curtailing the export of food produce to Russia. The resultant severe food shortage, described by some (erroneously) as a famine, highlighted the problems of distribution both between and within the republics. Entitlement to purchase the limited food supplies available has been organized on the basis of territoriality, with consumers in Moscow and Leningrad being required to produce passports or evidence of nationality and residence to access purchases. This has exacerbated the nationalism inherent in the Balkan States and in Russia and other republics and has increased the pressure which is threatening the very existence of the Soviet Union as a political entity.

It is not possible to predict at the time of writing what the outcome of these pressures will be, although a clearer position may emerge by the time this article is published. However, it does suggest that economic reform is going to have to deal with the demands made on the economy of the needs of reproduction as well as production, and that women's role as reproducers will have to be negotiated. Whilst the state guaranteed employment rights and basic social services, the sight of women queuing at all hours to secure the household food consumption was accepted as the outcome of inefficiencies of the system rather than inherent in the system itself. With these basic guarantees in question, if not as yet withdrawn, there is no buffer between the reproductive requirements and expectations of the population and the ability of the system as it is transformed to meet these requirements. The 'Woman Question' is therefore transformed from one which has been discussed in terms of the social and political emancipation of women, and the economic effects of reform on women (Molyneux, 1990) into one which reaches right to the heart of the formulation and execution of economic policy.

Notes

Ruth Pearson has written extensively on the impact of the global economy on women's work. She teaches in the Development Studies Unit of the University of East Anglia.

1 The trends referred to were (1) the potential of Eastern Europe as a site for foreign investment employing women in the labour-intensive manufacture of exports; (2) the growth of Eastern Europe and the USSR as a market for mass-consumption goods produced in the West; (3) the increase in regionalism and protectionism and the growth of regional trading blocks; (4) the growth of the 'informal economy'; and (5) the relocation of environmentally hazardous production to the East. See Pearson (1989).
2 The application of A. K. Sen's concept of entitlements to the discussion of the social wage in NICs and Eastern Europe is developed in Fitzgerald (1991).
3 The experience of trying to integrate such a critique into the analysis of structural adjustment policies in the Third World has been equally problematic; see Elson (1991).

References

CDSP (1990a) *Concise Digest of the Soviet Press* Vol. XXIII, No. 40, p. 25.
CDSP (1990b) *ibid.*, No. 10, p. 30.
DÖLLING, Irene (1991) 'Between hope and helplessness; women in the GDR' *Feminist Review*, No. 39 (this volume).
THE ECONOMIST (1990) 22 September.
ELSON, Diane (1991) 'Male bias in macro-economics: the case of structural adjustment', in ELSON, Diane (1991) editor, *Male Bias in the Development Process* Manchester: University Press.
ELSON, Diane and PEARSON, Ruth (1981) 'Nimble fingers make cheap workers': an analysis of women's employment in Third World export manufacturing', *Feminist Review*, No. 7.
FITZGERALD, E. V. K. (1991) 'Economic reform and citizenship entitlements in Eastern Europe: some social implications of structural adjustment in semi-industrialised economies'. ISS Working Papers, No. 95, The Hague, January.
McQUEEN, Matthew (1990) 'ACP export diversification: the case of Mauritius' *ODI Working Paper*, No. 41, August.
MOLYNEUX, Maxine (1990) 'The 'Woman Question' in the age of *Perestroika*', *New Left Review* No. 183.
PEARSON, Ruth (1989) 'Global trends in the world economy: implications for women in Europe'. Paper presented at the 5th Annual Conference of the European Socialist Feminist Forum, Göteberg, Sweden, November (mimeo).
SOUTH (1990) 'The big switch', April, pp. 13–15.

POSTMODERNISM AND ITS DISCONTENTS

Kate Soper

Towards the end of the 1980s, the decade in which postmodernist modes of thinking asserted themselves, and in so doing laid siege to a whole range of positions in theory which had grounded a socialist politics, 'actual existing socialism' collapsed under the pressure of popular revolution in Central and Eastern Europe. The net effect of this combined intellectual and political convulsion has been severely to disturb the equanimity with which many of us on the Left have in the past defined ourselves as socialists. In one sense this is paradoxical given that throughout the same decade many of us were also being extremely vocal in our denunciations of Soviet 'socialism' and working for an end to the old order in Eastern Europe; and given, too, that included among us were a number who were influenced by, and were themselves employing, insights derived from postmodernist theory. But if there is rather more sensitivity than previously now about the vocabulary of socialism, I think this is because theoretical and political developments have brought home more forcefully than ever before how difficult it is going to be to dissociate the socialist idea from what has been implemented in the name of it within the Soviet bloc. These developments have also made us more self-critical of the confidence, even at times complacency, with which we were wont to invoke the notion of an 'authentic socialism', as if this directed to us to a clearly desirable and obviously workable alternative to Communist orthodoxy.

However, then, we view the relationship between the post-modernist turn in theory, on the one hand, and the recent events in Central and Eastern Europe, on the other (and it is arguable that although the former was tending to a rethinking and undermining of socialist commitments in the West, it had little direct influence on the rebellion against socialism in the East), it is clear that their overall effect has been a dramatic alteration of the context which any form of socialist argument is now addressing. Indeed, so much has this

Feminist Review No 39, Winter 1991

changed, that it appears to pose the question not only of how socialists might pick up the pieces and think beyond their present crisis, but whether it is right that they should attempt to do so. In other words, one type of response to the present situation is to the effect that the Left should no longer attempt to salvage a philosophy which has been so doubly discredited. It should accept that what the postmodernists had been insisting upon in theory, namely that socialism is but another instance of domination dressed up as liberation, a 'grand narrative' credo bound to issue in totalitarian practice, has been proved all too true by events in Eastern Europe, and now that the whole historical aberration has been brought to a close, we should be prepared to forswear such grandiose schemes of social amelioration.

Yet, although we may accept that there is a certain wisdom in the counsel of theoretical modesty, there is also something too 'totalizing' about this response itself. Inspired though it may claim to be by the deconstruction of 'identity thinking', it actually collapses differences which need to be respected, since the situation in which we now find ourselves is much more complex than can be registered through a simple opposition of 'socialist' and 'postmodernist' perspectives.

In the first place, it fails to acknowledge the disquieting, even directly regressive, quality of much that has ensued since the heady days of revolution in 1989. Socialism may have been seen off, but the space it vacated has scarcely been flooded by that pluralist utopia of 'proliferating difference' to which the postmodernists have beckoned us in their assaults upon socialist theory and its 'totalizing' logic. On the contrary, it can be argued that what has been squeezed out and denied any serious political representation in Central and Eastern Europe are all those counter-cultural forms of dissent (feminist, ecological, anti-militarist, democratic socialist) which aspired to the establishment of some 'third way' transcendence of the Cold War binary opposition. In this sense, we have been witness not to the inauguration of an alternative logic to the capitalism versus communism antithesis, but to a developing economic and political momentum which threatens to absorb all oppositional difference within the 'identity' of the Western market society.

In this process, the peoples of Central and Eastern Europe have certainly reclaimed a form of 'civil society' and come to enjoy democratic rights which are by no means derisable. But they have done so at the cost of exposure to market pressures which will be experienced all the more intensely because of the second-class status of their economies; and the democratic powers they have gained in exchange will be as limited in their sphere of influence, as open to manipulation by business interests, no more a guarantee of the articulation and promotion of grass-roots citizens' concerns, or of the opening of their societies to a healthy, strongly oppositional plural political culture than their equivalents have proved in the West. In fact, it has long been recognized that democracy flourishes best upon the soil it creates, and that societies long denied its institutions are that much more susceptible to forms of chauvinist and demagogic opportunism. It would be quite wrong to assimilate the, in fact, rather differing societies which are emerging out of the ferment of revolution, but there are certainly developments within many of them which are now giving cause for alarm among elements whose liberal outlook made them radical opponents of the old socialist order. These societies, then, may be 'postmodernist' in the rather simple sense that they rejected 'socialism', but they do not promise at the moment to provide very fertile ground for the promotion of those more constructive forms of 'difference' politics which form the core of a left eco-socialist-feminist programme in the West.

To put the point thus is to direct attention to a second major reason for disallowing too ready an opposition between 'socialism' and 'postmodernism', which cannot, I think, be treated as labels dividing between the left-wing angels, on the one hand, and the neo-conservative or nihilist demons, on the other. For the impact of postmodernist theories on orthodox socialist thinking has by no means been wholly negative, and the revisions in our approach to science, power, subjectivity and language which they have influenced have been as important in their way as those earlier introduced through feminism (itself, in fact, a form of 'difference' politics).

The logic of difference

This is not to deny that there are very real and substantial distinctions between 'modernist' and 'postmodernist' approaches in social theory; it is rather to insist that what is at issue here cannot be viewed as a simple division between adherence to left- or right-wing political values, but is better viewed as a debate about how the political values which we do endorse are to be explained and justified. It is a debate between those who would insist that values cannot be treated in purely relative terms as products of discourses which are ungrounded in any universal or trans-historic claims about the quality of human experience and sensibility, and those who would argue that there is no extra-discursive justification of values, no transcendent 'rights' and 'wrongs' to which we can appeal in our denunciations of 'oppression' and aspirations to 'emancipation'. It is a dispute, to put it crudely, between a position in epistemological and moral theory which would hold that it is only in virtue of the discourse of 'rights', 'oppression', etc., that differences of experience emerge as differences *which matter* and are endowed with normative charge, and a position which would insist that it is precisely such differences of experience (as between suffering and its absence) that provide the meaning of moral discourse and distinguish its claims from those of arbitrary whim or subjective preference.

Now if we see the issue in these terms, it is clear that 'left-wing' values might be defended from within either perspective – either as a discursive product, a manifestation of the self-created norms within which our societies are currently immersed; or else as speaking to forms of exploitation and resistance which reflect more universal features of human experience and potentiality and are not simply discourse dependent. It is also clear, however, that if we adopt the first of these perspectives, we disallow that any privilege can be granted to our own (localized and historically relative) conception of 'progress' and 'emancipation' – which, in effect, is what the postmodernists are pointing out in their rejection of the Enlightenment faith in its own forms of rationality. The problem, therefore, becomes a problem of the internal coherence of a position which would defend 'progressive' values while so systematically undermining the discourse of 'progress' itself. How can a postmodernist perspective consistently present itself as 'liberating' while conducting such an unyielding critique of the metaphysics which have grounded all talk of liberation?

In other words, insofar as postmodernist theory presents itself as critical (critical of the failure to respect difference, critical of the potentially dominating conflations of difference legitimized by a collectivist politics), it is arguable that it subverts itself. In its deconstruction of 'identity' thinking and its binary grid of oppositional concepts, it directs us to a future in which we might be freed from the tyranny of constructed identities – and hence invokes the autonomy of persons even as it argues for their constructed subjectivity. It presents power relations as positive and productive, yet invites us to conceive of this modality in terms of the manipulation of desire, the co-option of souls, the working over of the body, and other moves which cannot be freed from the taint of oppression. It recommends forms of ethical or sensual or consumer self-expression to subjects who have theoretically been denied any autonomous presence or authentic selfhood. It has presented us as 'de-centred' and 'fragmented' subjects the validity of whose conscious experience must always be called in question – but only in that very process to submit us to conscious forms of self-scrutiny in the light of which we are supposed to cast off various forms of blindness about ourselves, re-organize our desires and adjust our behavioural responses.

It has finally, we might note, committed itself to a logic of difference which is theoretically incompatible with the logic of democracy, while continuing implicitly to rely on the latter for its critical force. For why should we 'respect' or 'preserve' the plurality of social actors (as opposed to simply recognizing an irreconcilable anarchy of subject places) unless we think it is right that they should be represented, and that in treating different persons or groups as different we are treating them more equally. In short, if we are obedient *only* to the logic of difference, we remove the grounds for any claims that different identities come with equal entitlements to the same forms of recognition: we deconstruct the grounds upon which any politics can conceivably be promoted. Some of those working under the deconstructive impulse have in effect acknowledged this when they have invited us to view all actual democratic practice as despotic, all 'authentic' democracy as no more than an obscure object of desire, impossible of realization.

Questions of value

It is precisely at this point, then, that we can demand that the 'postmodernists' show their hand, and admit either that they are not really advocates of any form of political change or programme whatsoever (which, in effect, of course is to admit to their conservatism), or else that they can only consistently present themselves as defenders of non-conservative political values by surreptitiously invoking the foundationalist positions in social theory they have explicitly rejected.

This dilemma of postmodernist theory has of late, one senses, been increasingly recognized by many of those who saw it as essentially friendly to the Left and a critical movement for advancing more progressive values. They have, that is to say, become more aware of the theoretical cul-de-sacs into which it leads, and begun to speak themselves of its impasse, and of the need to rethink the suppression of all foundationalist approaches to the value questions raised in social and cultural theory. In this sense, I think one can detect something of a return of the repression of value in the new mood abroad, or at any rate a more open recognition of the equivocation around value issues which has dogged the postmodernist exercise from the start.

If this is the case, then it may mean that new forms of communication are opening up across the 'realist' versus 'postmodernist' divide, and the stage set for the emergence of forms of argument which are informed and mediated by 'postmodernist' rationalities but at the same time much more ready to acknowledge the dependency of their critical force on a 'realist' approach to values. One might hope for this to be the case, since it is arguable that it is only by means of synthesis of this kind that one prevents a roll-back reaction: that a needed postmodernist self-criticism does not revert to a defence of the unreconstructed modes of thinking that were a legitimate target of the initial deconstruction. By way of making a little clearer what I have in mind here, I propose in what follows to indicate some of the ways in which this more tempered approach might affect the arguments we bring to bear in three key areas where questions of value have been most contested recently: those of socialism, aesthetics and feminism.

In the first place, then, as regards socialism, I would suggest that an approach of this kind invites a reappraisal of our former reliance on the 'pure' value of 'authentic socialism'. Rather than invoke the purity of that formation as a way of dissociating our commitments from the popular repudiation of socialism in Central and Eastern Europe, we should begin a process of rethinking. We should ask how far 'authentic socialism' depended for its political innocence on the reality of a history which always denied it the test of implementation, and address ourselves in more concentrated fashion to the task of specifying the economic and social forms which might realize its values. Instead of listing the virtues which the removal of capitalist relations would bring into harmony, we should accept that it is not capitalism which is responsible for the difficulties of reconciling liberty and equality, democracy and efficiency, cultural pluralism and social cohesion, national self-determination and international co-operation. Capitalism is one bad solution or irresponsible evasion of these problems. But the problems have to do with the intransigence of social reality itself, and cannot be wished away by demonizing an existing order. We have to show what other methods will work, and work better, and work better in part because they have built-in guarantees against the deformations to which attempts at socialist practice have fallen prey in the past.

Crises of our times

The present climate is by no means entirely unpropitious for addressing this task, for we are, I think, entering a period in which disaffection with what passed for socialism is going together with very extensive anxiety about the capacities of the untrammelled market to secure the 'good life' or offer any way out of the crises of our times: war, famine, ecological degradation, frightening exacerbation of the major global economic divisions, sharpening inequalities within the domestic economies. Political allegiances can no longer be so easily secured through the suppressions and ideological manoeuvres of the Cold War period, and we can henceforth expect, I think, that scepticism about the appropri- ateness for the future of either of its confrontational systems will become more acute. Symbiotic as they have been, the crisis of Commun- ism may also over time prove a crisis for capitalism, since it entails unprecedented exposure to its limits and contradictions. It would, in short, be wrong to equate distrust of socialist solutions which have hitherto been implemented with dissent from all forms of socialist value. There is no doubt that there is a great deal of commitment on both sides of the old-bloc divide to the ends of democracy, social justice, peace and ecological sustainability. But there is no doubt, too, that it will float in a vacuum above the arena of real politics, so long as it fails to put forward convincing programmes for the realization of these values.

Culture and politics

A second area where we need to appraise older value commitments in the light of more recent understandings is that of aesthetics and cultural studies. Certainly, I think it would be a mistake to sacrifice the gain that has come of seeing that a defence of the 'pure' value of artistic production has very often served as a cover under which art has been spared the scrutiny of other value considerations. There is no doubt that the appeal to intrinsic literary and artistic value has served legiti- mating purposes of a dubious kind: allowed 'high' art to deflect engagements with its ideological critics on the grounds that it is improper to confuse questions concerning the aesthetic merit of cultural production with questions concerning its ideological function or political messaging; by the same token, minority challenges to its canon have been resisted on the grounds that all such claims carry with them the taint of a political, therefore not truly aesthetic, motivation.

Yet we can be alert to the politics of value concealed in the immunization of art from politics, while still feeling that we do not want to, indeed cannot, dispense with any aesthetic discrimination altogether. Sensitive as we may be to the difficulties and potential élitism of judgements at that level, we may still feel loath to collapse cultural criticism into a purely relativist cultural history or sociology – still feel dogged by a sense that to opt out of aesthetic judgement is to deny the specificity of art while also, paradoxically, refusing to acknowledge its similarity to other practices to which we do not bring anything like the same hesitation in pronouncing upon excellence; where we are quite happy to recognize skill, superior performance, even beauty. In a sense I think we may even feel that the critical programmes which have problematized the canonical status of texts and invited suspension of aesthetics are themselves ultimately undermined in their purpose if we adhere too obediently to their recommendation: for are they not conducted towards the end of a more enlightened reading, the development of a more acute and educated aesthetic sensibility? Are they not driven by a sense that there is a distinctive and liberating pleasure in high-quality cultural production to which far more should have access than at present?

I do not claim, however, that the synthesis in this area is easily achieved, that the two sides of our thinking can be readily cemented. I rather think, in fact, that what we have here is what Adorno refers us to in speaking of the schism between avant-garde and popular culture: 'two torn halves of an integral freedom, to which, however, they do not add up'. But freedom seems the appropriate concept and the prospect of integration continues to beckon us.

Questions of gender

Thirdly, let me turn to some of the value considerations which are raised in the domain of gender relations. One way of looking at these is in terms of what might be called the 'utopian' question: the question of what it is that is wanted – of what constitutes progress in this area of human relationships, and how to achieve it. This question has of late acquired new dimensions and added complexity, in part because of the 'linguistic turn' associated with post-structuralist critiques, in part because of the collapse of the socialist regimes in Eastern Europe, which has perhaps forced us to confront more fully than before the fact that the cultural oppression of women persists across significant differences in social relations and female life experience.

In this context, I think one can draw a contrast (though it is obviously in some ways too simple) between an earlier phase of feminist campaigning which pursued its ends in the name of the 'liberation' of women and directed its energies primarily to the analysis and removal of the material – economic and social – conditions responsible for female subordination, and a later, more 'culturalist' orientation which has focused more on the symbolic negation of the 'feminine' and on the need for a general 're- or de-gendering' at the level of language and conceptualization.

In saying this, I am not for a moment denying that the earlier phase did not generate divisions, or that embedded within these there were not, in fact, considerable differences about ends (separatist strategies, for example, were frequently directed towards separatist 'utopias', liberal feminists were happy to settle for parity within an existing order, socialists by contrast saw liberation as intimately bound up with a more general social reconciliation and the removal of class antagonisms, and so on). None the less, these different wings of the feminist movement did have certain dispositions in common. They were addressed primarily to the experience of women in capitalist society. They viewed themselves as representing the needs of a relatively homogeneous category of women 'as such'; and they conceived emancipation in terms of the removal of quite tangible sources of oppression.

Now there is no doubt, I think, that the influence of poststructuralist theory, and the attention it has directed to the 'plurality' of subject places and experience, has been such as seriously to undermine the premises of this position. The feminisms which have developed under this influence have questioned the easy recourse to a universal category of 'women', the readiness to speak to a common set of interests or desires, and the resulting confidence in a single, 'totalizing' political strategy. They have also, in drawing attention to the role of language and symbolization in the construction of gender identities, and to the ways these are carriers of an oppositional and gendered conceptual system, come to focus much more on what might be called the metaphysical underpinnings of gender relations rather than on the socio-economic conditions of the sexes and the most immediately material and historically specific forms and institutions of male power. This, as I have suggested, has brought with it a significant shift in 'utopian' thinking. What is needed now, we are asked to believe, is not 'simply' changes at the material level since these, even if quite radical (a transformation in the mode of production) are consistent with the maintenance of a masculine Symbolic or cultural order and its binary gender system. What is needed, rather, is a cultural revolution which delivers us from the very modes of conceptualization within which we have hitherto constructed gender identities. We need to escape or transcend the binary gender grid as such.

There have been, I suggest, essentially two lines of argument pursued within this general perspective. Firstly, there are the Lacanian-influenced 'difference' feminisms. These have focused on the patriarchal definition of the 'feminine' within the Symbolic order, and have hence conceived the 'utopian' task in terms of a quest to register that 'otherness' or 'difference' which is not the feminine as spoken to within a 'masculine' culture. Since this is, in effect, to attempt to give voice to what has been defined as ineffable, the strains and stresses of this position are considerable, and they have tended to issue in theoretical moves which arguably do not break with the essentialism they explicitly reject. In other words, insofar as the 'difference' in question has been related to female bodily and sensual experience, with the emphasis falling on what is specific to women in virtue of their sexual being and maternal function, it can be said to reproduce conventional conceptions of femininity, though giving these a more positive charge. This may be an advance in some ways, but it reinforces the idea which other feminists regard as at the root of the problem, namely that there is some essential and identifiable quality of sexual difference.

Hence the inclination of the other wing of poststructuralist-influenced feminism, which is to resist the fixity of the binary gender system, and to argue that the only way out of this is by way of 'in-difference', a refusal to recognize ourselves in any of the categories of gender difference.

Now I think it is certainly true that any 'difference' perspective premised on the acceptance of the 'masculine' Symbolic promotes too rigid and narrow a view both of gender relations and of their cultural context. On the one hand, it invites us to think of all experience as gender marked, and hence fails to recognize any communality of speech and engagement, any overlap or gender-neutral space wherein men and women can register what is common in their responses to the world, their aesthetic appreciation, or their desires for the future. On the other hand, it fails to acknowledge that what is being termed 'masculine' culture is also the realm in which all non-conformity, rebellion and dissent from an established order of meanings and values has always and must necessarily find expression. It is in effect to opt for a form of feminism which rules out beforehand the possibility of its own effec-tivity, dehistoricizing culture in the process by denying its actual transformability and refusing to 'male' language its all too obvious mobility. This, it can be claimed, is not merely conservative but positively Canute-like: an attempt to stem the tide of gender transform-ation by denying it any fluidity. It is to have recourse to a form of nominalism, which by renaming as 'masculine' everything which subverts the existing allocation of gender roles and attributes can only in the end be understood as speaking to a nostalgia to preserve the identities of the old binary grid from all material transgressions.

That said, there is also, one can argue, a contrary form of conservativism in the recommendation to forget about feminine 'differ-ence'. For the risk then is that we adopt a theoretical position which abstracts from all the material transgressions which would be necess-ary to make a meaningful reality of the collapse of the old fixity of gender difference. If feminism gets too fixated on not recognizing a feminine difference, it could end up not making any difference: it could end up by overlooking what are still very offensive and oppressive dimensions of reality. For there are still many conditions of existence which are differentially experienced depending on which sex you happen to be, and in many ways these are peculiarly constraining on women.

'Utopian' projections

This brings me to some more general reflections on the 'utopian' projections associated with the 'in-different' perspective in Western feminism. We have been referred in this connexion, for example, to a more 'polysexual' or sexually confused future, to a society of 'proliferating difference', a society wherein there will be only 'bodies and pleasures', and so forth.

Difficult, if not impossible as it may be, fully to conceptualize such 'societies', these images, I suggest, are not without their attraction, and do capture something of what women, and increasingly men too, are now wanting. We are, I think, drawn by a vision of relations which are not lived out in a constant alertness to the difference which the difference of sex makes, and are therefore freed from the forms of possessiveness or limits on the possibilities of intimacy between the sexes which derive from the romantic, and highly sexualized, conventions governing inter-sexual relations. We want, I think, to get beyond this continual gender alertness for the further reason that only by doing so will our culture become more indifferent to sexual relations which are *not* heterosexual. In other words, I think we do aspire to a situation in which so-called deviant sexuality is not merely tolerated but not marked as different. This may well depend on significant changes in what we regard as possible or permitted in the way of heterosexual relations – a move which I am suggesting could in turn have quite enriching effects on relations between men and women, allowing both less angst-ridden forms of love and friendship.

I also think that there are many men and women now whose life experience is such that the existing gender stereotypes and cultural codings do a kind of violence to their own sense of identity and subjectivity. We live in a world today in which there are too many female breadwinners, male nurturers, feminist housewives and mothers, white, middle-class males teaching black, feminist literature, in short, too many transgressions or confusions of gender in our everyday engagements for us not to feel that much of the former gender narrative is perversely and even cruelly anachronistic. Our gender representations are already extensively out of joint with ourselves, and the de-differing of various roles and activities which this disjuncture has begun to set in motion will hopefully continue to the benefit of all, and certainly needs to be reflected in a continual updating of the normative content of feminist argument.

So in these respects (and I recognize that I have done no more than adumbrate their quality here) the idea of the sexually confused or de-differed culture does grasp something of what we want, and indeed of where we are already beginning to go. But at the same time, I think we have to accept that even as we welcome these de-gendering developments, we are also pulled by our existing identities, and not simply in the sense of feeling them to be an obstacle to modes of being which we think are more desirable; but also in the sense that a great deal of our excitement and erotic interest is dependent upon them. Or to put the point more crudely, if gender in-difference is construed as a neutralization or loss of gender then it has a distinctly dystopian and dampening feel to it, and we have to think through the implications of this dystopian 'feel' as integral to any considerations about our value commitments in regard to sexuality.

Let me only add finally that postmodernism, in my opinion, is no exception to the general rule that cultural movements must be viewed dialectically: as containing within them divergent and even contrary potentialities for change. In the case of sexuality, for example, I have sketched some of the ways in which the aspiration to de-differing or the proliferation of difference associated with postmodernist argument could prove progressive, by which I mean it could issue in more fulfilling relations and the erosion of some of the more painful structures of feeling which stand in the way of greater parity and reconciliation. But it could also encourage a more solipsistic and private conception of one's sexual being, in which the link between having a certain identity as a sexual person and experiencing certain bonds of love, erotic attraction and empathy with others becomes much more attenuated than it is at present. The idea of choosing one's gender which has been promoted by certain feminists, for example, as a desirable alternative to its social construction, may seem in many ways something to aim for. But it also seems to rely on the idea of a kind of radical autonomization of selfhood, in which all possible forms of dependency on others, and of others on oneself, are viewed as wholly contingent, something we select and change at will.

Perhaps this does not really offer us a very plausible scenario, and is therefore not one with which we should concern ourselves unduly. But just as I think new possibilities for reconciliation are opened up between the sexes, between social groupings, even between nations, by recognizing how different we actually are from what the gender system, and social narratives and nationalist ideologies would have us be, so one can detect many sources of strain and division in the assertion of autonomy and individuality which goes together with the stress on difference. There is a risk, in short, that under cover of the very respectable request that we acknowledge difference, we justify as forms of self-expression what we ought to denounce as modes of greed, narcissism and egoism which are all too little considerate of the basic needs of others; or that in challenging the political collective as a false form of humanism we grant legitimacy to what are actually very disquieting forms of tribalism; or, to be even more polemical, that in allowing an analysis of all the more ugly – racist, nationalist, sexist – tropes of our times as reactive reassertions of 'difference' induced by humanist discourse itself, we give the green light to a discursive neo-fascism. In other words, to grant all the rope to 'discourse' and none of it to 'reality', is to put the noose round those cardinal values of equality and democracy in whose name all serious struggle against oppression must be conducted. If it is socialist to make these points and to want to carry on that struggle, then so be it, let us be called socialists.

Notes

Kate Soper is a writer, translator, and lecturer in philosophy at the Polytechnic of North London. She is the author of *On Human Needs* and *Humanism and Anti-Humanism* as well as her latest book, *Troubled Pleasures: Writings on Politics, Gender and Hedonism*, published by Verso Press.

FEMINISTS AND SOCIALISM

AFTER THE COLD WAR

Mary Kaldor

The end of the Cold War was a heady moment for me. It was not just the excitement of being able to witness history, the joy on people's faces as they breached the Berlin Wall or swarmed into Wenceslas Square, although that was euphoric enough. I felt something more – that this was a personal triumph, a vindication of everything I had being doing politically and intellectually during the 1980s.

I was active in that part of the peace movement that advocated 'detente from below' – building links between movements in Eastern and Central Europe. This strategy was drawn from a specific analysis of the Cold War and of the nature of political processes. We argued that the Cold War was not a conflict between two different systems but an ideological device for sustaining two different systems. Both systems, the Atlanticist variant of capitalism and the Stalinist variant of socialism, needed a permanent external confrontation to legitimize power structures and maintain social cohesion. What is more, political parties, including the parties of the Left, were incorporated into the structures of the Cold War – hence the need for new social movements, outside the orthodox power structures, 'antipolitics' to use the term coined by opposition groups in Eastern Europe, working in both East and West.

The revolutions of 1989 seemed to be a kind of proof of this way of thinking. It was movements, not Western military might, that toppled the regimes in Central Europe. And the Western peace movement had played an important role, both in establishing a disarmament agenda which led to the INF Treaty and the talks about conventional-force reductions without which the Soviet Union could not have renounced the Brezhnev doctrine, and in supporting and assisting the fledgling peace and democracy movements in Eastern Europe in the second half of the 1980s.

It is true that the role of the peace movement was not mentioned in articles and television documentaries about what happened and this was irritating, to say the least. But what mattered, it seemed to me, was the fact that our arguments and language had been adopted by politicians. There were plenty of references to civil society, the importance of citizens' initiatives, the unification of Europe, a new peace order for Europe, a new security system in which the role of military force would be less important, the inherent link between peace and democracy, and so on. We had always argued that what was important for the peace movement, and indeed for antipolitics, was not whether 'our people' captured political power, but whether 'our ideas' were adopted. We were not interested in becoming politicians, we did not aspire to power, rather we wanted to change the nature of power, the relationship between politics and people, states and civil society.

One year later, the euphoria has almost entirely disappeared. The new democracies of East Central Europe face horrendous problems – economic, ecological and social. By and large, politics has shifted dramatically to the right; all sorts of new exclusivist political tendencies have emerged – anti-Semitic, separatist, antigypsy, etc; and the movements that were so important during the late 1980s have been marginalized in all countries, even in Czechoslovakia where a beleaguered Vaclav Havel remains President.

Worse still, we are, as I write, in the midst of a war in the Gulf. And within days before the outbreak of war, the Soviet military began to crack down on the Baltic republics. Was it coincidence? Some would say that the Soviet generals chose this moment when Western attention was diverted, and there is, of course, something in the argument. But, above all, these two events should be interpreted in terms of the end of the Cold War. There was bound, sooner or later, to be some reaction from the hardened cold warriors, if our analysis was correct. The scale of the reaction it can be argued merely goes to show how deep were the structures, institutions and ways of thinking that were associated with the Cold War. Whatever one's attitude to the war in the Gulf, it cannot be denied that the war has provided an ideal opportunity to scupper talk of the peace dividend, of a new global security system that does not rely on force, of politics in which war fevers play no role. Long before Iraq invaded Kuwait, there was talk of new enemies in the South which would replace the Soviet threat as a reason for armament. Saddam Hussein's behaviour substantiated that view. And, in the Soviet Union, the creeping military coup can be viewed as the Soviet army's recuperation from the Afghanistan syndrome and the loss of Eastern Europe.

One of the most remarkable characteristics of the post-Cold War world, as of February 1991, is its maleness. Turning on the television screen, I am continually struck by the serried ranks of men – male defence experts, male politicians, male soldiers, male hardliners in the

Communist Party of the Soviet Union. Even the representatives of the new democracies in Central Europe are all men. Occasionally, one catches a glimpse of a woman – Kate Adie (always described as 'indomitable'), Marjorie Thompson (Chair of CND, sometimes described as 'emotional'), a handful of American women soldiers, a nurse, a tearful Iraqi, an angry Israeli, the mother of a young man shot in Riga. The very fact that one tends to remember them all shows how rare it is to see a woman in the news. One of George Bush's personal advisers solemnly explained on television the other day that, after Vietnam, 'we had what we call a feminization of attitudes to war' but luckily he thought that this was 'all over now'.

Is it possible to explain the backlash against the end of the Cold War, the reappearance of violence and aggressive behaviour in gender terms? Can antipolitics, or the new social movements, be described as a female phenomena?

Clearly, there is a gender division and this is reflected in values and ways of thinking. The world of formal politics, especially formal international politics, is a male world. Politicians, diplomats and soldiers are nearly always men. In contrast, the world of informal politics, those engaged in everyday political processes, those who experience the consequences of politics, those who give their support to one politician or another, are just people, men and women. The media tend to focus on the world of formal politics. When we watch the endless Gulf War news, we see very little of ordinary people's opinions, and very little of the consequences of war – indeed there seems to be a conspiracy of silence about the Iraqi casualties.

This emphasis on formal politics, on the world of states, represented by presidents or foreign ministers, also entails a kind of abstract reductionism in the way that events are perceived and behaviour is legitimized. The so-called realist school of international relations views the world as a collectivity of states, each of which acts more or less autonomously and independently. Phrases like 'the United States is regaining its global leadership', or 'France is an unreliable ally, unwilling to shoulder its responsibilities' treat the state as a 'male' individual and exclude real political processes, involving complex relationships between groups of people.

Writings about gender often draw a distinction between abstract male types of reasoning and more holistic thinking which incorporates human emotions and intuition. Carol Gilligan, in her book *In a Different Voice* (1982) draws a distinction between male and female attitudes towards morality, between what she calls an 'ethic of justice [which] proceeds from the premise of equality – that everyone should be treated the same' and an 'ethic of care that rests on the premise of non-violence – that no one should be hurt' (174). She explains these differences in terms of differential attitudes towards attachment and separation that stem from different relationships towards the primary nurturer, the mother. Boys are more concerned about autonomy and their morality is based on a hierarchical ordering of rights or principles whereas girls are more concerned about relationships, their ideas about morality centre around a connected web of responsibilities.

I am sceptical about whether women are inherently less violent and aggressive than men, even if this is explained in terms of the conditioning of early childhood. Nevertheless, this ethical distinction does seem to reflect a real difference in the moral reasoning of formal politics and the more complex ethical positions developed in the sphere of antipolitics. In particular, Gilligan's distinction parallels the philosophical distinction between the just-war tradition and the perpetual-peace tradition. The former rests on an ethic of rights and allows one clearly to differentiate good from bad and to apply these categories to individuals, or in the case of war, states. The latter tradition is concerned with the way in which war hurts people and identifies a common interest in nonviolence on the part of the peoples of opposing states – hence the interest expressed by proponents of perpetual peace in schemes for international democracy. It is easy enough to see how this distinction applies to the Gulf War. Clearly Saddam Hussein is a dictator who has breached international law in unacceptable ways. It is rather straightforward to characterize this war as a just war. But if we take into account the victims of the war – the casualties who were also the victims of Saddam Hussein – as well as the complexity of politics in the Middle East and the West's responsibility for what has happened, the issue is no longer so clear cut. Kant argued that if one person is killed, who is innocent of the crimes of the state (which is certainly the case in Iraq), then the war is no longer just.

The same distinction dominated the Cold War debate. The Cold War was depicted on both sides as a conflict between good and evil of epic proportions, freedom versus totalitarianism, or socialism versus Western imperialism. Indeed the threat to use nuclear weapons required an almost infinite moral legitimization because it was such a limitless threat. The success of social movements in the 1980s was at least in some measure due to the denial of that good/bad characterization. It was the world of formal politics, of states and armies, that was viewed as responsible for the Cold War, and, in this sense, both sides were responsible. There were huge disagreements among opposition groups about who was most responsible. Western peace groups tended to identify the West as the worst offender, citing the establishment of NATO in 1949, the first-use nuclear strategy and the record of Western intervention in the Third World. Eastern opposition groups regarded the Soviet Union as the root of the problem, citing the interventions in Hungary and Czechoslovakia and the continuing history of oppression. What was important, however, was the mutual recognition that both sides were, in some degree, responsible and that oppositions shared a common interest in opposing military structures. Of crucial importance was the argument pioneered by Solidarity that democratization could only come about through an evolutionary process involving the reconstruction of civil society and not through violence. What was meant by civil society was autonomous organizations and institutions, ways of regulating social relationships that are independent of governments.

But even if this perspective can be described as an ethic of caring, as a female moral code in terms of Gilligan's distinction, antipolitics in Eastern Europe was predominantly male. Many of us in the Western peace movement were impressed by the way in which writers like Michnik, Havel or Konrad articulated ideas about politics and society that closely corresponded to our own experiences both in the peace movement and in the women's movement. The way in which they talked about 'human values' seemed to be exactly the same as what we had meant by feminist values.

It was therefore rather shocking to discover how hostile many of the proponents of antipolitics were to feminism. Havel, in particular, in a brilliant and moving essay addressed to the 1985 END Convention, entitled 'The anatomy of reticence' about the difficulties of the word 'peace' in Central Europe, included a quite unnecessary diatribe against feminism, which he described as a refuge 'for bored housewives and dissatisfied mistresses'. More recently, one of Havel's aides, a woman, was asked about the President's position towards women's issues. She replied, 'He likes women very much and treats us all very well' (Rosen, 1990).

It is very difficult to explain why these attitudes were so widespread. But it is important because it sheds light on subsequent events, on the male nature of the new democracies, and the virtual disappearance of antipolitics. The intellectuals who articulated the concept of antipolitics tended to come from relatively small groups of dissidents whose political careers could be traced back to 1968, the year of the student movement and the invasion of Czechoslovakia. Their ideas were actually very abstract; they were born of reason rather than practice. Where there were mass movements, notably Poland and the GDR, women were much more important, especially in the GDR. Likewise in the newer, younger movements, that emerged in the 1980s – the Dialogue group, the Danube Circle or FIDESZ (Young Democrats) in Hungary, or the Independent Peace Association in Czechoslovakia, women played a significant role.

The somewhat élitist intellectual groups like Charter 77, KOR in Poland, or the Hungarian Democratic Opposition saw themselves as representing civil society. Yet, although they were widely admired, they were not really part of civil society – they were brave, courageous individuals. Hence their puzzlement at how quickly their support evaporated after the revolutions and their strange construction of the new situation. Jiri Dienstbier (the Czechoslovak Foreign Minister) for example, used the widely quoted phrase that 'civil society is in power' – in my view, a total distortion of the notion of civil society, rather like arguing that the working class is in power because some workers win elections.

So what did antipolitics achieve in the 1980s? If the world of formal politics is back in control, even in Central Europe, was it all a waste of time, were we naïve? Or worse, did our efforts to end the Cold War provoke the backlash that we are now experiencing in the Gulf or in the Soviet Union?

If we suppose that there is really something inherent about male aggressive behaviour, that it is one innate component of human beings, then obviously it was a waste of time, war was bound to bounce back on to the agenda. But if we assume that these differential attitudes towards war are the consequences of the way politics is organized in our society, then we have to ask ourselves what was wrong with our approach. Is antipolitics actually a way of avoiding responsibility? It is much more congenial to be part of a social movement than to engage in the cut and thrust and inevitable compromise of formal male politics. Should we have entered politics more, engaged in some of the same tactics, tailored our views to public opinion with the aim of winning power? Were we behaving in a typically female way, retreating to the secure noncompetitive world of antipolitics or had we behaved more politically, would we have ended up just like the men? Doing what the politicians are doing now?

I cannot help thinking that what the Central European argued about personal integrity *is* important. Havel emphasized 'speaking the truth'. He said that we could construct a 'political force out of the phenomenon so ridiculed by the practitioners of power – the phenomenon of the human conscience.' That was important in 1989 – hence the backlash. The problem was that many of us believed that that was enough, we could bask in the victory of the human conscience. Unfortunately, antipolitics has to be sustained and reproduced – and since this is not a job or a career, since it is not part of the formal division of labour, that is very difficult. I do not believe we were wrong, but we celebrated too soon.

Note

Mary Kaldor is a peace and disarmament researcher, currently analyzing the economic consequence of the end of the Cold War. Her most recent book is *The Imaginary War* (Blackwell, 1990).

References

GILLIGAN, Carol (1982) *In a Different Voice; Psychological Theory and Women's Development* Cambridge: Harvard U.P.

ROSEN, Ruth (1990) 'Male democracies, female dissidents' *Tikkun* Vol. 5, No. 6.

SOCIALISM OUT OF THE COMMON POTS

Swasti Mitter

During my visit to India this summer, many of my Marxist politician friends asked me whether in the West socialism was universally believed to be dead. They sounded worried, and understandably so. With East meeting West in Europe, and 1992 looming large, the radicals of the Third World felt apprehensive about their international allies. The issue as they saw it was no longer whether to be Pro-Chinese or Pro-Russian, but whether to hold on to the principles of socialism at the risk of being called old-fashioned or to accept the so-called 'inevitable' march of the market economy and be hailed as avant garde.

In the middle of such despondence, I have also encountered dynamic searches for alternative economic strategies in India and in many other parts of the Third World. These visions of alternative strategies came not from the mainstream Marxist socialist movement but from the networks of vulnerable and casualized women workers. Because of the nature of the work they do, these women remain invisible to the mainstream labour movement and trade unions. They work from home-based units or small unregistered firms, or earn a livelihood as petty vendors or hawkers. Organizers of these casualized workers care less about the scientific definition of socialism but more about the need to be relentlessly active in order to create a society that is just.

The role of this alternative labour movement assumes a special significance with the rise of flexible employment even in the developing world. As in the West, the power of the trade-union movement diminishes as more and more jobs disappear from the corporate economy to the informal sector. The big companies concentrate on controlling the market whereas the production gets put out to smaller ones. The result has been a massive loss of formal jobs and a change in the gender structure of employment. In the declining formal sector men manage to augment their share of jobs; in the hidden or informal economy of the subcontracting units, in contrast, it is the women who become the major recipients. In the regulated sector of subcontracting units, employers are not legally obliged to grant maternity leave or to comply with regulations against nightwork. In these small firms, women thus form a cheaper and hence preferred workforce. The textile or the pharmaceutical industry in India typifies the situation.

The phenomenon of flexible employment has spread to Latin America as well. The changed management strategies partly explain the rise. But the proliferation of casual jobs arises also from the debt crisis which has compelled working-class women and men to accept extremely vulnerable jobs. The number of casualized workers increases as the Western aid going to Latin America changes in inverse proportion to the money going out in interest payments. The situation has deteriorated with the opening up of the Eastern Bloc. The US has already reduced its support to Latin America in order to allow emergency funds to flow into Eastern Europe. Similarly from the EC, in the next three years Poland and Hungary will receive \$20 per head, whereas it will be merely two dollars per head for sub-Saharan Africa over the next five years. Most of Africa's formal sector in the meantime has disappeared under the strain of having to pay interest and debts.

In the middle of these traumatic changes, women in the Third World are adopting a variety of strategies to take charge of their lives. It is difficult to cover them all in such a short piece – but they can be illustrated by a few examples. The most successful, and hence the most publicized organization is SEWA (Self-Employed Women's Association) which has organized nearly 40,000 casualized women workers in the Indian city of Ahmedabad around demands which go far beyond simple wage-bargaining. It has given confidence and dignity to a large number of casualized workers. The majority of them are untouchables or harijans. As one organizer so proudly put it: 'Maybe we are poor, but we are so many.' The September 19th Garment Workers' Union provides another example. It was the anger of the exploited seamstresses of Mexico City that gave rise to this very first independent union. It started in 1985 when, after the earthquake, the sweatshop owners of Mexico City tried to save their machines and profits with little concern for the women workers. Outraged at the employers' behaviour, the bereaved women got together. A woman from the union describes the process: 'We organized ourselves, more than 5,000 women, to fight for the defence of our fellow workers and to demand that our rights be respected by the companies.'

Women's demands in the labour movement very rarely centre on wage-bargaining. Issues such as childcare, sexual harassment, income-generating activities for the rest of the family, are always prominent ones. But these concerns play only a minor role in the mainstream trade unions. Women's excitement over the power of the collective in transforming their status, even within the family, becomes infectious. After starting their own informal all-women bank, a woman villager in Tanzania describes the way they are now keeping all their profits rather than having to hand them over to men: 'We women are getting clever. We did not do that in the past.' However, one should not get carried away by these success stories. In most cases, it becomes extremely difficult to sustain the energy and organizational zeal of the workers once the immediate reason for forming the group disappears. Activists find it hard to keep the group spirit going unless the goals of the organization get broadened, or they get linked with movements beyond their own localities and specific issues.

In broadening the horizons of their struggles, the grass-roots women activists from the Third World look for support from national and international movements of women workers. They need it for a show of solidarity as well as for improving their managerial and financial capabilities – without which no organization can survive in the long run. The link is also necessary for providing a forum where activists from different parts of the world can exchange their experiences of struggle.

The future of socialism depends, to quote Sheila Rowbotham, on devising ways of organizing the unorganizable. A close look at the experiments and initiatives in this direction in the Third World may well benefit the labour movements of Europe. The spread of street vending and the hidden economy in Poland or in Hungary reminds one of the informalization of activities in Latin America or in Africa. The disturbing rise in flexible employment in Western Europe also demands innovations in labour mobilization. There is thus a renewed need to link up the workers' movement internationally beyond the narrow boundaries of mainstream unions. In forging and sustaining such a link, however, we need to shed some of our Eurocentric bias.

A couple of years ago, a young man came to see me from a television company to discuss a programme on debt-crisis. To put hope and optimism in his otherwise rather bleak script, I suggested that he include some novel forms of organization of poor workers from shanty towns of Latin America. I mentioned how in Lima, for example, working-class mothers now fed their children and their families by buying and cooking communally around what they call their 'common pots'. These 'ollas comunes' – much in the tradition of Peruvian working-class resistance – had been taken up again as a powerful expression of solidarity by poor women. Members organized numeracy and literacy courses around these common pots; those who met in the collective kitchens became vociferous about their rights as workers. In the middle of extreme adversity, the collective strength lent these women dignity and some amount of economic power. Could these common pots, I mused, herald a new type of movement for the workers? There was bewilderment in the young journalist's face. Throughout his extensive travels in Latin America, he had neither seen nor heard of these 'common pots'. Then came a faint recognition: 'Are you talking about soup kitchens?', he asked.

A symbol of solidarity of casualized women workers in the Third World often appears no more than a 'soup kitchen' to our comrades in the First. But perhaps it is out of these common pots of women workers in Asia, Africa and Latin America that a new socialist ideal may emerge.

Notes

Swasti Mitter is a Senior Research Fellow at the Centre for Business Research at Brighton Polytechnic. As a researcher and as an activist, she has been involved in grass-roots women workers' movements internationally. She is the author of *Common Fate, Common Bond: Women in the Global Economy* (Pluto Press, 1986).

This is the script of the talk delivered at the socialist conference 'Freedom, Democracy and Socialism: An International Debate' on 17 November 1990, Manchester Town Hall, UK. The statements of Third World women are taken from the forthcoming book entitled *On Empowering Women in Casualised Trade*, edited by Sheila Rowbotham and Swasti Mitter.

1989 AND ALL THAT

Beatrix Campbell

1989 was the year when the dialectic of the anti-Communist communist died. Communism is dead, long live communism! Did anyone say that after 1989? So many communists, inside and outside communist parties, lived within a culture of critique that enabled them, like everyone else, to celebrate the collapse of communism.

But any piety – it's OK, we've hated these regimes since 1956 anyway – surely soured in 1990. When the triumph of Tiananmen Square turned to tragedy, it still looked like post-Communist Eastern Europe was going to be one of the most interesting places in the world. But the triumph of protest then became a tragedy of politics: the legacy of their *ancien régimes* left societies that were not only nonrenewable as socialist societies, but nonviable as anything else either. If not before, the word 'communist' was contaminated.

Glasnost inaugurated the Eastern spring of self-knowledge. Soviet citizens were glued to the televised sessions of their Deputies in debate, millions of people re-engaged in their society, and journalists, in particular, began to give the people back their history. The pleasure of self-discovery across Eastern Europe, however, turned into rage and humiliation and worse, a new kind of paranoid purging. Eastern Europe's *glasnost* came up with such bad news and evidence of such bad faith, that 'socialist self-determination' bled to death.

Here at home, Trotskyists and Stalinists found each other once again; perhaps discovering that the cultures they shared had more in common than either of them had with revisionism, they constructed their own historic compromise to defend the relics of 1917. The historic war between reformism and revolution returned. This time as farce. A feminist friend with a Trotskyist past confessed, 'I've become a tankie' during a conversation about the fall of the Berlin Wall. She was shamed to invoke the Soviet invasion of Czechoslovakia in 1968, which liqui-dated socialist renovation in Eastern Europe. Forced to face the unpopularity of socialism in Eastern Europe, she, like those regimes themselves, retreated into a bunker to defend not socialism, but socialist *power*.

Mesmerized by the market

Clearly, the crisis was caused by the Soviet Union's retreat from the Red Empire – the promise of noninterference by the Soviet Union allowed the people of Warsaw Pact countries to protest against their own regime.

Then when the border between socialism and capitalism was opened, and the citizens of socialism surged across it, a good many socialists in the West seemed so much more mesmerized by the triumph of capitalism than the collapse of communism that they found themselves scolding the people of Eastern Europe for succumbing to the plastic bag and the lure of filthy lucre.

Western socialists were, in the end, defending the frontiers of their own fetishes. The *market* was being restored in Eastern Europe, they gasped. All those people scurrying into the West just to get their hands on *things*! But wasn't it clear that the abolition of the market and the absence of things was itself part of the crisis in Eastern Europe? If coercive political systems could not empower the people then the least they could do was feed and clothe them efficiently. They didn't. The systems of production, distribution and exchange were frozen, antique, undemocratic. They did not encourage equality or efficiency. Worst of all, they were immunized from political pressure, because there could be no political pressure to improve on the primitive laws of supply and demand.

In any case, the abolition of the market simply meant that many of these societies had their own marginal market systems anyway. It was this that provided the clue not only to endemic economic corruption, but the corruption of thought and language which contaminated the language of socialism in socialist societies beyond redemption.

What had felt thrilling about 1989 was the drama of self-discovery. But that moment also exposed the extent to which these societies, in which everything apparently was politicized, had actually de-politicized their own populations. These were societies wrapped in silence. No society can know itself if it doesn't know how many people commit suicide, how many babies die, or how people manage to live on wages below subsistence level.

A Russian woman of my own age, well read about Western politics, including feminism, said in 1989 that she'd spent 27 roubles sending telegrams to lobby her Deputy. 'This is the first time I have taken part in my society', she said. Like everyone else she was fascinated by the wall-to-wall televising of the country's new parliamentary process. She was learning a new vocabulary of democracy, both personal and political. Her contemporaries in the West are the generation which created a new kind of politics in the last three decades, it created a cultural revolution in the 1960s and 1970s, it created the Women's Liberation movement, black civil rights, a new consciousness of ethnicity and nationality, ecology, sexual politics, it tried to change the relation between direct and representative democracy. Initially, it lived largely outside the institutions, but latterly blurred the boundaries between the mainstream and the margins of political society by occupying both. That generation is a paradigm of the active citizen.

Its cohort in Eastern Europe possessed no less sophistication, stamina and generosity than their Western contemporaries and many more qualities, too, which derived from their national cultures and from the stoicism induced by system. The democratic generation was defeated at the end of the 1960s in Eastern Europe, once again a graveyard of heroism. What should then have been both a process of renovation in Eastern Europe, and a process of dialogue between Western and Eastern progressives was quelled. And so, processes and peoples were simply sent into a kind of coma.

Stalwart qualities which should have described the national cultures of Eastern Europe, became instead endemic inertia. The society's services were characterized not by socialist service but by bad temper. The powerlessness of public servants, be they bureaucrats or salespeople, produced a culture in which people were abused, day in day out by clerks, drivers, shop staff. There was barely any democratic discipline of public service, and increasingly the collective ideal ended up just that, an ideal. Or worse, an ideal that failed.

Capricious shortages and sudden supplies of goods, together with the byzantine difficulties of everyday life, produced an ingenious and sometimes obsessive consumerism. It wasn't always the self-realization-through-consumption syndrome of the West, it was the vigilante's response to a political culture which has made ordinary access to food, clothes, paint, toilet rolls, screws, spare parts, anything you want to think of, extraordinarily difficult.

Equality also became a contaminated concept. Equality for women meant extra exploitation – they work an 84-hour week, 41 of them paid.

The people have been told that equality is what they've got. What concept, then, had any utility for women, for Jews, for non-party members, for 'criminals'? What were intellectuals to feel in a society where workers' power was often an alibi for philistinism, cultural poverty and paranoia? Was it surprising that a kind of class contempt for what they call the 'simple people' would survive?

'Patriarchal' modernism

Eastern Europe's collective self-discovery was also a Pandora's box in other senses: racism had not only survived socialism but had been deployed by it; sexism not only survived state socialism, it structured it.

The crisis lay in their history as experiments in modernity that were always more or less patriarchal or sexist in the broadest sense.

The relentless rigidity of the megaplan and the banishment of civil society – that space of benign chaos in which people actually live their social lives – meant that people lived remarkably private lives, that people had no room in which to develop legitimate alternative al-

legiances and cultures. It also left no space for personal or local
initiatives to meet the society's needs where the party or the plan failed.
The disregard for the consequence of productionism in both personal
and physical ecologies produced unhealthy societies. Eastern Europe
has some of the most polluted terrain in the developed world, and one of
the worst measures of social health – infant mortality rates – in the
developed world. The political crisis of Eastern Europe was a crisis of
reproduction – the means by which society reproduces itself biologically
and socially. Women were drawn into the prioritized productive world,
but the Party did not reciprocate when it came to reproduction: the
neglect was palpable in childcare, in education, in housing, in health
care, in the countryside, in food distribution.

Soviet minds could turn to relocating lakes, flying into space, but
not to contraception, carrot distribution, refrigerated trucks, cafés. It
was the crisis in the spheres of reproduction which enabled Gorbachev
to consign women to their pre-Bolshevik destiny, the home. Somebody,
somehow, had to deal with the difficulty of daily life. Women were, thus,
to do what society could not or would not.

The Soviet mentality celebrated the muscular masculinity of The
Worker, a cult of sacrifice rather than self-expression, a culture of
dominance and control rather than self-determination, whether personal or public.

Structural sexism was also expressed in the suppression of a
politics of subjectivity, the assignment of private life to the unreconstructed family (a family which reproduced the rights of men and the
responsibilities of women, a family in which masculinity was felt to be
both a power to be prized and a vulnerability to be protected by women);
in the dominance of class as the sole category by which exploitation or
expression could be understood, to the exclusion of a system of power
associated with gender; in the syntax of dictatorship, dominance and
conquest which suffused the society, a grammar derived not only from
the tradition inaugurated by the Communist Manifesto (and the
dictatorship of the proletariat) but also the cultures of masculinity as
conquest and control.

For all these reasons and more, the absence of the market, of laws of
supply or demand, of civil society, and perhaps most important the
absence of popular politics, froze the society, left it cold to the challenge
of the majority of its population, women.

For me, a communist and a feminist, the state socialism have
always produced alienation and apology. It was feminism, crucially,
which clarified a critique of faustian Communism, which wasn't a
retreat into conservatism. By conservatism I mean either Leninism (ah!
if only Lenin had lived then it wouldn't have gone wrong!) or capitalism.

But 1989 changed my disposition from alienation to excitement and
then to despair. I was in Poland and the Soviet Union in 1989 and the
evidence of everyday life showed societies that were both politicized
afresh and yet also by now listless, depressed, tired, humiliated. By
1989 it was all too late – the extraordinary experiment begun in 1917

was both heroic and doomed by its undemocracy. The discoveries of *glasnost* made it all seem so much worse. And if communism could not be redeemed then it was because the system had been so much worse than had been thought.

Dead and gone

So, is communism dead? As we have known it, yes. Is socialism dead, too? Well, socialist cultures worldwide are in crisis. Having presented themselves as the solution to the world's problems, we have to face the fact that, like capitalism, they may also be part of the problem and not yet the solution. And patriarchal politics, although everywhere dominant, are everywhere contested.

The mind turns to a third way, the co-operative culture which used to be a bastion of popular socialism operating *in* the market not against it, which built massive institutions of production, distribution and exchange. Who knows why it died? Amidst its imperfections, it pre-figured none the less a third way between Bolshevism and social democracy. No doubt its time is past. But it may just remind us that socialism didn't begin in 1917 nor did it end in 1989.

Note

Beatrix Campbell is a working journalist.

IN LISTENING MODE

Cynthia Cockburn

The effect of *glasnost* and *perestroika* in the Soviet Union, and even more the revolutions in East and Central Europe in 1989, has been to throw me into listening mode. All of a sudden we could hear at first hand what women from behind the Iron Curtain felt and thought and wanted. Listening genuinely, I found, meant shelving the Forward Plan. An uncomfortable doubt settled on me and remains. And that is why this article is full of question marks.

The big thaw in the East came at a time when, as it happened, I was well positioned to take up new contacts. I was just beginning a research project that had a Europe-wide dimension and involved women from ten countries, including the USSR. I had, besides, been involved in fostering a newly emerging network called the European Forum of Socialist Feminists – an initiative started in 1985 by Danish and German women. It seemed as though, in the late 1980s, my own life was more open to Europe at the very moment Europe was more open to us.

Only looking back now can I see how big the change has been for me. The early eighties were devoted to besieging missile bases, linking arms round perimeter fences, sitting on damp tarmac. Our message to those who pointed their weapons towards the East had been, more or less, 'Don't tell *me* who my enemy is'. Arrived Gorbachev, and little by little we found ourselves free to meet and befriend those from whom the missile makers and shakers had so long and so effectively divided us. We could sidestep the state, their state and ours, and meet the women we'd rhetorically named our Soviet sisters.

Anastasya Posadskaya wasn't the first Soviet woman I met. But our encounter was the most symptomatic, for both of us, of the new moment. I'd made her acquaintance briefly in the Soviet Union some months before, enough to know her as warm, enquiring, a feminist. In 1988 she was sent from Moscow to work in Austria for some months. She posted me a card from Vienna. 'I'm in paradise', she wrote. 'I have a flat with two rooms. Come and stay!' I hardly knew her. I had too much work at the time. How could I afford a holiday? But then again, how could I refuse an invitation to begin the conversation we all of us, each side of the divide, owed each other, the conversation that would begin to recover the last seventy years?

So I flew to Vienna for a long weekend. We embraced joyously, linked arms, and set off round those Middle European streets, in and out of baroque churches, looking at Klimt, but seeing nothing. Because on this historically prepared neutral ground we began to listen to each other's past and future. Her childhood and mine, my family and hers, her path to feminism and the one I took.

Quite soon, though, we found our smiles stiffening in anxiety. And the trouble, to my surprise I think, wasn't feminism. It was socialism. 'But what do you mean exactly by a market economy?' I'd ask her nervously. 'But what do you mean exactly when you call yourself a socialist?' she'd ask, in dismay.

A good question that. I began by thinking agreement could be reached (and surely we were bound to agree, she and I?) by redefining our terms. What I meant could stand, provided I found new words for it. Or 'socialism' could remain, so long as I meant something different by it.

I came back from Vienna not so sure of these things. Inventing a new label, or recasting the resonances of the word 'socialism' isn't enough. To be true to this conversation, I began to understand, I am bound genuinely to rethink and reshape my politics. We can't go on putting down all the ills of the world to 'capitalist class processes' or to 'the profit motive'. But a similar obligation, I still believe, bears on Asya. To be true to our conversation she has to rethink and reshape her faith in the capitalist market economy, free competition, consumer society. She may even have to begin to believe a little of the propaganda about the West she's been force fed. That's hard when your political identity has come through resisting it.

I was always one of those socialists who wouldn't join a party. Perhaps it was due to being distant from British politics at an age when other youngsters were cutting their teeth on student rebellion. When my contemporaries were in university I was a shorthand typist. At the time they were joining IMG I was in the Far East (as we unquestioningly called it in those days) earning a living and patching together a self-taught anti-imperialism. It was in the lull between the French and American phases of the Vietnam War. Who was this man Ho Chi Minh whose ascetic, intelligent face I uncovered, on a photo at the back of a cupboard in the British Information Services office? So my socialism was invented and idiosyncratic. Oddly, this doesn't make me hang on to it any less fiercely than those who acquired theirs in a political party. Indeed, perhaps it makes me identify with it more.

Later, in 1970s London, the grass-roots politics of community action immunized me against the style and ethos of the Labour Party and labour movement. We were 'reproduction' to their 'production'. We were about consciousness-raising, they were about a line. We were socialist but we were libertarian.

Of course, the Soviet Union had nothing to do with our kind of socialism. Our hands were clean of Stalinism. And yet . . . red was our colour. 'And yet' . . . the language of contradiction and troubled consciences. Didn't we celebrate the Cultural Revolution? *Fan Shen* was our Bible in the early seventies. Didn't we fly off to Cuba in supportive groups? Weren't our heroes the fatigue-clad founders of communist Third World states? And don't we (or do we?) love them still? For all the bad company it keeps, socialism is a very malleable thing. You can shape your own dream out of it. It becomes a personal charm, less important for its shape than as a talisman to ring one round, define out all that is evil: capitalism, consumerism, conservatism, nationalism.

What the explosions of Eastern Europe have done to me is to oblige me to look inside this charmed circle, to scrutinize more searchingly the contents of my socialism. I've had to pick over the bits and pieces, re-evaluate them, reaffirm some, throw others out. I've had to admit to a certain guilt. Not guilt by association with the Soviet system, but guilt by political idleness. I have condemned individualism, for instance, while loving my highly individualistic life. I've condemned the politics of the family, while thriving in one. I've admired collectivity, while finding it intolerably uncomfortable to put into practice. When I heard what a Moscow childhood in a 'collective flat' really meant – five rooms, five families, shared kitchen and bath – I saw more clearly. The little bit of my life that's non-family, vaguely collective, sort of 'socialist', is the luxurious pinnacle of a pyramid of conventional Western wealth and choices.

This process has led me to recognize something I should have seen some time ago. What I meant by socialism has long been, more or less, what I mean by feminism. A certain generous, well-worked, twenty-years-mature, feminist perspective encompasses a great deal. Non-violence, an end to exploitation, participatory democracy, fair shares. A rationality of care. Full value for the scorned and neglected three-quarters of life: reproduction. Respect for sustaining and sustainable systems – social, economic, natural. Good listening, a hearing for every voice. Creativity and fun. An acknowledgement of difference, the difference that provides the only basis for alliances.

So far, so good. But the test is still to come. When we hold the next conference of the European Forum of Socialist Feminists, Anastasya and other new participants from Eastern countries are going to say, I know, 'if you take us seriously, please rethink the title: drop the word socialist'. Why does that make me feel panicky? Is feminist enough? Can it say everything I mean? Does the revolution in the East mean that feminism has to come of age?

Note

Cynthia Cockburn is a researcher and writer based at the Centre for Research on Gender, Ethnicity and Social Change at the City University, London. She is currently engaged in a Europe-wide project on the impact on gender relations of new technology.

WOMEN IN ACTION:
COUNTRY BY COUNTRY

THE SOVIET UNION

In this section we have included two important documents of the new women's movement which emerged in the Soviet Union at the end of the 1980s. The first is the Declaration from the founder members' meeting of the Independent Women's Democratic Initiative, known by the acronym NEZHDI; in Russian this means 'DO NOT WAIT!' The meeting to launch NEZHDI was held on 24 July 1990, and was attended by more than seventy women from five cities in the USSR. The interview which follows helps to place this initiative in context. It is with Anastasya Posadskaya who took a central role in drafting the NEZHDI manifesto. She talked to Maxine Molyneux last September while she was staying in London, about NEZHDI and about the problems and opportunities women are facing in the Soviet Union today. Cynthia Cockburn introduces the second document, the concluding statement of the First Independent Women's Forum of the Soviet Union, held in the town of Dubna, on 29–31 March this year.

Feminist Manifesto: 'Democracy without women is no democracy!'

Declaration from the Founder Members' Meeting of the
Association
INDEPENDENT WOMEN'S DEMOCRATIC INITIATIVE

We, the participants in the seminar 'Women in Politics and Politics for Women', recognizing that the process of social renewal cannot be truly democratic without an active, independent women's movement, have taken the decision to establish the association Independent Women's Democratic Initiative – NEZHDI.

NEZHDI is an association of independent, democratically run women's groups, societies and individual women, coming together with the aim of providing moral support, advice and other help to members of the association, and also joint action in solving problems of general interest.

NEZHDI acts as an independent women's platform.

NEZHDI is the transformation of women from passive recipients of favours and tips into active, self-reliant creators of their own lives.

NEZHDI is the creation by women of a spiritual environment of co-operation, solidarity and creativity, the overcoming of bitterness, aggression and mutual alienation.

Tasks of the association

1 Economic independence via mutual aid

NEZHDI believes that a woman's economic independence is the foundation of her dignity in society and family. By conjuring up the horrors of approaching unemployment, attempts are being made to get us to return to the home, 'protected' by allowances and part-time work. But this is only part of the truth. Along with these 'rights' we also acquire obligations, the greatest of which is unpaid housework instead of paid work, the obligation to submit to economic dependence on husband and state.

NEZHDI is *for* the raising of family values in society, for women as well as men having more opportunities for high-quality leisure, for contact with family and friends, for bringing up children. But we believe in a strong and economically independent family, whose fate depends on the productive labour of its members, and not on the charity of the state. We are against society hypocritically using its failure to establish family values as a reason for forcing women out of the sphere of paid and visible labour into unpaid and invisible labour.

NEZHDI considers that the past seventy years of socialism have propagated one of the most dangerous myths – the myth that women have been over-emancipated. How can one speak of the liberation of one sex if in our society the individual, the family, the town and the republic have not been emancipated? Or has the state been only half totalitarian, only for men? NEZHDI is convinced that in reality there has been no emancipation, that there is a patriarchy which is expressed at the level of social production: women's professions and occupations are the least prestigious, the worst paid, women's work is to carry out orders, routine, heavy and uncreative; even in 'female' occupations the directors are men. In the new sectors of the economy – joint ventures, firms, corporations – at best we are graciously invited to be secretaries, translators, etc. The widely advertised reduction of the administrative apparatus in ministries and institutions has been in more than 80 per cent of the cases carried out at the expense of women! We can only ask a rhetorical question: how many of those people were the ones who took the decision, the ones who really controlled things? And the remaining high-ranking men discovered a fine consolation for the reduction in the number of their subordinates: they divided those people's salaries among themselves.

NEZHDI considers that our government statistics more readily conceal the true situation of women than reveal it. This is particularly intolerable now in a period of transition to the market. We are in favour of the market, we recognize that our present difficulties are the reward for years of incompetent and criminal administration. But we want to know what price women will pay for the curing of society's problems. We want to know, so that we can act. NEZHDI supports the full and systematic publication of all social statistics affecting the situation of women.

Among the association's tasks are:

- the provision of legal, advisory and financial support to women's organizations whose aim is women's independence;
- the organization of business and management schools for women and assertiveness-training courses [courses in psychological and social steadfastness];
- the organization of campaigns against the preferential sacking of women in the reorganization of industry and the reduction of staff;
- solidarity and also financial and legal support for members of the association who find themselves in a crisis;
- the establishment of an insurance fund to support women living in poverty;
- the exertion of pressure on the new economic structures to stop or prevent discrimination against women;
- the mandatory inclusion of women on a proportional basis in both state and local schemes for professional training and retraining of specialists;
- the revision of pay scales and wage rates in 'women's' occupations, according to the quality of the work.

2 Social and political tasks

'Puppet-women' in representative organs of power and 'iron ladies' in the director's chair, women elected by no one but appointed by one or other state institution, obedient to the will of the bosses and always ready to carry out any directive issued from on high – thus has a negative image been created of the woman director, the woman political leader. They have built an invisible and unappealing barrier for women as candidates in the reformed soviets, which every female candidate felt and which allowed only a handful of individuals to win.

For decades the political system shamelessly used female

qualities such as discipline, conscientiousness, women's emotional nature, their readiness to suffer together and offer assistance, expecting nothing in return. We formed the majority of those engaged in so-called public work, many of us were rank-and-file members of the Party and of various public organizations. Even during the period of *perestroika*, the stillborn organism of the women's councils [*zhensovety*] was formed from our ranks, under the nominal leadership of the State Committee of Soviet Women, which no one had elected. However, we were permitted to share the thing men value most – power. The central feature of that power, which has brought the country to the brink of economic and social catastrophe, is its domination by a militaristic consciousness, the urge to use force to resolve all social conflicts, the infringement of the interests of the individual in the service, allegedly, of the public interest. In such an environment, the men who created it destroy themselves under the constant pressure of incompetence and mutual conflict.

Yes, we lost the elections. Yes, today we are outsiders in high politics and local politics. At present the vast majority of those who formulate and discuss political issues and take the decisions over our heads and on our behalf are men.

But this is not *perestroika*'s last word. NEZHDI considers politics to be a matter for women as well. There are thousands of our female compatriots who are well qualified and ought in future to enter the institutions of power – women who exercise the highest degree of responsibility towards the people who elected them, and possessing a political culture rooted in competence, openness, goodwill and commitment to the interests of the individual.

NEZHDI will support those female political leaders who uphold the values of humanity.

NEZHDI will support women's democratic political clubs and organizations.

NEZHDI will facilitate the organization of schools for women in political leadership.

NEZHDI will advocate the involvement of independent women's organizations in issues of military politics: for social security for servicemen and their families – soldiers and their mothers and fathers should not have to pay for the incompetence of their generals. For the transfer to a professional army – a professional army is cheaper than a nonprofessional, as professionals make fewer mistakes for which we have to pay. Better 600 competent generals than 6,000 Mukashovs [incompetent leaders]! Let us have a woman as minister of defence in the RSFSR! There must be a conversion not only in words, but in deed – and that includes a conversion of ideology.

The association advocates a democratically elected committee to observe the Declaration forbidding all forms of discrimination against women and to implement the UN Nairobi guidelines. Women in the USSR ought to know what sort of report the government makes about their situation to international organizations and who produces these reports.

NEZHDI is opposed to a one-sided protectionism that demeans women, and it will support a policy of equal opportunities.

NEZHDI is convinced that no one will help women if we cannot help ourselves. We have been organized 'from above' for so long, have we really lost the ability to do it ourselves and for ourselves?

3 Information

One of the foundations of patriarchy, men's power, is the monopoly on information. Therefore NEZHDI intends to set up a Women's Information Bureau (ZHIB) which would collect and disseminate information about:

● women's movements, groups and organizations;
● the situation of women in various countries, regions, social and political structures;
● academic research and publications on women's issues;
● conferences, seminars, symposia and also information which will help women acquire the essential knowledge to integrate themselves into the process of social renewal and the stabilization of the country during the transition to a market economy.

Information will be collected and stored in a computerized data bank. ZHIB will publish a bulletin for the association's members, arrange for the sale of information to nonmembers of the association and publish a newspaper, *Woman and Democracy*.

4 Research support for the association's work

NEZHDI considers that one of the reasons for the lamentable situation of women has been the long-standing belief that the 'woman question' had been solved, which made it impossible for systematic and unprejudiced research to be conducted into existing problems.

An independent women's movement must be able to depend on independent research. The association supports the setting up of centres of research, education and information on women's (gender) issues; it will develop links with equivalent centres abroad and facilitate the exchange of students and scholarship holders.

The Centre for Gender Studies, which has joined the association, will undertake research to monitor the situation of women around the country, summarize the experience of other countries, make its data base available and prepare a report for the association's annual conference.

In this way we confirm our intention to be subjects and not objects in the transformation of society, to participate on equal terms in the construction of the country's democratic future. We, the participants in the founding meeting of the NEZHDI association, call on the entire independent women's movement, groups, organizations and individual women to join the association and prepare for its first conference early in 1991.

Note

Feminist Review is grateful to Linda Edmondson for translating the NEZHDI document.

INTERVIEW WITH ANASTASYA POSADSKAYA (25 September 1990)

Maxine Molyneux

Anastasya Posadskaya has been centrally involved in several initiatives within the emerging women's movement in the USSR. She was a founder member of the LOTOS group (which stands for 'liberation from social stereotypes'), whose members have campaigned, among other things, against the re-domestication of women and for a greater awareness of gender inequalities in Soviet society.

In 1989, she helped to establish the first Centre for Gender Studies in the USSR, which is based in the Institute for Social and Economic Problems of the Population of the Moscow Academy of Sciences. In that year she wrote, with two other women from the Centre, Natalya Zakharova and Natalya Rimachevskaya, a critical feminist analysis of women's subordination in the USSR. Following its publication in the party journal Kommunist, *she and her co-authors were invited to submit a position paper for policy on women to the Congress of People's Deputies, the executive equivalent of the former Supreme Soviet. They were subsequently invited to play an advisory role in the committee which has responsibility for formulating policy with regard to women, the Committee for the Protection of Maternity, Childhood and the Family. Anastasya Posadskaya has now been appointed Director of the Centre for Gender Studies.*

MM Socialism has always been identified with ideas of women's emancipation, and many feminists, both socialist and liberal, have been inspired by elements of Marxist theory even if they were critical of its class reductionism. The collapse of the 'Soviet model' has made three things clear; first that no socialist alternative to capitalism can be said to exist any longer; secondly, that the vast majority of people in both 'East' and 'West' reject what they think of as socialism, and thirdly that most women who lived under communist-party rule considered that the

Anastasia Posadskaya (left) and Maxine Molyneux

gains of formal equality and full-time employment were outweighed by the severe strains of living under a system that did not work. In this light, what would you say as a feminist to those who claim that socialism failed, and in particular failed women?

AP   There are very different views on this depending on whether you are from the West or from the so-called socialist countries. The Western view tends to be that there are different kinds of socialism and that what we experienced was either not socialism or was a distorted form. In the West socialism usually means socialist values – good values, an alternative to capitalism. But for people from my country what we had *was* 'existing socialism'. They wouldn't think, since it wasn't really socialism, let's now have the real thing. On the contrary, they would be more likely to say, we did have socialism and we are fed up with it; we want something different.

It is difficult for feminists from East and West to understand each other on this point. We are often very attracted to each other personally but very disappointed politically in these terms; it takes us a long time to work out some kind of understanding about this.

MM   Do you think that the socialist project for 'women's emancipation' was misconceived?

AP   One of the problems is that the solving of the so-called women's question under socialism never actually happened. The idea was that women's emancipation would occur through their mass incorporation into social production, and the 'socialization' of domestic labour, while the Party worked at changing people's attitudes. But some of these aims did not get translated into policy. So can we say that the ideas were wrong? First of all the practical implementation of a socialist alternative in the concrete circumstances of Russia failed, and this led to the failure of other aspects of the attempt to bring about the general transformation of society. Only now can we really pose and resolve this issue of women's emancipation (which also concerns men). We need more information than we have had till now. The statistics concerning women's place in society concealed more than they revealed. Now we can freely use the results of our sociological surveys whereas before the data were restricted and not published. so it is time to reopen the women's question and probably also to open the socialist question again.

The danger now, however, is that we cannot use the old language because it was discredited by hypocritical usage; wonderful concepts like equality, emancipation, solidarity, can no longer be used. They were used to describe a reality which was quite their opposite. We were always told 'you have equality, you have emancipation'. 'Solidarity' was for years our Party's favourite word. Now this language is discredited, it is associated with a particular party structure. But what language do we use? We have a real linguistic crisis, and this affects our ability to communicate.

So it's really not a failure of socialism, if socialism means a socially just society – because ours was never a just society. Our progressive democrats say let us get rid of the labels, let us get rid of these names, capitalism, socialism, because nobody knows what these terms mean. I think that makes sense because we spent seven decades playing with labels and ignoring the real problems.

MM To return to the record of the existing socialist states with respect to women, while there has been a formal commitment to women's emancipation, with formal legal equality and the entry of women into education and employment, this has always gone along with considerable inequalities between the sexes. It would also be true to say that the inefficiencies of the command economy devolved heavily upon women themselves in a number of ways – poor working conditions, scarcity and queuing, for instance. How would you summarize the effects of this kind of system upon women, and of course on the family, where women have a particularly important role?

AP You are right that this commitment to equality has always existed. But it was absolutely formal and absolutely instrumental, it was not a commitment on behalf of women as such but was pursued only to achieve other goals, economic or demographic. We did have one of the highest rates of women's participation in production, 82 per cent, and this was always used to demonstrate the Great Achievements with regard to women. But what did this figure mean? Very little. There were certainly some prominent Soviet women and some 'heroines', who through their wonderful achievements showed that our women could attain everything they wished for. But behind these heroines stood the majority of women with very narrow life perspectives, and hard lives.

So this formal commitment was discredited and along with it some good things. The representation of women in parliament for instance, was previously guaranteed under a quota system allotting 33.3 per cent of seats to women. In reality the state was more concerned to have obedient women in parliament than women representing women's interests. These women were seen as people who raised their hands from time to time, so as a result the idea of women in power or women in elected bodies, or indeed any women in positions of power, is now discredited.

MM   This history creates special difficulties for feminist movements, yet there have been some positive developments. You yourself, along with other members of your new Centre for Gender Studies, have served as adviser to the government committee which formulates policy affecting women, and you have, with others, taken a major step in launching NEZHDI, the Independent Women's Democratic Initiative. How did this come about?

AP   We wanted to go beyond putting pressure from above. Although this is important, we couldn't rely on the top really being committed to women's issues. Much more interesting and more important for us was the development of what we call the informal women's groups. So in the spring of 1990 we began to hold a seminar at our new Centre for Gender Studies under the broad title of Women, Politics and Policy. We wanted some discussion of our position paper while it was still in the process of being written to enable those outside the academic milieu to be involved at the very beginning. We began to meet every month and eventually, by July, there was a core of women representing informal women's groups. So we thought, let's not turn the Centre into a kind of academic patron which sponsors the seminar, invites participants and suggests a subject for discussion. We decided to develop our own policy and agenda as a group of women.

Another reason for founding the association was that we didn't want to repeat the mistakes of the *formal* women's movement, organized by the Soviet Women's Committee and currently quite active. They have changed their name to the more neutral Union of Women (no socialist, no Soviet). It's very similar to what happened in Hungary and Czechoslovakia. We criticized them in our position paper because they are not elected by anybody, they do not represent anybody. So now they want to hold elections. Yet they are still organized by the state. They really should have independence to be capable of formulating policy, making it known to other people. They should acknowledge that they represent only themselves, not all soviet women.

MM   Would you favour the closure of the Union of Women?

AP   The formal women's movement is there, let it exist; if they help at least one woman, then fine. There is the question of how much they cost us – which is quite a lot because they have party money, a wonderful building in the centre of Moscow and about a hundred staff. They have resources, they can invite foreign women and can go abroad, the state will pay for them. But why should women be organized in this way? One of the phrases in our NEZHDI manifesto which I like very much is that we have been organized by somebody else for too long – why can't we organize *ourselves*?

MM You decided not to call your association feminist. Why?

AP There are two reasons for this. One is that feminism is like socialism – another label. It's seen as a bourgeois trend and caricatured as selfish, and stupid. Feminists are thought of as terribly worn and dreary women who look like men, who demonstrate on the streets, and hate men. Most women who are in the association and who are presumably going to join do not know what 'feminism' is other than this stereotype. They could be feminists in our own particular soviet way. But they do not call themselves feminists, and it would be difficult to attract them with this name. We want our organization to be an open one; not the kind of so-called open organizations which were imposed from above in which nobody was really involved or committed, and everything was planned from above. That is why in the title the key word is independent, which means independent from party control or state-organized control. The word democratic also has a special signifi-cance, it means both anti-party, and pro-public. And in Russian the acronym for our association, NEZHDI, means 'do not wait'.

MM The NEZHDI manifesto does not raise the issues of reproductive rights or sexuality, yet the LOTOS group has spoken out about the need to take these questions up in the public arena.

AP Yes, we also left out those issues concerning maternity provision and birthing. The conditions in hospitals are terrible in terms of the lack of anaesthetics, medicine, dirty linen, and so on. This should be a point of concern, and I wonder why, during our six-hour discussion of the manifesto at the conference, it did not come up, and why, as the one who was very much involved in drafting the manifesto, I did not include it. Perhaps it was because we had already included these questions in our position paper for the government. The name of that government committee talks of women in terms of Maternity and Childhood, and it required us to speak about those issues. But for my own part, I always resist tying women to motherhood and children. Although women are, of course, the main subjects of these concerns they should be seen as social concerns, matters for state policy, as well as for men. When we wrote this manifesto, I just didn't want to touch these problems because I was fed up with them. At the same time I now think I was wrong. It is women who will have to protest about these things because men will remain silent.

MM Sexuality clearly is a problematic area for people in the Soviet Union, first of all because of the previous, officially imposed, puritanical morality, and secondly because of the practicalities of being able to organize your sexual life without among other things, adequate contraception. Did you feel that these issues were difficult to phrase in political terms at present?

AP Yes, sexuality is difficult. There is no publicly articulated concern about this, either by men or women themselves. We know that so-called normal sexuality, and the heterosexual family, don't exist free from problems for the majority of people. Many people suffer on account of being different from this norm, but there is still no discussion about this. A few groups have appeared. There was a gay demonstration in Moscow, and there is a group in our association called SAFO (Sappho), and while there are many lesbians in this group they have not made sexuality a political issue. In fact, there were several women from this group at our founding meeting and they approved the manifesto but didn't raise these issues.

MM   How do Soviet feminists feel about the current fascination with pornography in Eastern Europe and the Soviet Union?

AP   I am not representative of the current view. We had a big discussion in the LOTOS group about what attitude to take towards pornography, and to the objectification of women in advertisements and the beauty contests. It ended with my tears and anger at other women; I ran out of arguments and I was absolutely in the minority. But to me state control or state censorship are at the moment a greater threat; I believe that we should not permit the state to get too involved here. Pornography is like chicken-pox; people should develop their own immunity to this kind of thing, they should not have to depend on the 'medicine' of the state.

MM   What about moving on, inevitably perhaps, from pornography to masculinity. Tatanya Tolstaya (the novelist) has argued that Russian women do not need equality with men. She claims that it is women not men who have the real power in Russian society. Men were broken by war and repression, they now die younger, they drink themselves to death; women were spared by the strength of their attachment to the home. What is your response to this view?

AP   I cannot really disagree with that, because we do not know enough about our women and men. The methods our sociologists use, these big quantitative surveys, do not reveal the inner life of the family. I am in no position to comment on this idea of the matriarchy of family life and patriarchy of public life. Two years ago when I wrote a manifesto for our LOTOS group I argued that the matriarchy of family life and patriarchy of public life was one more problem socialism had to overcome. Now, two years later, I'm not sure that that is true, I think it should be studied more. In reality gender relations were so deformed by the society we had, and people had such unusual strategies for reaching their goals; for instance, some women used marriage as a way of getting a flat, or having a child. Once they achieved this they just got rid of the man. Is this matriarchy, or patriarchy – a consequence of the fact that men have more independence in economic terms? While he can buy himself a comfortable flat, she never can. It is very complicated. What is the man's strategy? To create a wonderful egalitarian family with communication and co-operation as the main values between the members of a family, or is it to have unpaid supporters for his other interests, public or productive? Whose power is that? I would leave this question open, because I do not know the answer. We are planning to do research into these issues at our Centre.

MM   In light of this, do feminists in the USSR see men or certain kinds of men as possible allies in their struggles?

AP   I used to think men would be our allies because they are oppressed in the family too. I wrote an article called 'Invisible tears', about men's tears, which talked about the fact that men cannot realize themselves personally, particularly in the family. I thought that men would understand this and there would immediately be a men's lib movement. *Moscow News* quoted me saying this, and I was dubbed the advocate of men's lib. But I have still not seen these men. Maybe they will appear, who knows. One large group which would support giving women and men the same opportunities in society are the fathers of children after divorce. At present they suffer discrimination in seeing their children. Another group is men in non-traditional professions, those who would like to be teachers or health-workers, or work in kindergartens and nurseries. I've just learnt that gay men have sometimes been allies for Western feminists, but we have no contacts of this kind.

MM   Is there a real danger that there might develop in the Soviet Union a neo-conservative backlash which would feed on the anxieties about 'social decomposition' and strengthen the currents favouring the re-domestication of women?

AP   Yes of course, I think anything could happen in the USSR. It has been a society flattened out under a heavy weight, it was just smashed flat like a plate. This weight is now lifting, and the shape of society is changing, it is becoming more rounded, more transparent. Now there will be something of everything in this society.

But with respect to the return to the family, we are against women having no choice in the matter, but we are not against the family as an institution. Our views probably differ from those of Western feminists who regard the family as something which tied women and alienated them from real life. In our country all institutions were actually destroyed by the state, including the family in many respects. The realm of the private, or personal, life was regarded with suspicion – even some songs were prohibited during the Second World War on the grounds that 'love distracted the soldier from the great communist future'. At the very beginning there was the idea only of the unity of a socialist society which struggles against imperialism. The private sphere was so persecuted that now we see that new political forces play on this. It is the same in Poland, and very strong in the Baltic republics. Our progressive people, our democrats, all say that the family was destroyed by the state, that women lost their natural femininity and became masculinized; so it is seen as progressive to recreate the family which the state destroyed. This complicates the position of feminists. My point here is always that we are absolutely not against the family but that the need of any person to have a private life should not be used hypocritically, in order to divide the sexes. It is very dangerous in our country to be anti-family because you are immediately condemned as pro-state or pro-party.

MM   The problem will be how to prevent policy changes which effectively restrict women's choices. You have supported the idea of a quota system to guarantee women's representation in the new organs of government. Is there a danger that this idea will be rejected as 'old thinking'?

AP Things are changing, and this issue is much debated at present. In our position paper we suggested a new kind of quota system, one which was not formalized or imposed from above because that wouldn't work, but one which would be adopted voluntarily after discussion within the particular body. The quota should also be competitive, which means that there should be preferential treatment for women only on the basis of equal ability and proportionality.

MM Would you see the republics agreeing to a quota system even if it were to be agreed by the central government?

AP Most republics would reject the idea. If the central government has a quota system, they would want to do the opposite. My concern is that we should understand political policy as a creative process. There should be no single recipe for all the republics. All the republics, including Russia, rejected the idea of union because it involved a kind of primitive commune in which the whole suppressed the parts. Policy should be creative, different and not derivative of the centre.

MM How does NEZHDI see its role in relation to women in the Caucasus and Central Asia?

AP This is an important problem – should we simply say let them be, let them cope with their own problems? Should we leave them without any contacts and without any arena or platform for debate? The same problem arises with women from the Baltic republics who are facing 'return home' tendencies. I think we women should support each other, we should create through conferences, through networking, a common atmosphere of discussion to share ideas and problems, but not impose on everyone the same views.

MM In a context where the national question has become so dominant in the republics, and where the particular form of nationalism is so antithetical to feminist ideas, what hope is there of a strong women's movement emerging?

AP Now we come to the question of what is a feminist perspective and whether it can develop in the republics. First I would say that we are talking about starting a dialogue, perhaps initially quite a restricted one. It has, I am sure, already started, and there are women in every part of our huge country who need and want it. We already know women from Central Asia, from the Baltic republics, from the Tartar autonomous republic and from the other areas, who need this dialogue, and they have contacts with our association. They do not represent all the women of their particular area and that is good because it is difficult to represent all of them. Why good? Because for decades all we heard about was 'all soviet peoples', this notorious phrase. Now when we speak at meetings we speak as individuals, it is very important to have a real personal participation and an ability to express your own personal concerns.

'DEMOCRACY WITHOUT WOMEN IS NO DEMOCRACY': Soviet Women Hold their First Autonomous National Conference

Cynthia Cockburn

In a Russian town called Dubna on the icy banks of the Volga river in late March this year, women organized a conference that many of them feel was a historic event. It brought together more than 170 women in the 'First Independent Women's Forum' of the Soviet Union. Never before had there been a major, publicly advertised, conference on women's issues that was not under the aegis of the official Soviet Women's Committee.

In the Soviet Union the official Communist Party position has always been that the simple fact of women's engagement in the paid workforce, combined with a formally stated policy of sex equality, had been enough to solve the 'woman question'. Women themselves perceive a very different reality. Women continue to be grossly under-represented in decision-making positions, to be confined to low-paid, routine and often monstrously heavy and unhealthy work, and to carry with little help from men all the responsibility and labour involved in domestic life. These things have been represented, in the official view, not as systematic oppression but as simple inequalities due to delayed development, wrinkles in the socialist programme that would soon be ironed out.

The *glasnost* and *perestroika* launched by Mikhail Gorbachev since 1985 has been ambiguous for women. The new openness has enabled them to speak out against their continuing oppression. The economic restructuring has, however, threatened women disproportionately with unemployment. The ensuing shortages of food and consumer goods have increased their workload. Finally, a new orthodoxy about women has begun to replace Marxist-Leninist theory. It is a return to the old patriarchal 'truths' about women being essentially different from men, best suited to care and nurture. Men are thought to have been

The Dubna Conference; March 1991

effeminized by women's multicompetence. The idea of women 'returning to their natural duties' appeals to a government wishing to increase the (white) birth-rate and achieve many redundancies from employment without social disruption. It also appeals to many women desperate to get some respite from the double load.

Defining a workable feminist position for the new era, in which women are neither in the frying pan nor the fire, has taken time. In early 1989 an article appeared in *Kommunist*, the official journal of the Communist Party of the Soviet Union, authored by two women, Anastasya Posadskaya and Natalia Zakharova, working in a social research institute in Moscow, and by the institute's director, Natalya Rimachevskaya. The article broke with all precedent by proposing a principle of autonomy and choice for women – women should be the active subjects not the manipulated objects of Soviet policy. Men, this time around, should take their share of responsibility for resolving the crisis of overwork in women's lives. The authors pressed for quite practical policies. The various child and family benefits should be offered to either sex, not to women alone. Incentives should be offered to enterprises to make them less likely to throw women out of work first in the economic restructuring.

While feminists in social research were developing this approach, other women were taking advantage of the more liberal climate of *glasnost* to regenerate a feminist culture. Natasha Filippova, a chemistry graduate working in Moscow University, was facilitating a growing network of small feminist groups called SAFO. In Leningrad, Olga Lipovskaya, a poet, was publishing *Women's Reading*, a *samizdat* journal typed at home and circulated in an edition of thirty copies for other women to reproduce and pass along.

By late 1990 women were talking the language of a 'women's movement', and the time seemed ripe for a national conference. The organizing committee of the Dubna Women's Forum included Natasha Filippova and Olga Lipovskaya, together with Anastasya Posadskaya, Valentina Konstantinova and other women of what had by now become the Moscow Centre for Gender Studies. Olga Voronina and Tatiana Klimenkova of the Institute of Philosophy of the Soviet Academy of Sciences were involved. The committee also included an energetic group of women working in the Institute for Nuclear Physics in Dubna, who were able to offer the Institute's conference facilities.

The conference was widely advertised and any woman or women's group was invited to write in. Applications were accepted on a first-come, first-served basis. The result was an extraordinary mixture of interests and backgrounds. Participants came from twenty-five different cities and forty-two women's groups or organizations. There were women, like Valentina Konstantinova, who have had many years of acquaintance with feminism beyond the borders of the USSR. By contrast, there were women from industrial women's councils, such as those at the huge Kamaz automobile plant in the Tartar Republic, for whom the idea of autonomous organizing had dawned only the previous year. The range of interests and approaches to women's issues was very wide. There were women from the Leningrad Women's Party, who believe in an essential woman with a civilizing mission. There were student groups and businesswomen's groups. There were working-class women from Minsk, women from the striking miners' community in the Kuzbass. Some women represented environmental groups, there were women from the area affected by the Chernobyl nuclear accident, groups of 'women with many children', single mothers, university women, disabled women. Individual women had heard of the conference and made their way to Dubna from the Baltic republics, Siberia, the

The Dubna Conference: March 1991

Urals, Georgia, Kazakhstan. There were, however, no Muslim women's groups and indeed few from Trans-Caucasus or Central Asia.

And where were the official Soviet Women's Committee of the USSR? Perhaps astonished by not being recipients of a formal invitation, they had failed to apply till all the places had been allocated. A late request for three seats at the conference was turned down, along with late applications from other groups. The organizers saw no reason to afford the Soviet Women's Committee favours they would not afford to any woman. At the last minute however the Soviet Women's Committee delegated a representative to come to Dubna, regardless. She arrived without even an overnight bag, complaining that she had not had time to tell her husband of her departure. She found a room and attended the conference as an extra, with no privileges to set her apart from the remainder of the participants. This was certainly a first.

The plenary sessions at the conference focused on selected themes. Anastasya Posadskaya spoke on women as an emerging subject in the process of the social transformation of the USSR. Natasha Filippova spoke on 'the women's movement – an inside view'. One paper addressed the failure of the USSR to act on the United Nations Convention on the Elimination of All Forms of Discrimination Against Women. Olga Lipovskaya talked about the use and abuse of women as objects of consumption – from beauty contests to pornography. And Zoya Khotkina talked on the implications for women of a shift to a market economy. Other themes dealt with in plenaries or workshops were women and business; women and democracy; women and the arts; and women and the media.

There had been twenty-six of us non-Soviet women, from eight countries, present as guests and observers. On the third day we were asked to give our responses to the Soviet discussion and to compare our experience with what we knew of theirs. Although the women's movement in other countries has been an inspiration to Soviet women, it is important not to overestimate this. They have a clear sense of their own contemporary needs and circumstances. It is however taking time to recover a sense of their own history of women's activism in the nineteenth and early twentieth centuries.

From a British perspective, I found myself interested by particular aspects of the discussion. First, I was impressed by the apparent degree of autonomy of these women, not only from the official Soviet structures but from the new democratic political movements. Issues were not fought out along the sectarian lines of the (mainly male) democratic and socialist opposition groups. Despite clearly being active in oppositional politics, women didn't appear to come with party briefs. The starting point was women themselves.

A second phenomenon was the strong interest in helping women gain management skills and become entrepreneurs. There was a feeling that the market economy was going to be a playground for men, that a priority for women was to get in on the act. This was perhaps not surprising given the direction of *perestroika*: business was seen as a way of coping with threatened unemployment. All the same, it was reassuring that some women were talking of 'an ethical market' and 'management with a woman's face'.

It seems likely, however, that the great majority of women will continue to be employees of state or private enterprises. At first I was surprised therefore by the almost complete absence of discussion of themes which, a year ago in a conference on women's employment I attended in Naberezhnie Chelny, had seemed to be of all-consuming importance to working women: discrimination in jobs and training, low pay, poor conditions, appallingly heavy and dangerous work. In short, exploitation. Related topics that are undeniably of vital importance to women in the USSR and that did not feature large in the programme of the conference were women's health, housing conditions and childcare. The reason for these absences, some women said, was that women did not want to dwell in Dubna on the problems they talk about every day. They did not want to represent women as victims. Rather they wanted the conference to focus on the potential for women to take control of their own lives.

Thirdly, it was interesting to see the way sexual politics was handled at the conference. Two themes that have been central to the women's movement in Britain are still felt to be scandalizing in Soviet society. One is rape and other forms of violence against women. The second is women's own definition of their sexuality, in heterosexual or lesbian desire.

The issue of rape was not on the conference agenda. Instead the organizing committee raised it incidentally in a plenary session and invited women to attend an unscheduled workshop on violence against women, which was quite well attended.

The issue of homosexuality had already, as it happened, almost wrecked the conference. Two days before the event was due to begin, an article appeared in *Moskovski Komsomolyets*, a sensationalist daily paper. Announcing a conference in Dubna on 'a woman's right to free love', it featured a Moscow gay man making a false claim to be on the organizing committee of the conference and implying the conference would be about and for gays and lesbians. The lurid treatment of homosexuality in the article drew widespread adverse attention to the conference. People in Dubna expressed fear that their 'children would be put at risk' by an influx of 'deviants' to the town. The Deputy Director of the Institute of Nuclear Physics withdrew permission for the conference to be held on the Institute's premises. Only two days of furious protests, explanations and recantations saved the Forum from disaster.

Not surprisingly, then, at the conference the organizing committee, whatever their own individual sexual identification or views on lesbianism, treated the subject with kid gloves. Olga Zhuk, a Soviet lesbian researching lesbian issues, and Julia Dorf, a US lesbian who is in Moscow helping to organize for later this summer a joint demonstration of US and Soviet gays and lesbians ('Turning Red Squares into Pink Triangles'), spoke briefly, but there was no formal session on the theme.

The matter was not included in the final statement. Its importance was, however, underlined by a member of the organizing committee in a spoken preface.

Some of the organizers believe the *Moskovski Komsomolyets* article to have been used by the KGB, possibly even inspired by the KGB in the role of *agent provocateur*. It was felt there was a certain connexion between the official women's structures and a phone call known to have been made to the CPSU, who had in turn complained to the relevant Ministry which had leaned on the Institute of Nuclear Physics to stop this all-too-feminist and autonomous event. Certainly two men identified as from the KGB attended all three days of the conference. A few years ago the move to suppress the conference would have succeeded. Now, despite reverse trends in *glasnost*, the momentum of the women's movement and the democratic movement is, it seems, too great for this to happen.

The conference ended with the agreement of a final statement (see below). Important clauses expressed the need for the creation of a public body to ensure the implementation of the UN convention on women's equality; a development of specifically women's forms of democratic politics; support for women's economic activity; an end to the sex-stereotyping and objectifying of women in the media; and fair shares by men in domestic work and responsibility.

Although some women stressed the need for a co-ordination centre for the emerging women's movement, other women felt this would risk reproducing oppressive structures. In the event, a simple information network was agreed. One great achievement of the conference was unanimous agreement (but for two abstentions) on this final document. A second was that it now seems possible to speak confidently of 'feminism' and 'the women's movement' in the Soviet Union in a way that just two years ago would have been impossible.

The following is a draft translation of the final document, which was agreed by the Forum at Dubna. The organizing committee emphasize that the statement was drafted hurriedly and has yet to be refined and finalized. This translation is also provisional, and was made by Valentina Konstantinova with the help of Cynthia Cockburn.

Concluding Document of the First Independent Women's Forum of the Soviet Union (Dubna, USSR, 29–31 March 1991)

We, the participants of this Forum declare that:

● The attitude towards women in our country can be defined as one of discrimination – economic, political, sexual and cultural. Woman, by being included in the process of production, has not avoided continuing to bear full responsibility for bringing up children and serving the family. As a result she has a double burden – paid employment and unpaid work in the home.

- Women are accused of being to blame for many social problems, such as the increase in the divorce rate, juvenile delinquency, prostitution.
- The mass media and social sciences actively perpetuate a myth of 'women's natural functions', that women have a purely biological, predestined role. This makes it difficult for women to have freedom of choice and to realize their individual, intellectual and creative potential.

The Constitution proclaims the formal equality of the sexes, but equality does not exist as a reality. It is therefore necessary to unite all our efforts to achieve real equality of women in all spheres of human activity.

With this aim, Forum stands for the following proposals:

1 Human rights
Taking into account that the United Nations Convention on the Elimination of All Forms of Discrimination Against Women was ratified by the USSR in 1981, it is necessary:

- to stimulate widespread awareness of the convention in our society and to set up a public body to ensure its implementation in the USSR.

2 Politics
Ignoring the interests of women, a huge social group, is a sign of an undemocratic and backward society in a humanitarian and political sense. We therefore believe:

- in all institutions of parliamentary and state power at every level the interests of women and men should be represented proportionally, without gender bias;
- we should establish independent women's political organizations, movements and initiatives and look for new, non-traditional, women's forms of politics;
- we should appeal to the relevant commission of the Supreme Soviet of the USSR and the Russian Federation to exempt public women's organizations from liability for tax.

3 New economic conditions
In the light of the intensifying economic crisis and its consequences for women, and sharing the view that business should carry social responsibility, Forum believes it is necessary to generate independent economic activity for women:

- setting up a data bank of commercial information for women entrepreneurs;

- setting up a fund to support women's businesses;
- establishing a system of training for women in business;
- establishing alternative state employment opportunities for women who become unemployed.

4 Family

In the interests of society as a whole we need real democratization of many social institutions, genuine transformation rather than a revival of traditional, clearly obsolete, models. We should encourage and support a new type of family, one based on a principle of partnership with equal participation and responsibility of both parents in childrearing, domestic labour and emotional well-being of the family. The key principle is that all the members of the family are individuals with equal rights.

5 Culture and knowledge

The social understanding of women is seriously distorted today. Our society desperately needs cultural renewal. One of the causes of the crisis is the almost complete exclusion of women's spirituality from the processes of cultural and historical creativity.

We should work to end the stereotyped representation of women. The catastrophically low level of sex education, the increase in pornography, widespread encouragement of beauty contests – all these tend to reinforce stereotyped views of women. We need campaigns against the practice of representing women purely as sex objects. We should have alternative education programmes that take into account the achievements of Western feminist thought.

Existing statistical information about women does not give a complete and accurate account of the position of women in the USSR. We should develop our statistics to make them correspond with international norms.

In order to implement this programme we believe educational developments are necessary. We need a range of special training courses to facilitate the development of an alternative, women's, perspective on social and cultural problems. We should set up a system of feminist research, and women's studies should be taught in secondary and higher education.

For development of an interactive and effective women's movement in this country, Forum believes the primary task to be the establishment of an independent women's information network.

We, the participants of this First Independent Women's Forum of the Soviet Union express our solidarity with all women in this country and around the world!

DEMOCRACY BETWEEN TYRANNY AND LIBERTY: Women in Post-'Socialist' Slovenia

Milica G. Antić

There have been feminist groups in Yugoslavia since the mid-1970s. Today it is possible to speak of a number of women's movements developing in Yugoslavia, but each defines itself in relation to the specific republic in which it is active, rather than in relation to the increasingly contested national entity of Yugoslavia. This section contains material from two such movements; from Serbia, and from Slovenia.

In international law, Slovenia today is still a part of Yugoslavia, although it seems that it won't be so for much longer.[1] But this is not the theme of this article, which is limited to Slovenia. This is because of the nature of the subject I'm trying to present.

Although it is true that women throughout Yugoslavia are oppressed in all manner of ways, nevertheless they confront very different problems, arising from their various general and specific situations. Women in Zagreb (Croatia) face essentially different questions from women in the patriarchal village of Klinčina (Kosovo). Questions such as the representation of women in parliament and the constitutional right to abortion, which are now debated in Slovenia, are not even on the agenda in Kosovo, where Serbia has dissolved the regional assembly (parliament) and imposed its own Constitution. People in Kosovo are struggling for mere day-to-day survival. Almost every family of the majority Albanian population faces the constant threat of physical harassment and of police invasions of their home. Even within Slovenia, the situation is complex and differentiated, so I shall restrict myself to certain 'key' questions.

The end of the old regime

Self-management socialism – as we called our attempt to make a society without social differences – has failed in Slovenia, as throughout Yugoslavia. But the transition from a communist to a noncommunist regime was in many respects different from those in other Eastern European ex-state-socialist countries like Czechoslovakia, Poland or the German Democratic Republic. It was a step-by-step transition, without any kind of revolution. Slovenes don't like revolutions. One was more than enough, as the saying goes. The transition was effected by means of the institutions of the existing system. No communists were put on trial, there were no overnight transformations.

The end of the old regime began with the opposition in civil society to the death penalty and to the infamous Article 133 of the federal penal code (verbal *delicti*). The issue of refusing conscription (conscientious objection) became an important focus of democratic opposition, as did ecological and peace movements, and subcultural movements like punk.

In 1989 – known as the Slovene Spring – it seemed that the coming period would also bring liberation for many potential political subjects, or rather social minorities and marginalized groups. A widespread fascination with the process of democratization turned into disappointment with democracy (which as yet barely exists) when the interests of so called 'social minorities' were proclaimed to be less important than the interests of the newly arising nation-state.

Once again we have a hierarchy of big and small, important and unimportant questions and problems. In 'socialist' society everything was done in the name of the working class. Neither individuals nor their interests existed. The only recognized subject was the working class, which of course was genderless. There were no declared differences inside this group. Legally, all of us, women and men alike, enjoyed equal rights. But actually we didn't possess many of these rights, especially in the field of politics. We should not, of course, decry the social rights we did have (welfare provision, health insurance, close-to-full employment), but all those rights arose from work; there were almost no rights of citizenship. Dictatorship of 'work and workers' was a sacred institution which veiled the Communist Party state. So we had been hoping that by establishing democracy we would win the rights of citizenship without further conditions – like being a member of the working class or being a member of the nation.

Our hopes have already been disappointed in regard to non-separation of 'big and small' questions; in regard to the nation we have yet to see. Now we have a new big subject – the Slovene nation. According to majority opinion in Slovenia it is endangered by other Yugoslav nations – especially by the Serbs. Everything must be done to protect it. The main problem is to establish an independent Slovene nation-state; all other problems not connected with this one are seen as unimportant.

Women and the nation-state

The problems of women – the 'largest minority' – in establishing a new democracy have once again not been discussed. What is going on with women throws a bad light not only on the 'process of democratization', but on certain democratic processes too. So far women have been almost entirely marginalized as political subjects.

The first step in establishing a new democracy was the 'democratic and free' election of April 1990. But this did not bring any improvement in the position of women. On the contrary, their position in the field of politics became even worse. Formally, there were no obstacles to the participation of women in politics. But neither the parties nor the electoral law in Slovenia incorporated any mechanism to enable or encourage the greater involvement of women as candidates. Women were very poorly represented on the lists of candidates, and even fewer were elected. The proportion of women in the Parliament of the Republic of Slovenia is now barely 10 per cent, whereas the figure in the former parliament was almost 25 per cent. There seems to be an iron rule about power which dictates: the more the power, the fewer women. We only have two women in the government and no one in the five-person presidency.

Some people will shrug their shoulders and reply that even so, the percentage is higher than in some so-called West European countries. It is true that in some of these countries the representation of women in parliament is very poor, but what I would like to point out here is a specific and important difference. Whereas in most Eastern European countries – although by no means in all – the percentage of women in parliament is rising, in Slovenia it is decreasing.

It seems that women figure only as an electoral body and not as active individuals and political subjects. They are still treated as unpolitical beings who do not have their own opinions about politics and are too emotional to be involved in politics. It's pointless to argue (as a recently conducted survey revealed) that this is not true: that women in Slovenia mostly have their own opinion about politics, are informed about political affairs, and are very rational about political life.

To confront this situation, a group of women, with some help from certain opposition parties, managed to establish a Parliamentary Committee for Women's Issues.[2] This offers an opportunity to engage with women's special problems and their political articulation in a relatively organized and professional way. Yet what remains unsolved is the question of who will be the Committee's interlocutor in the government. For there is still, despite all the requests, no women's ministry to which the Committee could address initiatives, demands, suggestions, proposals and opinions about issues that are important for women.

New constitution

The second important step of making democracy in Slovenia is connected with the initiative for a new constitution. We are aware that the Constitution is a very important document, determining the place of each individual and group of individuals in society. And what will the proposal for a new constitution bring to women? Overall it is written for male adults and in male gender (as a matter of language). Women are mentioned only as mothers. Yet again, motherhood represents a special, highly appreciated value. A mother's place is, of course, with the children in the family, and here I'd like to point out that the proposal for a constitution privileges the family above any alternative patterns of living. The family is becoming the only pattern of life worth living.

It has happened again that women are subsumed within the patronage of a bigger entity. This time that is the family, which is treated like a subject with its own rights. (The draft legislation proposes to grant a government allowance to families; the bigger the family, the bigger the allowance.) Women are once again not considered as political subjects as such, they exist just in the private sphere and their biggest concern is children. When we are talking about children, it is about Slovene children, of course, who are very precious because the Slovene nation is 'endangered' by other nationalities living in Slovenia who will eventually outnumber it. So women have to give birth to more and more little Slovenes. (In a government white paper on a new population policy, there is even a proposal to levy a solidarity contribution from employed people without children, which would be redistributed to large families.) That's why motherhood is such an important function, not only in the Constitution but in everyday life too. The Christian Democratic Party has gone so far as to propose that mothers with three or more children should receive wages and pension rights for their work in raising a family.

The effect is to expel women from the public into the private sphere, and so increase their political passivity and their dependence on men. Just when they almost became citizens!

Tied in with the conceptualization of motherhood is the *right to abortion*. In Yugoslavia women have the right to demand an abortion till the tenth week of pregnancy without any constraints.[3] But such liberal salvation from the socialist period is now seen as a great hazard to the future of the Slovene nation, which, according to most of the parties in the governing coalition, is on the brink of dying out. (Women in Slovenia give birth on average to 0.8 girls. This figure is around 10–20 per cent higher than in the so called West, but for the Slovene government it is a very worrying trend.)

In the preamble to the Constitution there is a clause about the sanctity of life being a basic value of the society (of the postmodern society – according to the author of the preamble). Sanctity of life should not (again according to the author of the preamble) be directly connected with abolition of abortion rights, but should just mean a new context for the question of life as a whole. National-conservatives, however, see in that formulation the basis for excising from the draft Constitution the stipulation about free decision over childbearing in the existing Constitution.

Today, we face more and more pressing demands for the total abolition of this right (the maximalist option) or its enforcement with some exceptions on the basis of medical or social reasons (the minimalist option). These demands come mainly from circles around the Christian Democrats, and other nationalist parties. The most worrying recent development is the announcement by some doctors that abortion is an immoral act; gynaecologists above all are very loud in their insistence on a doctor's right to refuse to perform an abortion, because of his or her conscientious objection. For these doctors, women's right to demand an abortion either does not exist or it counts for less than a doctor's right to refuse it. (The loudest advocates of illegalizing abortion claim that just as legislators gave the right to women, so they can take it away.)

All options, however, have arisen from the concern over the allegedly 'dying out' Slovene nation. In this concern, nation as the supreme subject is superior to the individual, and women are put in the position of adolescent, immature subjects. According to those who would like to make abortion illegal, women should not have the right to make decisions concerning their own bodies, but should leave this decision-making to someone else – a doctor or a committee. In the contest between pro-life and pro-choice movements, the general atmosphere favours the former.

The reaction of women

In Slovenia nowadays, women are not simply passive observers of all these events, but there is not a large women's movement. Women's reactions differ according to age, social status, religion, interest and political conviction. Some think there is nothing to be done, others are satisfied, others again are not satisfied and are organizing themselves in more or less small but active groups – either independently or as a part of their party (e.g., the old Communist Party). And some of them are trying to establish an umbrella organization, although they face an uphill battle.

However, it must be stressed that politics is still largely considered to be 'man's business' in these regions. Parties did not even think about being more open for women members, or including provision for 'equal opportunity' or 'equal status' in their manifestos. One of the instruments which would ensure women's equal political participation and representation in parties' bodies is a policy of gender parity. The demand for introducing such a policy, however, was posed only by Liberal Democrats, where possibilities of women playing a more important role in party politics are the strongest.

In spite of the fact that democracy in our country is threatening to become the democracy of the nation, one represented by male adults with women only more or less noticeable as observers, some women in Slovenia still remain hopeful that through building various women's activities within all fields we will eventually avoid this danger. With this goal, at least some women will neither neglect strictly political ways of dealing with these problems (elections, the parliament, party politics), nor fail to pressurize public opinion through activities from below.

Notes

Milica G. Antić is a teacher of Sociology at secondary school in Škofja Loka. She is a member of the group Women for Politics formed in Ljubljana. Her current research is on women's entering in the field of politics.

1 Yugoslavia is a federal republic. It has six republics (Croatia, Bosnia, Montenegro, Macedonia, Slovenia, and Serbia), and until 1990 there were two autonomous regions within Serbia (Kosovo and Vojvodina). It has four different main languages, three different main religions, and many ethnic and other minorities with their own distinct languages and religions. Slovenia is, inside Yugoslavia, the most northern part, and the most developed part, of the state. But it is small. It only has 2.2 million inhabitants, and among them 90 per cent are Slovene, the others are from other republics, or are Italians or Hungarians. Slovenia is an ex-communist republic now. In the 1990 elections it was the DEMOS coalition (six parties) which won. But the ex-Communist Party is the biggest oppositional party, and its leader, Milan Kunan is the freely-elected president of Slovenia. The transition from communist to noncommunist regime was peaceful and democratic.
2 This Committee has members among women MPs as well as women who are experts on women's issues (sociologists, historians, philosophers, psychologists), and women from different women's groups.
3 It is a part of the 1974 Constitution, Article 191, and a part of family planning law from 1977.

A WOMEN'S POLITICAL PARTY FOR YUGOSLAVIA: Introduction to the Serbian Feminist Manifesto

Cynthia Cockburn

In early November, just before the Serbian national elections, a group of women in Belgrade took the bold step of forming a women's political party. Two months later it had five hundred enrolled members, a committee of twenty and a shared leadership of nine. It was also getting a great deal of media attention. The party is called ZEST – short for Zenska Stranka, the Women's Party. The word itself, as in English, suggests a positive force or energy. As an acronym it combines other meanings: the Z stands for women, E for ethics, S for solidarity or co-operation, and the T for tolerance.

Yugoslavia today is beset by economic crisis and riven by internal dissension. Indeed, civil war is now imminent. What the Women's Party stands for, as much as a platform for women, is a platform for peace. Although their manifesto is clearly by, for and about women and women's rights and freedoms, it is also an intervention for the nonviolent resolution of differences among the Yugoslavian national groups.

As with Green parties, there is a danger in women's parties that they fail to generate a programme that has more than single-issue scope. ZEST puts forward a thorough-going policy for active govern-ment, democratic, Green and social. They propose a decentralized and non-authoritarian democratic structure, an independent judiciary, a mixed economy, free- and high-quality health care, educational reforms, environmental protection, and democratic and accessible media. They thus offer a new form of politics that transcends what they see as a outworn left/right dichotomy.

I met with six of the initiating group: Marina Blagojević, Vesna Gojković, Maja Korać, Andjelka Milić, Zarana Papić and Lina Vusković. I asked them whether they had been criticized by any feminists in Yugoslavia who might condemn intervention in the political process as reformist, 'liberal' feminism. Two things deflect this criticism, they believe. First they have formulated the Party in such a way that it goes beyond 'rights' for women to broach extensive societal change. Second, ZEST's primary aim is not winning elections but energizing a women's movement at the grass roots. ZEST is, yes, a bid to take power, in order to change it. But even more it is a consciousness-raising tactic, a stimulus to organization in a country where the women's movement has till now been a scatter of small, local groups usually focused on some practical project. The Women's Party is not organized as conventional parties, on a territorial basis, but on an interest principle. For instance, there will be a group in a school with a strong interest in education, one in a hospital concerned particularly with health issues. 'We want the state to evacuate all spheres of our lives. We want women to know they've the strength to change things for themselves.'

A good example of the consciousness-raising effect has been their intervention in the presidential election. They have put forward a proposal for a 'job share' involving two ZEST candidates, one man and one woman. Although they've been ruled out of order, they are defending the constitutionality as well as the evident fairness of their proposal. Meantime the idea has 'surprise value', they find, and is generating a good deal of debate.

The party to date is largely Serbian in membership and activity. Serbian women are not immune to the class divisions and ethnic rivalries that fragment Yugoslavia. Can a small group of highly educated women (and a few men) based in Belgrade claim to speak for 'women' in Yugoslavia? Their answer is that they believe women in all communities and of all classes will be attracted by practical policies that are clearly relevant to them and appeal to interests women can be shown to share. Marina Blagojević's statistical research shows, for instance, that in all republics of Yugoslavia it is gender far more than ethnicity that determines women's disadvantaged position in the labour market and their low wages. Discrimination by sex is greater than discrimination by nationality. They also believe that most women want a peaceful resolution of ethnic differences.

Throughout Eastern Europe women who organize around women's issues today are being condemned as 'selfish'. These women have not encountered that in the course of their campaign. Women, they point out, are not a small interest group. They are half the population and the workforce of Yugoslavia. Seventy per cent of the unemployed are women. This is not a minority problem but a fundamental one in Yugoslav society. None the less, 'nobody will solve these problems but us.' In any case, they point out that 10 per cent of their membership is male and men will not be precluded from representing this Women's Party.

Public reaction has, in fact, been very positive. When they went to register the new Party at the relevant ministry, the woman clerk responsible for inscribing ZEST was so delighted to hear about it that she duplicated the Party's programme at ministerial expense and circulated it to all women employees. Men have been supportive too.

'Men find patriarchy heavy. There's a universal appeal in our ideas.' Where they anticipated animosity and indifference, then, they've met with warmth.

Other political parties have responded by hurriedly putting forward women candidates themselves. The dominant Socialist Party (formerly Communist) led their Serbian electoral campaign with a poster of a young woman and the words 'equal rights'. Several parties invited them into partnership. Indeed some claimed in the media, quite without justification, that ZEST was in coalition with them. 'They thought we came on a plate'. ZEST do, however, find it preferable to keep the word 'feminism' out of their publicity. As in many countries, the term has been anathematized. When asked, 'are you feminists then?' they turn the question around, and ask 'what do you mean by feminist?'

The decision to form a party, rather than some less formal initiative, was not taken lightly. After long discussions they came to feel that women simply 'needed a legal space in the power system'. The experience of two decades of the women's movement was, 'we've always been marginal, always put down'. They felt they should go now directly to where the power lies. 'To change anything you must get in there.' They are sure that throughout Eastern Europe this is the right moment, indeed a decisive moment, for women to enter formal politics autonomously, to take a part in deciding the future.

Their own future bodes a lot of work for already over-committed women. Funds are inadequate for the campaigning and recruitment they need to do. They are desperately short of potential women candidates with the necessary time and experience to compete at the polls. They will enter as many as they can in the next round of local elections. They will eventually contest republic and federal elections, and keep pressing for their job-share presidents. More importantly, however, they want to see, in five years' time, 'a women's organization active in every location in Serbia' and growing activity too in all other localities of Yugoslavia, not as party branches but as a women's movement.

The Women's Party Charter of Intentions

By this Charter women of the Steering Committee of the Women's Party make known to all women and the general public their resoluteness to take an active part in the resolution of the ongoing social crisis. Women make up half of the population, almost half of an active and employed labour force, one third of the educated and skilled population and half of the electorate. This is an enormous and undisposed-of potential.

The Women's Party appeals to all who feel socially marginalized. All feeling expelled from the public scene and willing to change that, could find themselves in the ideas of the Women's Party. Female situation is the first symptom of a sick situation and its suppression of individuality, neglect of particular human desires, powers and potentials in the name of abstract and imposed 'higher' goals. As a half of humankind, women have to engage themselves in the change of this state of affairs, and the way to accomplish this is but one – affirmation of all still-hidden and disregarded human qualities and potentials.

Why a Women's Party?

The prolonged economic and social crisis of Yugoslav society has only worsened the already imperilled existence of women. Although legally equal and free, women have for decades been living the life of second-rate citizens and unrealized and subjected individuals in the family and society alike. Instead of real progress, the prevailing part of society, and within it women in the first place, has been deprived of its right to independent political thinking and organization; unemployment and the accompanying economic emigration, an inadequate educational system, poor living standards, despicable family conditions, bureaucratized institutions uncaring for citizens, their self-centredness – have been affecting women as the most neglected part of the population. And besides, women have never ceased to be subject to the repressive influences of a backward patriarchal social conscious-ness, which recognizes and appreciates woman only as the sexual and reproductive object, with the outcome of her ever more tragic susceptibility to physical and psychic maltreatment and exploi-tation in the family and society.

In the existing situation the Women's Party will act in conformity with the following urgent goals, claiming no right to voice the interests of all women:

- It will promote women's self-confidence and their faith in their own abilities, strength and maturity to fight independently for legal rights and genuine interests of their own;
- It will support the emergence and further development of the women's movement as the firm guarantee of continuity in accomplishing the equality of the sexes and social reform processes leading to that end;
- It will act so as to facilitate the unveiling and recognition of the forms and holders of authoritarian consciousness and be-haviour who hardly care for the genuine democratization of society, overwhelmed with lust for power and dictatorship over human needs.

Association principles of the Women's Party

The Women's Party is a voluntary, independent political organization. It enrols women and men approving its programme, regardless of occupation, education, religious or national affiliation.

The Party will initiate various forms of association and gatherings of women on all levels – from territorial all the way to interest and professional organizations of women in economic, cultural, educational, scientific and technical and health-care spheres, in arts and creativity of all kinds.

The Party will advocate dialogue and co-operation with all existing and new forms of female organizations and associations determined to further the spread and strength of female self-consciousness and their influence in all the domains of social work and decision-making.

As the political party of the *by far most numerous social minority*, the Women's Party will initiate and propose changes on behalf of marginalized social groups. To this end the Party will co-operate with associations of citizens and institutions engaged in solving the problems of all deprived groups and individuals in the society.

Principles of Activity of the Women's Party

By this Charter, the Women's Party obliges itself to stick to the following principles of organization of social life and relations in its public declarations, political activities, electoral campaigns and parliamentary engagement:

1 For democracy and against all forms and aspects of discrimination and authoritarian power and authority in society.
2 For peace, tolerance and co-operation among nations and peoples.
3 For quality of life as a crucial aim of development.

At this moment the Women's Party has the following PROGRAMMATIC GOALS:

- The creation of a system of mixed economy with different forms of ownership; stimulation of development of small and medium enterprises; rational use of human and natural resources; orientation towards regional development; stimulation of self-employment; development of clean technologies; stimulation of private initiative in all spheres; a unified tax system; direct and progressive taxation of enterprises and citizens; control of budget spendings;
- An independent judiciary as a guarantee of functioning of the legal state and responsibility of those holding public posts for

the passing and implementation of laws and decisions; laws that won't endanger individual freedoms and will ensure and protect the integrity and dignity of personality;

- Good essential health care, compulsory and free, based on minimal deductions from personal income;
- Struggle for a healthy environment as the imperative of the future; stimulation of research and introduction of clean technologies and use of alternative sources of energy; preservation of natural goods and development of ecological consciousness;
- Radical reform of the educational system not only regarding curricula, but also organization of life and work in educational institutions which will provide for the development of individuality, creativity and solidarity of pupils and teachers; change of stereotype notions of sex roles; development of alternative forms of upbringing and education on all levels;
- Realization and improvement of quality of family life; establishment of equality in relations among its members; equal participation in housework and the upbringing of children and social recognition of household labour, as a condition of further development of emancipated and creative personality; individual freedom to choose, according to his/her needs a form of community of life and equal legal treatment of different forms of community of life;
- Autonomous culture and adequate cultural policy as the only genuine protection of critical consciousness in creation and communication of cultural values;
- Equal opportunities for communication, implying access to media and participation of all citizens; right to answer; right to information quota for women and children; change of stereotype mass-media notions of women and men.

Editor's note: This Charter of Intentions is in the English version prepared by its authors.

CZECHOSLOVAKIA

INTERVIEW WITH ALENA VALTEROVA, founder of the Political Party of Women and Mothers (Prague, November 1990)

Mita Castle-Kanerová

At the end of 1990, the year of dramatic changes for the whole of Central and Eastern Europe, Czechoslovakia alone had thirty-seven registered women's groups. They represent various interest groups, pressure groups, single-issue campaigns and social clubs for women and organized by women, such as Prague Mothers, Gypsy Women, Women in Science and Technology, Association of Women in Management, Single Mothers, Social Democratic and Christian Women's Unions, etc.

The Political Party founded by Alena Valterova is, however, the only one of its kind. This is because it is the first of the newly emerging groups which is both independent of the old political structures and feminist in its aims. The specificity of this Political Party lies in its interventionist role, hoping for 20 per cent of its membership to reach parliamentary representation. There is now a well-established network of 250 women throughout the ten regions of the Czech and Slovak Federative Republics. They communicate by correspondence to enable wide participation, paying a great deal of attention to the fact that not many women caught up in the double burden of family and work can travel to meetings or spend long hours in public debates.

Alena has a clearly worked-out vision of the new Party.

In your terminology, we belong to an autonomous feminist movement. Most of our women are between thirty-five and fifty. Forty per cent of the membership are single mothers, childless women are an exception. Most of them live in regional towns and villages, which is good because it gets us away from measuring the gravity of our problems purely from a city perspective. Our main emphasis is on changing the legislation and the customs through which women's discrimination has been perpetuated.

We will not organize knitting or cooking classes. That belongs to a sphere of social initiatives. However important these may be, we want to move on. The old Women's Union was a social club that was comparable to a club of stamp collectors. Most of their representatives were members of the Communist Party and, if they wanted to defend women's rights more vigorously, they ran the risk of cadre screening.

Our programme starts from the heritage of the past – too many broken, what we call incomplete families, with women's needs and interests unmet and undefended. Our constitution calls for new family legislation; stricter legislation on maintenance; considering woman's overall standard of living; possibility of a 'pension' for those women who have completed the upbringing of their children; educational reform with smaller classes; shorter working hours in line with other European countries; a woman's right to choose her GP; the right to choose how many children she wants; but also limit marriages below the age of eighteen and a restriction on the number of marriages during one's lifetime.

All our women in this country need more information about their rights. People do not know their citizenship rights all that well. We need to break women's passivity. The elections are over, and in the new parliament there are 10 per cent of women. This is less than half of the old system of representation. Besides, what kind of women are they? It is highly unlikely that they will have personal experience of living with their kids on the brink of poverty.

One of the most difficult problems currently in Czechoslovakia is that old neglect of women's issues risks being combined with a potentially even greater neglect due to the current economic changes towards a market economy.

Our aim, in the first phase of our political activity, is the defence and representation of the socially weak and disadvantaged. At present, every fifth woman provides alone for herself or for her children. In 1988, official sources indicated that roughly 650,000 people lived below the poverty line. By 1989 the numbers had grown to 900,000. At the same time, the number of households with inadequate income has increased. All in all, we have about 3 million citizens who belong to the socially weak category. Out of that there is over ½ million 'incomplete' families, predominantly headed by women. That is in a country of 15 million inhabitants!

These people are predominantly women with children, so they don't have time to sit in meetings. They are worried about their future. They feel the increased insecurity at work. They don't understand the workings of the parliamentary system. They live in fear because they have no reserves. They can't strike like the miners, nor do they know what awaits them since they cannot determine any of the events or partake in the decision-making.

The Political Party of Women and Mothers is clearly a voice for those who were the silent section of the population in the old regime and who are in danger of remaining silent in the present climate. It is very definitely a new type of political organization.

Alena is critical of Civic Forum, the broad political movement that led the way in the downfall of the old authoritarian regime in Czechoslovakia.

Civic Forum has a rather negative attitude towards the women's movement. We stated as long ago as last January (1990), that we have little in common with Civic Forum and with the old official Communist Women's Union. That position still stands. Our relationship with the trade unions is more hopeful, since we share a similar position with them. We didn't have and still don't have access to decision-making, to legislative plans and the new proposals that are now being made. If the trade unions defend the rights of working people, we shall have something to share with them. There will be discussions about the new labour market, working opportunities for women, the removal of discriminatory practices as far as wages or qualifications are concerned, the provision of services, support for single mothers, provisions for after-school activities for children, etc.

If we think about the implications of marketization for women, we must be aware that politics is the extension of business. Business means the market. And the market cannot be democratic because what prevails is the might of the strongest and the best placed.

Women are being removed from the labour market in great numbers. With the restriction of employment opportunities also comes the restriction of their educational opportunities. In Czechoslovakia at present, about 50 per cent of women work because of financial necessity. They will become economically dependent on their partners. Their entitlements to pensions and loss of qualification will be in doubt. They will be socially isolated because of the lack of provision of services. Others will have to make a choice not to have any children. At the same time, most of our women have been brought up not as mothers but with a view that a person is valued according to his/her economic activity. Now, the talk is of women staying at home with their kids for at least ten years.

Legislation is in chaos. There are a few good-sounding pieces of legislation that theoretically give, for example, single mothers certain rights and securities. In practice it is different. In the case of maintenance from a self-employed father, there is no guideline as to what or how the contribution should be calculated because of lack of knowledge about his anticipated income.

I am afraid that women and the poor have not had much say so far in our 'velvet revolution'. In the time since the changes of 1989 and since the elections in June 1990, it has been evident that the revolution is an affair of those who have the time, the means and the opportunities to take part. It has been a male affair. Who wants to hear of women's problems? There are too many other more 'interesting' problems to solve. If we don't speak for ourselves, if we don't let everyone hear us, we shall be faced with the same situation for years to come. If we look at any photographs from public meetings, from parliamentary sessions which clearly show the absence, the invisibility of women, we shall see that men have made a grave mistake. We were offered by them for example the 'freedom of choice' to watch striptease even before the resolution for a new law on political parties was debated. Our organization is here to redress the balance. In the past, the woman's question was of course debated in Czechoslovakia but only superficially, and only in reference to their position as economically active members of the society. Now is the time to break the new ground of political activism. We have had a situation where women's questions have been neglected in our society just as much as ecological questions.

It's time to learn that leaving certain issues for the distant future will not work. It's also time in Czechoslovakia to connect with women's movements elsewhere. It may not be easy to network as the specific problems in each country create their own agendas, and very often there is also the now-realized difference in using certain conceptual categories to describe the specific conditions facing East European women. (Eva Eberhardt working at the EEC points at the conceptual lag in some of her documents.)

Women in the West, although they have the 'luxuries' that we are after, like part-time work, higher living standards, shorter working hours, no shopping queues, nevertheless experience stress, have a similar percentage of neurosis, give in to alcoholism and are generally not satisfied with their position. Therefore, to merely model ourselves on Western culture, to take over Western social arrangements will mean that women's positions here may change but they will not improve!

In my opinion the main problem is that women lack self-confidence in their own abilities. In the old Eastern European context, this is particularly relevant, as the image of the paternalistic, protective and intrusive state was all pervasive. Thus, what remains to be done is to learn from each other, to prevent distorted viewpoints about the 'West' as well as to learn to understand the causes of historical developments in the 'East'.

We, in Czechoslovakia, because of our geographical position, may play a role of something like mediators between women's political initiatives in East, Central and Western Europe. It would be good if we could manage that.

At the end of my talk with Alena Valterova, I was left with the thought that the culture of the women's movement has hopefully arrived in Czechoslovakia.

I also hope that the women's movement in Britain will offer every help so that Alena's Party can succeed.

One of her current concerns is to be able to publish a new networking journal within Czechoslovakia, 'Woman 91', that would list pro-

grammes, initiatives and contacts of other women's groups there together
with information about new legislation, issues around the labour
market, and social and family concerns. Equally, the journal wants to
bring information about social-policy issues concerning women in other
European nations.

Postscript

Alena Valterova came to London at the end of June this year (1991), so it
seemed appropriate to ask her about the situation in Czechoslovakia
now. She was adamant that her interview should not go out without this
postscript.

My main criticism is of the rejuvenated Czech section of the
Women's Union that survived after the dissolution of its federal
structure. Despite the talk of a new leadership and orientation, they
have retained access to government sources of information, to the funds
of the old Women's Union (their property totalling something like eighty
million Czech crowns), and to the membership throughout the republic.
The end result of their activities is starving other initiatives of financial
support, fragmentation of the women's movement, lack of cooperation
and a privileged relationship with the key Ministries. Out of the eight
main new women's organizations that were given government grants
from the old Women's Union funds, four are still subservient to the old
structures and mentality. They can do profound damage because of
their undemocratic practices.

The Women's Union has been invited to take part in government
discussions concerning women's issues, particularly issues of employment and social policy. This means that no other women's organization
can have a say at this important level. As far as I can see, they have been
invited not because of their mass membership but because of the
manner in which they work, that is by rubber stamping the dominant
views of the government. They have not shed their centralist structure
either, misinforming some of their rural members about the new
possibilities of organizing women.

But all in all, one can see that the women's movement in
Czechoslovakia has its potential, perhaps starting to bear fruit in some
two to five years time. Its strength could lie in the fact that some twenty
per cent of all women voters are now involved in one kind of women's
initiative or another. That is not a bad ratio, is it?

Note

Mita Castle-Kanerová is a sociologist who left Czechoslovakia after the events of
1968. She teaches at North London Polytechnic. In spring 1991 she spent three
months teaching at Charles University in Prague.

HUNGARY

HUNGARY: A Loss of Rights?

Maria Adamik

After the events of 1918–19, 1945, and 1956 this is now the fourth attempt this century to bring about a basic change in the Hungarian social structure. These attempts at social change and their failure may be characteristic of an insufficient democratic tradition, and the lack of a middle class. Nowadays the real issue is again how to achieve a well-balanced development that is accepted and supported by the majority of society, how to avoid the sources of new dangers and the artificial solutions which have been tried so often in our history.

Although, in comparison with neighbouring countries, Hungary has had a relatively long time to form a multiparty system, the previous regime collapsed before the new parties managed to establish themselves. This is why the old traditional parties from before the war have been trying to revive and the various dissidents among the intelligentsia had to organize themselves into parties. The fall of the Communist Party (MSZMP) and the subsequent extreme rejection of the previous political and social structure meant that there was no left-wing political force still active. This is itself a sign of unbalanced development: the Marxist baby has been thrown out with the Stalinist bathwater. With respect to women, for instance, it is probably the case that the last forty years of so-called socialist women's emancipation is associated with the previous regime and therefore discredited and rejected – while it itself provided an excuse not to let even the thought of feminism into the country. In spite of growing impoverishment, words like solidarity and equality are still not really acceptable.

Although people are generally more active – and associations and social organizations have many women members – and a certain redistribution of political and economic power has taken place, politics still play an excessively dominant role in civil society. However, living conditions are steadily deteriorating, and so people have very little faith left in party politics. The very low participation in the local government elections held in October showed this quite clearly. The last and, in fact, the only recent political event that generated public enthusiasm and a feeling of national unity – and then only for a short period – was the rehabilitation of the 1956 revolution. However, sooner or later it will turn out that the official recognition of 1956 is not a sufficient source of strength to solve our present economic problems. The conflicts of interest are getting sharper and sharper. There are no mechanisms for dealing with and absorbing the conflicts between the winners and losers in the present situation, nor have the techniques of discussion developed between those in power (government) and civil society. Decision-making is enormously complex, because not only are there interests confronting each other like the winners and losers of the move to a market economy, but also the conflict between economic rationality and the long-frustrated desire for historic justice and compensation.

With respect to women's participation in the process of political change, it was typical that during the election campaigns even the parties for whom no argument was too extreme did not think of promising anything for women, although they could have won many votes for themselves (and also by opposing a campaign for the abolition of abortion rights that was running at the same time).

In 1980 the proportion of female representatives in parliament was 33 per cent, in 1988 it was 21 per cent and after the first free elections in 1990 this proportion decreased to 7 per cent. This means that there are currently only twenty-eight women in the Hungarian parliament, among whom single and divorced women are over-represented. We still do not know the proportion of women in local government bodies, but it is also expected to be low. This will have a direct effect on women living in regions where the infrastructure is historically underdeveloped, the resources have been withdrawn by central government, and social problems and employment difficulties have begun to show a steep increase.

There is a saying in Hungary that 'We have a Swedish tax system, an Austrian [or sometimes Swiss] price system, and a Third World wage system.' The average wage in the state sector is 250DM per month, and at the same time some basic foods, clothes – and most recently petrol – have reached, or nearly reached, world market prices.

Alongside increasing impoverishment, social inequalities are growing to an unexpected extent. Enormous incomes – generally unregistered and untaxed – are being earned by some citizens, mainly outside the state sector, and this offends ordinary people's sense of justice.

From the social-psychological point of view, what is happening is causing a huge amount of stress, for some generations it may be the second crisis of adjustment they have had to go through since the war (most people are having to work out and come to terms with their relationship to the previous system and at the same time to find a new place within society – all of which takes up a great deal of time and emotional energy) and yet the present period is one which requires the maximum effort from the Hungarian people.

Since the long-neglected health system is not able to provide for the population in its generally bad mental and psychological state, unfavourable tendencies can be expected in morbidity and mortality rates, suicide, alcoholism, etc.

State social policy is now withdrawing from community provision and prefers to transfer the burden to local governments and individual families.

The newly elected local-government bodies do not have the resources even for the maintenance of schools, kindergartens or crèches. Nonprofit organizations and voluntary associations – with the exception of those established by the Churches – are either nonexistent or not ready to operate. At the end of the eighties the number of families with children was over-represented in the lowest income bracket even pushing out the pensioners, who are also in an extremely bad situation. There is also practically no provision for single-parent families – 80 per cent headed by women, and raising 13–15 per cent of children under fifteen – despite the fact that even families with *two* breadwinners are not economically secure.

Besides the number of homeless people, and of elderly people selling their last rags or searching through dustbins, the extent of child poverty is also set to increase.

I have already mentioned that the parties have no interest in women's issues, and what a tiny proportion of women there is in parliament. The present situation is hardly more favourable with respect to other areas of interest representation. There is no committee dealing with women's issues either in parliament or in the government (not a single member of which is female).

The former Hungarian Women's Council – an organization which was set up by the last regime to provide an official – or rather artificial – voice on women's issues, is largely discredited, despite an attempt to reform itself by changing its name in 1988. This is nevertheless the organization which represents Hungarian women at the international level. Any real grass-roots movement will have enormous difficulties finding resources (even the basic infrastructure such as premises, telephone, etc.), since it will have no access to power, and will be operating in a society where the bitter struggles of everyday life isolate women from each other and make the growth of real sisterhood extremely difficult.

After a period of fighting each other, the former official trade union and the new alternative trade unions are now willing to co-operate (as in a recent taxi-drivers' demonstration) but one attitude they have so far shared has been not to take any account of the vulnerability of women in the labour market.

Whatever the case may be, these initiatives unfortunately cannot be seen as a real counter-balance to the traditional and conservative influence of the Churches – mainly the Catholic Church – and the Christian Democratic Party within the governing coalition, a member of whom has been appointed the new Welfare Minister. All these bodies are in fact hostile to women, although of course not explicitly.

It therefore looks as if the near future could be a period of a loss of rights for women. Some people say that women shouldn't be sorry, since the last forty years didn't give them real emancipation anyway, only a formal one. This statement is true for a lot of other socialist 'achievements'; there are a number of basic contradictions that have still not disappeared, proving that it is not enough to change laws and declare new values if everyday life and the values held by ordinary people do not move in the direction of democracy.

1 The basic contradiction for women is that they did not get emancipation as citizens but as a right to work, together with certain advantages as members of the labour force (which can be manipulated to meet the demands of the economy), and as mothers (who can be made responsible for the nation's demographic situation). In Hungary the famous childcare grant and allowance cost less than either good-quality institutions for children or a reasonable level of unemployment benefits.

2 Stereotypical prejudices against women have lived on and may, in parallel with the increasing flood of pornography, get even worse: on the streets, in the mass media, in the press, in cabarets, and other cultural events.

3 Women's relative disadvantages as regards prestige and wages have continued at work, and it has become clear that, although the overall educational level of women is higher than that of men, the structure and content of their education is less favourable, so that every year tens of thousands of young girls leave primary school – which is compulsory – without completing their studies.

4 More and more facts are becoming available about violence within families, rape and child abuse. However, the public does not want to face the problem, no academic research is dealing with it, and there are no shelters for battered women and children. Reproductive technologies are being applied without official supervision or even public attention, women are completely defenceless when in medical care, and there are no alternative services available.

In addition, a very strident antifeminist movement has emerged during the last decade – and cannot even be regarded as a reaction to feminism since the latter did not even exist. This movement blames women for the increasing mortality of middle-aged men, the rising divorce rate, the falling birth-rate, and the generally decreasing stability of families. That women really did have guilty feelings about this phenomenon is demonstrated by the fact that, even up to the present day, they have not been able to bring about any substantial changes in the domestic division of labour, i.e., housework. This last is an important factor because the promised service sector has not developed in Hungary, and what there is, is far beyond the financial means of the average family.

It is interesting that both official population policy and the sociology of the family as a science have focused on the crises of the nuclear family, without considering that the generally unsatisfactory state of interpersonal relationships might be the source of the problems rather than the family itself.

Seventy-five to eighty per cent of Hungarian women are in employment (90 per cent among the younger generation). Particularly in the countryside, the range of jobs available for women is not very fulfilling. However, from the point of view of women's economic independence and participation in society, these jobs remain very important for them.

There are now powerful interests calling for full-time motherhood to be an officially recognized occupation. This well-known reaction to unemployment, i.e., political and economic problems, may soon join forces with a revived Christian morality to compel women back into their traditional roles. There will no doubt also be a wish to replace the disintegrating social services and health system, and the minimal levels of social benefits, with the unpaid work of women. With these new – but actually only too familiar – regulations, women will be left anywhere but in the Europe towards which the government and the rest of the country is allegedly striving.

We should bear in mind that there are at present probably more similarities between the women of Eastern Central Europe than between other groups. I think it is very important and I would like to suggest that a network be established in this region to serve a number of purposes.

We could for example appoint an equal opportunities unit of Eastern and Central Europe, which could help to solve our common problems in this area and set about introducing the legal requirements and norms of the equivalent institution in the European Community.

Another function could be to collect and register relevant information about women's initiatives from all over the world.

A third function could be to serve as a kind of East–West women's trade union that would organize training courses in new skills and technology for women from all parts of Europe.

Note

Maria Adamik is a sociologist at the ELTE University in Budapest. She has written on the impact of Hungarian social policy on women. She is co-founder of the Hungarian Feminist Network.

DECLARATION OF INTENT

Feminist Network of Hungary

During the past forty years, just as before the Second World War, women have not been able to play an active role in social and political life. In the countries behind the Iron Curtain women could not join in the positive and progressive actions taken by women's movements around the world. Despite the recent political changes that have taken place in Hungary, women still must face their virtual nonrecognition as full citizens.

The founding of the Feminist Network demonstrates the persistence of needs long declared nonexistent. The Feminist Network aims to achieve the recognition of specific female interests and points of view, the participation of women in public life and decision-making, the realization of women's and men's real emancipation, and the abolition of all kinds of discrimination. We intend to change the political, economical and employment practices that have been perpetuating women's current disadvantageous situation both in society and in the family. Through dialogue and public debates we wish to reshape the structure of interests so as to make possible a real, rather than a forced and false harmonization of interests.

We will fight for the improvement of our life conditions, our right to work, our autonomy, our health and for our basic and broadly defined existential security.

We hope to join in a united Europe, and we are convinced that these specific women's interests are also the values of a civilized society, serving women, men and children.

The 1949 Constitution recognized women's emancipation. In practice, this was reduced to the right to work, and under the given economic conditions this right became a necessity. This emancipation granted by the state without any previous public discussion or grass-roots organization in a basically conservative society with a double standard of morality has only succeeded in producing deeply uncertain and self-doubting women prone to accept the scapegoat role they are often given.

In order for this situation to change:

● The impact of the last forty years on women's roles, status, and self-conceptions of male–female relations, and on family, must be analyzed and these analyses must be widely disseminated.
● The current efforts of the renewed and strengthened conservative religious groups, aided by the mass media, to secure the dominance of their moral views in society must be opposed.
● The parliament, with its overwhelming majority of men as members, must be prevented from making decisions in haste and without social debate, especially such decisions that can have particularly far-reaching consequences for women.

If these tasks are not accomplished, the great majority of women – surrendering the few positive developments of the past forty years – will have to choose resignation and submission in order to survive. The former omnipotence of state power, disabling or deforming all members of society, destroyed support communities and exploited the natural forces of human life, including human relationships. Women, men and children have been forced to bear their burdens alone. Women have become a bad but cheap workforce. State social policies have made them responsible for the size of the population. With the degradation of human relationships they have become sexual objects. The lack of decent educational institutions and service infrastructure has ensured both that they remain unpaid household servants, and that they do not have an equal chance with men in the world of paid work.

Those few women who have been in sufficiently favourable situations to become independent modern women, have seldom found similarly modern men to be their companions. Authoritarianism and paternalism, in addition to their everyday burdens, have also made men vulnerable (rising mortality rates) and distorted their personalities. The consequences of their inability to renounce their privileges and dominance shapes private and public life in Hungary even today.

The Feminist Network commits itself to the goal of extending to children, women, and men equally opportunities for self-realization with regard to gender, religion, nationality, racial origin or social class. From this it follows that our understanding of emancipation is universal and is directed toward the whole of society. To this end, the Feminist Network demands that effective steps be taken against unemployment, that the employment structure which is so disadvantageous to women be changed; that the formation and operation of strong trade unions with proportionate numbers of women in leadership positions be facilitated within all ownership sectors of the economy; and that the introduction of new technologies not be permitted to force women into jobs with low prestige and obsolete technology. Legal opportunities should be created for flexible working hours and part-time work for both men and women.

The concept of work must be redefined so that the work required to care for family and children and the tasks needed to sustain everyday life should be included within the sphere of important activities deserving social and material recognition. Men and women must be assured equal rights and obligations to participate in these activities. A high-quality system of childcare institutes and family services must be created out of public funds. A free and high-quality health system, including a more enlightened women's health network, is essential for the entire population. The availability of abortion must be legally guaranteed and contraception must become a responsibility of men as well as women.

Social and moral constraints which penalize forms of cohabitation outside of the traditional marriage and family must be struggled against and must not characterize state policy. The possibility for participation in social insurance must be created for and extended to every man and woman regardless of family status. Strong efforts must be made to increase society's tolerance of all otherness – whether cultural, sexual, racial or religious – and its acceptance of mentally and physically disabled people, and of pensioners. The books and activities of nurseries and schools must be examined critically in order to prevent the continued propagation of obsolete and destructive prejudices regarding gender roles.

We protest against violence within families against women and children, which is widely known about but not discussed. Now is the time for it to be given the public attention it deserves, for only with public education can this tragic situation be ameliorated. We urge stricter and stronger judicial handling of such cases, as well as the creation of refuges, telephone and taxi crisis services for those suffering from such violence.

The feminist movement is an organic part of Western democracy. The political activity of feminists is aimed at overcoming those aspects of male-female relations which are based on a relation of unequal power. We too are working for the real – not simply formal or legal – equality between the sexes in every area of social life. We hope finally to free the word 'feminist' from the misunderstanding and uninformed prejudices under which it currently labours.

Feminist Network
Szerb utca 8
1056 Budapest

ABORTION, CHURCH AND POLITICS IN POLAND

Hanna Jankowska

At the beginning of 1991 when the abortion debate in Poland entered its new stage, many women still didn't realize what was going on. Women parliamentary deputies who met recently with workers from some female-dominated factories were astonished at their ignorance of the issue. Women have no time to follow parliamentary debates, no time to read newspapers. Many of them still think that the outlawing of abortion can't pass because it is absurd and stupid. And it is important to note that many of those women use abortion as the main means of birth control.

Another feeling is predominant in some intellectual and professional circles: that the Unborn Child Protection Bill is inevitable. The Catholic Church is the main winner and the most influential force in present-day Poland. You can't resist, you must find a compromise settlement. And the Pope is coming in June, you know . . . The Bill must be passed before his visit.

Speaking about women's rights seems to be ridiculous in Poland. The word 'feminism' has bad connotations. For a long time it was (and still is) mocked in the Polish mass media. The emancipation of women is associated with the overthrown regime; many people consider it as one of the relics of the Communist system. In the process of major political and social changes stress is put on a return to old values, to national and religious tradition.

In fact, there was no tradition of an independent women's movement fighting for women's rights, because emancipation was given to Polish women 'from above' by the state-socialist regime. During the past decades Polish women didn't feel that their basic rights could be endangered. Inequality existed, but it was difficult to describe and define. It was a classical example of a glass ceiling. And it must be emphasized that Polish women were and still are terribly tired because of problems of daily life, daily food supply, lack of household services. Many of them associate 'emancipation' and 'women's rights' with being forced to work outside the home because one salary (of a husband) is not enough to feed the family.

During the last two centuries of stormy Polish history a model of victimized, self-sacrificing woman has developed, a woman fully devoted to her family (or homeland) who doesn't know her own happiness or pleasure, indeed who was taught that she has no right to be happy as an independent individual. That feeling is deeply imprinted on the minds of many women.

For example, almost every interview with a career woman must contain a question about her family and whether she is a good cook: first of all, she ought to confirm her value as a family servant, in order to be making a career.

This is the social context within which the abortion debate is taking place. But it didn't start in 1989. The pro-life and pro-choice options had already clashed in the early thirties. It accompanied discussion of the new penal code in Poland which had regained its independence in 1918. Polish democratic intellectuals struggled against the 'Women's Hell', as they called botched, back-street abortions. The name was invented by Dr Tadeusz Boy-Żeleński, well-known writer and publicist, a pioneer of birth control in Poland. Thanks to his efforts, the penal code draft was liberalized. According to the code of 1932, induced abortion was allowed in cases of rape, incest or medical indications. It was more liberal than some current proposals discussed in the parliament which don't include any medical indications except direct threat to the mother's life.

The penal code of 1932 was in force until 1956 when abortion was legalized by the Abortion Admissibility Law of 27 April 1956. Under the executive provisions of 1959, abortion in the first trimester of pregnancy is allowed on demand for a woman who gives a statement about her difficult economic or social situation.

The pro-life lobby (mainly Catholic groups) made several attempts to de-legalize abortion or to restrict access to it. A scrupulous reader of the Catholic press would have noticed that the issue was always present. They attacked the 1956 law from the very beginning. In the seventies they found some support from the state authorities. Edward Gierek, the Communist leader at that time, wanted to build a strong populous Poland. The state mass media propagated the so-called '2 + 3' family, i.e., having three children. The issue of changing the Abortion Law was also raised but the debate didn't last long. Economic crisis was looming.

The historical compromise between the Church and State has always made its imprint on birth control in Poland and the state's attitude towards the Society of Family Planning (member of IPPF). The better Church-State relations were, the less subsidies were given to the Society. In 1981 even its name was changed: the Society of Family Planning became the Society of Family Development. But it didn't save the Society from harsh attacks by Catholic circles.

In the interim period, before the great democratic changes, the abortion battle really started.

A draft of the Unborn Child Protection Bill was published in a Catholic newspaper in March 1989. It was prepared by experts of the Episcopate and did not allow abortion in any circumstances. A woman *and* the doctor who helped her could be sentenced to up to three years of prison. At first, almost nobody took it seriously. Almost nobody knew that it was an official legislative initiative signed by seventy-six deputies. The draft was discussed in the Seym (parliament) commission in April and May 1989. The discussion was accompanied by mass-media coverage and huge demonstrations in Warsaw, Poznań and Bydogoszcz. Women's consciousness awoke at last. As Dr Renata Siemieńska said, public opinion became aware of the fact that there are issues which apply directly to women. New independent women's organizations began to emerge: Polish Feminist Association, Pro Femina, Women's Self-Defence Movement, Democratic Union of Women.

les femmes
ne sont pas
des machines
à faire
des enfants

NON!

kobiety
nie są
maszynami
do robienia
dzieci

NIE!

Women aren't machines for producing babies. VOTE NO!

The Seym commission decided to start 'general public consultations' on the issue. But the parliamentary elections on 4 June 1989 brought major political changes. Solidarność won, a new parliament was formed consisting of two chambers (the Seym and the Senate). The antiabortion bill ceased to evoke interest for some time.

The next stage of the abortion battle took place in the Senate where the pro-life lobby had an influential majority.

In December 1989, a group of thirty-seven senators (among them three women), appealed to the parliament to renew the debate on the Unborn Protection Law. Since then, on 30 April 1990, new regulations of the Ministry of Health limited access to abortion. A woman who wants an abortion on social or economic grounds must make written application and consult four specialists: two gynaecologists, a psychologist and an internist. The psychologists are nominated by the chief local administrator. After all this procedure, the doctor can still refuse to perform an abortion. The woman can appeal to a special commission of doctors in her district. It is obvious that such a procedure is rather difficult to execute in small towns and villages.

As a result of the new regulations, the medical staffs of three state hospitals (in Sieradz, Kraków and Myślenice) decided to refuse to perform abortions. A statement of a women's organization condemning this decision was read in the parliament on 19 July by Mrs Anna Szymanska-Kwiatkowska, MP and vice-president of the Democratic Union of Women.

On 20 July 1990, two commissions of the Senate approved the draft of the Unborn Child Protection Bill. It was prepared by a group of senators headed by Mr Walerian Piotrowski (a lawyer from Zielona Góra district, member of the Christian Democratic Working Party). It stated that a woman who has an abortion would not be punished, but other persons who kill the 'unborn child' or help to do it would be sentenced to up to three years in prison. A person who forced a woman to have an abortion could be sentenced to up to eight years of prison. No medical or criminal grounds were taken into consideration. As for rape, the pro-lifers argued that 'we cannot sentence an innocent child to death because of the crime of his father'. After some amendments, the draft was approved in the Senate plenary session on 29 September 1990. The cases of rape and direct threat to the mother's life were taken into account as grounds for abortion. Doctors or other persons performing an abortion can be sentenced to up to two years of prison.

The plenary debate was rather stormy. Some well-known senators spoke against the law, among them Dr Zofia Kuratowska (vice-president of the Senate), Mr Andrzej Szczypiorski (a famous writer) and Mr Zbigniew Romaszewski (head of the Human Rights Commission, well-known defender of human rights during the previous regime). All of them enjoy respect in intellectual circles in Poland. Unfortunately, the pressures were stronger than moral authorities. Fifty senators voted for the draft, 17 were against it, 5 abstained. It is important to emphasize that two days before the plenary session the draft had been rejected by the Senate's Commission on Human Rights headed by Mr Zbigniew Romaszewski.

The debate was accompanied by a demonstration called by all women's organizations. There were also participants from the Alternative Society Movement, Socialist Democratic Party, Polish Socialist Party, free thinkers, anarchists and many individuals. One of the most popular slogans was: 'The Senate is impotent'. The mass-media coverage was favourable to pro-choice groups. It caused a nervous reaction from the bishops who sent a rough letter to the chief of Polish TV. It represented direct intervention in the state's TV affairs.

The Pope paid tribute to the decision of the Senate and stressed once more his concern for 'unborn life'. It confirmed rumours that the parliament intends to promulgate the Unborn Child Protection Bill as a gift to him. And in fact, Vatican sources affirmed it. Dominik Morawski wrote from the Vatican (*Solidarność*, No. 43, 26 October 1990): 'The issue of antiabortion law proposal is treated here in a more serious way than some circles in Poland can imagine, I mean those circles which make it a matter of political manipulation. I am entitled to believe that the visit of John Paul II to Poland in June next year may be cancelled if the matter is not resolved in a favourable way before spring 1991.'

It seems that Poland is going to be converted into a model Catholic state, implementing all Vatican teachings which concern human reproduction. The pro-life lobby has launched a campaign against all methods of family planning except so-called natural ones. 'Pornography and contraception are forms of aggression against life', says their declaration of 10 March 1990. A director of the state hospital in Suwałki district, Dr Tomasz Soszka, who started to implement a family planning programme supported by WHO, became the target of coarse attacks by priests and the Catholic press. He was accused of an 'attempt on the fertility of the most healthy group of Polish women', i.e., of peasant women. Yet his true goal was to diminish the terrifying number of abortions in the Suwałki countryside . . .

It is necessary to stress that abortion remains, unfortunately, one of the main methods of family planning in a country where the level of sex education is very low as a result of the activity of the Catholic Church. Three years ago, under the pressure of Catholic circles, the Ministry of Education withdrew from circulation in schools a manual on family life which contained a chapter on sex education. Only 11 per cent of Polish women use modern contraceptives. Well-known Polish demographer Professor Marek Okólski calls this situation 'a case of forced contraceptive recklessness'. The less efficient methods of birth control are the most often used: natural method (Ogino-Knaus calendar) – 35% of couples; *coitus interruptus* – 34%; condoms – 15%; the pill – 7%; chemical spermicides – 2.5%; IUD – 2%.

The low level of sex education is accompanied, as usual, by a high level of prudery and bigotry. A woman in her late thirties from Warsaw told me that for several years now she has used an IUD, but can't tell her husband about it. He is a bigoted Catholic and believes only in 'natural methods'. Both are university graduates.

The number of abortions according to the Church's sources is estimated as 600,000 yearly. It may be exaggerated. The real number remains unknown because the statistics of the Ministry of Health register only abortions performed in state hospitals and co-operative clinics (excluding private clinics). According to these official statistics, the number of abortions is clearly decreasing: 137,950 in 1980; 105,300 in 1988; 80,100 in 1989; 59,400 in 1990. The supply of contraceptives is now better than before (at least in big towns), but the main problem is lack of information and consciousness.

The latest stage of the abortion debate began in January 1991. On 15 January the Constitutional Tribunal dismissed the motion of the ombudswoman, Professor Ewa Letowska. At the request of the Polish Feminist Association she had appealed against the restrictive regulations of the Ministry of Health concerning abortion. On 25 January, the first reading of the Unborn Child Protection Bill took place in the parliament. One day before, it was announced that fifty MPs would speak during the session. But it didn't happen. After Mr Walerian Piotrowski had presented the draft of the Bill, one of the independent MPs proposed a vote on rejecting the Senate's proposal of continuing discussion on it: 124 voted for rejecting, 213 for continuing. After that a hot discussion began about points of order, there were many statements and counter-statements, the debate was interrupted many times. Finally the parliament decided to form an extraordinary commission which would continue discussion on the law. The commission consists of 46 persons, 50% women, 20 of whom are of the pro-choice lobby (among them 68% women), 24 from pro-life (among them 33% women), two of unknown attitude. The 'extremists' of both sides are in the commission, so it is difficult to imagine how it will be able to work and to prepare any proposal. In the first meeting they decided to do research on public opinion (so-called 'consultation'. The pro-life activists were against it, but it was approved by voting (20:18). From 15 February until 31 March all citizens and organizations were able to send their opinions to the parliament.

Public opinion polls conducted by independent centres in November 1990 showed that about 60 per cent of citizens are against the Senate's draft. In general, interest in the abortion issue has diminished. Most of the people including women themselves, are actually rather passive. Only two hundred women and men took part in a pro-choice demonstration in front of the parliament on 25 January, although the time and place were announced in most popular mass media. In spring 1989 and in September 1990 there had been thousands of participants. Bad weather can't be the only explanation. People are tired of the problems of daily life, disgusted by political quarrels. Many people still don't realize what the 'protection of unborn life' means in practice and what will be the consequences. The most widespread positions are: that the antiabortion bill is so absurd and stupid that it can't be passed; or that *they* will do what *they* want; we can't resist it. (*They* – '*oni*' in Polish – means the government or the authorities, regardless of their political character). The second attitude is prevalent at the moment.

The pro-life lobby don't stop at the Unborn Child Protection Bill. A draft of the new Polish Constitution is being prepared in parliamentary commissions and it is inevitable that a paragraph concerning the protection of unborn life will be included in it. The last proposal (of the Senate!) states: 'The Polish Republic recognizes the natural right of every human being to life from the moment of conception and guarantees its legal protection.'

Whether the Bill is passed before the end of this parliament's term or not, it will be a hot topic of parliamentary elections which start in autumn 1991. For many people the abortion issue means something more than a purely women's concern: it is a question of freedom of conscience, of individual rights, of separation of Church and State. The parliamentary elections will represent a decisive clash between two options: the populist clerical and the democratic one.

Appendix

What the public thinks about abortion

Attitude	Youths			Adults		
	1989 %	*1990* %	*Difference* %	*1989* %	*1990* %	*difference* %
for right to abortion	20.4	27.7	7.3	52.8	45.3	−7.5
against right to abortion	60.0	50.4	−9.6	31.3	39.6	8.3
'it's hard to say'	17.4	19.6	2.2	15.9	14.7	−1.2

The polls were conducted by the Centre of Public Polls (a state institution) in spring 1989 and spring 1990.

Some quotations of the main candidates for the presidential post

Lech Wałesa: 'You know that I am a devout Catholic. My faith is not a playing-card. For many years I have worn the Holy Virgin in my lapel. I don't play with my faith. You may like it or not, but my opinion on this matter [the abortion issue] can't differ from the opinion of the Church I belong to. Of course we ought to help women in a difficult situation, we ought to think about social needs and what to do in order not to harm anybody.' (*Słowo Powszechne*, Catholic daily, 15 October 1990)

'You can blame me, I can lose all presidential posts but I will never change my opinion. I have eight children and I wish the same to everybody. And if anybody needs help, we can help!' (rally in Tarnów, 3 November 1990)

Tadeusz Mazowiecki: 'Abortion is a serious social disease. Human life ought to be protected from conception until death. It is a matter of my Christian principles. The parliament will decide the final form of the Unborn Child Protection Bill.' (from his official programme published in *Rzeczpospolita*, daily, 8 November 1990)

Note

Hanna Jankowska is a Middle East specialist in Warsaw. She is an active member and a spokesperson for Pro Femina, a mixed group campaigning for a woman's right to abortion.

WOMEN IN POLAND: Choices to be Made

Małgorzata Tarasiewicz

Some people say: let us first establish our democracies and then we can work out the details (meaning the rights of women). But if these two things do not go hand in hand, not only will women remain second-class citizens but also our societies will remain backward civilizations, limiting themselves only to talk about democracy. Without the partici- pation of women in changes in Poland and without their being involved in political, social and economic life, democracy will never be achieved. The new situation creates new conditions in all spheres of life. Economic competition and new routes to political posts mean new opportunities for women, opportunities to take positions in which they will have a chance to influence the society they live in.

Eastern Europe is in a transitional period. This period is marked by a struggle of ideas, which is especially important since whichever ideas emerge as dominant are going to influence the lives of more than one generation.

Some years ago, an unofficial organization in Poland received a letter from somebody who had a paint-sprayer and wanted to write slogans on walls but did not know what to write, so asked for advice. It is a present-day reality in Poland that where government positions are at stake, the only groups that can make any gains are those that are well organized and experienced in using political pressure. Women are definitely not such a group. They are like the person with the paint sprayer; their problem is how to exert their rights.

Over the past forty years women's organizations were treated instrumentally, and though the legal system could have been con- sidered pro-feminine, in Poland, as in other Eastern European coun- tries, there was a great discrepancy between the legal system and social reality. 'Front' women's organizations, with a conformist membership, have created a destructive and demoralizing image of what a women's organization is like. The stereotype that originated in this way is now very much predominant within the society. So new attempts to establish a women's group are often discredited as the second Women's League, as the communist organization was named. Moreover, issues like abortion are used instrumentally during political turning points like the parliamentary elections in the spring of 1989 or the presidential elections in the autumn of 1990. All the major political forces are playing on the issue of abortion for their own ends. Catholic fundamentalists reject any kind of discussion of the topic and support the criminalization of abortion. Ex-communists, surrounded by some remnants of the Women's League, advocate the right to choose. The alliance with the Church makes it rather awkward for other major forces to speak up about this issue. Because of this, popular consciousness identifies pro-choice attitudes with the corruption of the past forty-five years. The strong influence of the Catholic Church makes society stick to the traditional vision of the female role, limited to a wife and mother stereotype.

The political climate is dominated by traditional values. With the growth of unemployment there are government plans to send women home from their jobs in order to improve the situation on the labour market. Moreover, women see staying at home as new and progressive (Rosen, 1990). The only point of reference for Poland is the pre-war period, which is the only model of the social organization of an independent Polish nation. It is viewed with nostalgia and among other things it provides the image of what a family should be like and what the feminine role is. Polish pre-war society, dominated by Catholic ideals, definitely cannot be a model for a completely different post-totalitarian country aspiring to a free market economy, with all the setbacks and benefits that such a situation brings about. The most visible advantage consists in transforming the image of work. In the communist period, work was not considered to be a source of independence. Low wages became a kind of substitute for social welfare. In the new situation women will probably develop a new attitude towards gaining professional skills. The most common danger that women, like the rest of society, will have to face is unemployment.

By the end of October 1990, women constituted 51% of the one million unemployed. It is important to stress that among young people more women than men remained unemployed. By the end of October 1990 there were 37.3% unemployed women for one vacancy compared with 9.5% men. In six regional districts there were over a hundred women for one job vacancy (and in one district as many as 1,398). For 97.3% of registered unemployed women there was no offer of a job at all. Women, because of their double duties, cannot compete with men on the labour market. Women's situation will get even worse with time and advances of restructuring in those branches of industry – like the textile industry – that employ mainly women. At the moment, employment in some textile enterprises is kept stable but, in order to avoid mass redundancies, women are sent on unpaid leave or work only two days a week, earning 500,000 zł, which is well below the poverty level.

Economic recession and the urge to cut costs has led to degradation of the value of women's work. According to data from 1988, almost two-thirds of Polish women worked outside the home. However, the motivation for most of them was not the hope of fulfilling career ambitions or the intentions of being financially independent but a much more mundane need to make ends meet. This situation led to massive participation of women in the labour market. Since all consumer goods were scarce in Eastern Europe women had a second full-time job running the household. The difficulty of obtaining goods forced many women to take part-time jobs. Now it is often this kind of a job that disappears first. Polish women are also less qualified than men and as such are easier to dismiss. Another reason for dismissing women is a cultural one: it seem to be generally accepted in Poland that a man needs a job more than a woman.

In an opinion poll carried out at the end of 1990, 45% of working women's husbands thought that women should not work outside their homes. The same opinion was shared by 53% of men whose wives did not work professionally, by 35% of working women and by 47% of house-wives.

It was a common belief that as soon as we got rid of communist rule the aid and investment would start pouring in from the Western countries. This turned out not to be true. The majority of Western businessmen interested in Eastern Europe are interested in quick profits only. They do create some jobs, but on their own conditions: no trade unions, no complaints about work conditions, low wages. That is why few men want to work there; women have no choice, no matter how big the health hazards are. Women's co-operatives and the training of women managers are discussed both in the Ministry of Labour and the trade unions, but as funding is insufficient and women are not adequately organized it only remains in the domain of wishful thinking. The conditions of work that are offered to unskilled workers are often unacceptable and the pay too low for men.

A woman's position on the labour market is perceived as more flexible due to the predominant image of woman as wife and mother whose main life goal is to support the family. Escaping the social pressure to become a mother of the traditional type and 'finding alternative forms of female identity' are among the most important women's issues in Poland. This adds to the problem of unemployment. The traditional role models determine women's position in public life, resulting in male domination in all spheres of social and political activity. Women's internalized negative view of themselves leads many women to reject institutions aimed against existing inequalities. Recently, hearing about the possibility of creating a ministry of women's affairs, one woman was shocked and said she felt human first and foremost, so why should such an institution be needed at all?

Besides an internalized negative view of themselves, there is another factor responsible for women's denial of the existence of discrimination in our society. This other factor is pride in being a Polish mother and in preserving the patriotic values of the Polish nation. That is why women's problems are crucial in the transition period in Poland and Eastern Europe. George Konrad, a writer from Hungary, in his book *Anti-Politics* explains how, during the last forty years, the private sphere was the only place where people could retain their soul and resist the intrusiveness of the state. The importance of the private sphere – which was mainly women's domain – made the role essential to all forms of resistance to the communist system. Now the uniqueness of the private sphere is much diminished as the civil society establishes itself. When men join public life women are left in a less valued sphere of life. Long associated with the home, women are simply not seen as part of the new civil society.

In the immediate future, the main things to be achieved for women's benefit will lie in two spheres. The first is concerned with the better circulation of information between Eastern Bloc countries, so that particular solutions can be found together. The experience of Western countries is equally valued, as it can be applied to Polish conditions so that we do not have to break through an open door. The information should cover such questions as ways of retraining women, of creating new jobs and legislative problems. The other sphere of activity consists of what may seem to be more abstract, that is, changing the stereotype of a woman. This would involve a broad range of activities including work with the mass media and revision of educational systems. In this respect, too, we will need extensive support from our more experienced peers.

Note

Małgorzata Tarasiewicz worked as Women's Officer for the Solidarity trade union in Poland. She resigned after a year and five months because of disagreement with the leadership on the issue of abortion (Solidarity is 'pro-life') and because of her reservations about the union as being undemocratic. She is president of Amnesty International in Poland and active in women's grassroots organizing. Before joining Solidarity she was a member of the oppositional Freedom and Peace movement – a human rights and anti militarist group.

References

DOBRACZYNSKA, Małgorzata (1990) *Dilemmas of Polish Women – Let's Work?* Paper given at CSCE Women's Conference, Berlin, November 1990.
ROSEN, Ruth (1990) 'Women and democracy in Czechoslovakia – an interview with Jirina Siklova' *Peace and Democracy News* Campaign for Peace and Democracy, New York, Fall, 1990.

ILGA: Lesbian delegates to the 1989 World Conference in Vienna

REPORTS

THE INTERNATIONAL LESBIAN AND GAY ASSOCIATION

Lisa Power

Europe was the birthplace thirteen years ago for the International Lesbian and Gay Association (ILGA). It is still the arena for many of our most successful campaigns and of our greatest support and, with the emergence of the autonomous Eastern European movements, still rapidly growing in strength.

Founded in 1978 in Coventry, England, ILGA has from the start engaged with international bodies which neglect lesbian and gay human rights as well as individual countries which persecute us. We have fought a long campaign for inclusion in Amnesty International's definition of prisoners of conscience (not yet successful) and for exclusion from the World Health Organization's definition of disease (we won). In Europe, we have worked with growing confidence and success with both the Council of Europe (CoE) and the European Community (EC). Our members have forced landmark decisions from the European Court of Human Rights (ECHR) and taken a high profile in the Citizens Assembly of the Conference on Security and Co-operation in Europe (CSCE) – the new body incorporating Eastern Europe.

Lesbians and gay men have very few rights or safeguards in international human rights law as it is currently interpreted. Only in Europe have we established even the basic right to existence. Although law is often seen as a gay male area, since it is most often used against them as individuals, it is frequently also invoked against lesbian or mixed organizations and also allows the social persecution of lesbians.

In Europe, ILGA has pursued the twin aims of strengthening our human rights and also strengthening our own organizations. Our supportive role in the growth of the Eastern European movements is one of our most proud achievements. Eager celebrants of the Westernization of Poland, Czechoslovakia, East Germany and others would do well to remember, however, that the 'liberalization' process has been a double-edged sword to the emerging lesbian and gay groups. Only in Russia and the most repressed dictatorships have Western attitudes to homosexuality been a straightforward improvement. The rise of Catholic dogma and fascism, most notably anti-Semitism, have brought new threats and new chances for repression.

A feature of these Eastern groups is the strength of the lesbians; not always numerically, but certainly in character and depth of involvement. Feminism takes new forms and some of the dogmas dear to Western hearts fall on stony or simply uncomprehending ground.

ILGA's annual European Regional Conference is the primary meeting place for Eastern and Western groups to exchange information and offer support. In 1991 it will be held in Berlin at the end of December; our optimistic lesbian members in East and West Berlin offered a jointly hosted event before the reunification had happened. In Berlin, we expect to hear reports from Copenhagen on a European project on lesbian visibility; from Utrecht on the Iceberg Project which monitors discrimination in Europe; from London on an EC-sponsored survey of employment conditions; from Cyprus on their fight for legalization; from Prague on the Citizens Assembly and from Moscow on their court case against *Pravda*, the state newspaper which linked a lesbian and gay group with bestiality and necrophilia. We'll also discuss racism, sexism and other ongoing areas of concern for the movement.

Notes

ILGA is a worldwide federation of lesbian and gay groups from more than fifty countries.

For information on the European Lesbian Visibility Project, contact LBL, Knabroestrade 3, 1210 Kobenhavn, Denmark.

For information on ILGA throughout the world, contact the Information Secretariat at 81 Rue Marche au Charbon, B-1000 Brussels, Belgium.

For UK information and membership, contact the ILGA London Support Group, 141 Cloudesley Road, London N1, England.

BLACK WOMEN AND EUROPE 1992

Elizabeth Szondi

This one-day seminar was held at the London Women's Centre, on 24 February 1991. It was organized by the Women's and Equality Units of Camden, Hackney, Haringey and Islington Councils. Some two hundred women (mostly of ethnic origin) were in attendance, drawn from voluntary and statutory organizations from all over Britain.

In the past eighteen months all types of interest groups in Britain and in Europe have woken up to the implications of Europe 1992. Black, migrant and refugee organizations across Europe and Britain have come together to fight racism, discriminatory internal controls and to have the rights of non-European Community nationals upheld on an equal basis with other European nationals. Campaigns such as European Action for Racial Equality and Social Justice have been established to develop a network across Europe.

Following a meeting with grass-roots workers and European migrant representatives in Hackney, a Migrant Forum was launched in Brussels in November 1990 with funding from the European Commission. The Campaign Against Racist Laws (CARL) has produced a Charter of European Community Rights in wide circulation.

The established women's organizations in Britain and in Europe have not been idle either. In September 1990 The European Women's Lobby was launched in Brussels. In Britain, its 'wing', the National Association of Women's Organizations (NAWO) was also established. It covers one hundred organizations and five million women of whom the vast majority are white middle-class professionals.

The community groups and organizations set up to redress injustices to the black community have given little space to the perspectives and concerns of black women. Nor have the white-dominated women's movements served their interests any better. Their preoccupations have centred around gender issues of most concern to white middle-class women. Officials responsible for social policy in Britain and in Europe have also excluded black women. Valerie Amos, in her opening address, pointed out that neither the Equal Opportunities

Commission (EOC) nor the Commission for Racial Equality (CRE) keep separate statistics on black women.

Judi Bashir (NALGO trade unionist) reported her experience in applying to the European Commission's Directorate-General for funding to invite black, migrant and refugee women from Europe to the conference. The rejection letter read:

> This conference is certainly very interesting but our second action programme on equal opportunities does not include financing seminars for immigrant women . . .

It was against this backdrop that the conference was organized. Its main aim was to make black women officially visible by developing their collective voice through networking, carefully planned campaigns and strategic alliances with other relevant organizations both in Britain and in Europe.

Issues highlighted during the day included:

● The potential of the single European market for increasing the division between highly skilled workers, and the informal sector of the poorly paid on the margins – consisting mainly of black and migrant women. The importance of access to training for black and migrant women was emphasized.
● The creation of the category of 'third country nationals', which will mean that many British citizens will have fewer rights of settlement within Europe than other EC nationals.
● The rise of racism and xenophobia within Europe.
● The restriction of the right of entry for refugees.

Action points arising out of speakers' discussions

European level
Black, refugee and minority women must:

● familiarize themselves with the legal framework, organizational structure and political sources of influence of the European Community;
● ensure that EC training programmes (currently restricted to European nationals) are made accessible to them. Such training initiatives should encompass assertiveness and confidence-building;
● the positive action managerial programme New Opportunities for Women (NOW) should be extended to cover black women in the United Kingdom;
● link-in with migrant groups in Europe campaigning for the same rights for refugee and non-EC nationals as those enjoyed by EC nationals;
● lobby for greater representation of black, refugee and migrant women at decision-making level within the European Commission;

● lobby also for their representation in the organizations responsible for dispensing funds.

National level
● lobby: the CRE, EOC, local authority race units, TUC, CBI and central-government departments on behalf of the interests of black women;
● link-in with, and seek to influence, all other voluntary and community-based organizations campaigning on European issues;
● encourage black women's organizations to join NAWO, particularly its training unit;
● encourage Training and Enterprise Councils (TECs) to undertake positive action training initiatives to prepare black women for 1992.

At the end of the conference five networking groups were set up, each one covering the key areas covered during the course of the day: racism/Fortress Europe, education and training, immigration, refugee/asylum seekers, and women's rights. Each one is being co-ordinated by an authority volunteer drawn from the ranks of the women present. These five groups are responsible for finding funding and progressing the action points. The conference organizers also plan to produce a comprehensive report as a basis for raising finance to stage a major event later with participation of black, refugee and migrant women from all over Europe. It is hoped that this, in turn, will lead to the establishment of a vibrant, effective Black Women In Europe Lobby capable of working in parallel with the European Women's Lobby for People with Disabilities.

Conclusions

The conference discussions clearly highlighted that (at least working-class) black women in Britain are caught between racism on the one hand and sexism on the other. This would appear to strengthen the view that they have need of *both* the women's movement and the black movement although, of necessity, the black liberation struggle must assume centrality, in my view.

Many speakers appeared to acknowledge this reality by repeatedly stressing the need to avoid polarization between 'black' and 'white' women. The establishment of an autonomous black women's organizing facility was not to be construed as a competitive threat. White women should rather regard it as a means of fostering mutual respect – a mechanism for delineating the parameters of autonomous as well as collaborative action.

For such co-operative and collaborative action to become a reality, white-dominated women's movements must review their organizational structure, ideology and practice. They must come to a greater understanding as to the reasons why they fail to accommodate the experiences and perspectives of black women, particularly the most disadvantaged.

Can the women's movements, as presently constituted, be developed realistically into an active, campaigning force for *all* women, including the black migrant and refugee women who are fast becoming the new exploited underclass of Europe? After careful review the honest answer may be that it cannot be done. In which case, in my view, the best way they can assist the black women's liberation struggle is to support and encourage their efforts to establish their own independent organizations.

Notes

Further information is available from: Ms Annette Johnson, London Borough of Hackney Women's Unit, Dorothy Hodgkin House, Reading Lane, London E8 1DS.

Elizabeth Szondi works in the Education Section of the Commission for Racial Equality.

REVIEWS

Against the Grain:
A Celebration of Survival and Struggle, Southall Black Sisters, 1979–1989

Southall Black Sisters

Southall Black Sisters: London 1990, ISBN 0951 570 404 £7.50 (Institutions) £4.50 (Individuals) £1.50 (Unwaged)

'Like all our work this bulletin has been written in the heat of the moment' – that throwaway line in the introduction of *Against the Grain* prepares us for all that is stimulating and disappointing about this booklet.

Marking the tenth anniversary of the founding of Southall Black Sisters (SBS), the booklet consists of a series of separate articles arranged in three sections: a brief introduction in which women who belonged to the group in the late seventies and early eighties describe their experiences; a central section which is essentially the stories of a series of battles fought and won (or at least not lost) by SBS – against fundamentalist Muslims, conservative Asian organizations, male antiracists and so on; and a brief concluding section by women recently involved in the group.

At a time when the feminist movement is producing very little which tells of day-to-day activism, *Against the Grain* is a welcome and refreshing contribution. With a striking honesty which makes events described ring true even to those of us who have never been to

Southall, it tells us about the horrific murders of women by their husbands which but for SBS's agitations would have been ignored even in the Asian community, the role of the family in controlling and abusing women who demand even the most basic independence, the pomposity and hypocrisy of community leaders who tried to do SBS out of its funding, the difficulties of black women allying with white radical feminists . . . And it tells us this not merely for information but in the course of describing specific struggles against various forms of oppression.

Running through the booklet are two main themes that any activist fighting for the most basic human rights and dignities for black women is likely to face hostility from those who claim to represent the community: 'We are constantly told that to raise our experience in public is to invite a racist backlash and to weaken the primary struggle of black people against racism. Yet we find ourselves having to confront the daily experiences of women, violence, sexual abuse, rape and harassment on the street, in the home and at work. And linked to this the question which crops up with predictable regularity. How to afford safety and protection to women and children by making demands of the police, the judiciary and the welfare system but at the same time recognize that these very institutions have been at the forefront of attacks on black people in this country since the 1950s.'

But what happens next is not really dealt with; the issues are raised but the argument which one expects to follow is missing. And so while the problem is clearly stated – the difficulty of making these particular decisions and creating strategies against a backdrop of the intense racism of Thatcher's Britain – the reasoning behind these decisions and strategies is never touched upon. Missing too is any explicit analysis of either the history or the nature of forces which have created a situation where women's oppression can flourish on such a scale. We are told, for example, that 'community leaders' who are against all interventions in domestic violence have been willing to co-operate with the police when it suits their interests, but we are never told who these 'community leaders' are: what is their class and history and, most significantly, what is their role for the British state?

Similarly, antiracism is frequently mentioned, we are told of its 'heroic [i.e. macho] tradition', of the 'left and anti-racist perspective of black youth as the progressive face of the community' and yet antiracism itself is never clearly defined. Readers not in the know may easily get the impression that antiracism is more or less the same as multi-culturalism. Coupled with this is a reluctance to distinguish between the politics of various protagonists – between the antiracism of funded and nonfunded groups, of black Marxist individuals and local councils, and so on. Even though there are clearly issues on which all these groups and individuals need to be challenged, is it useful to lump them all together? Should not our strategies and even our tactics in dealing with them be affected in turn by their relationship with the British state, by courtesy of which all these injustices occur or are allowed to occur? For much of the book I found myself asking whether SBS regards itself as part of the antiracist move-

ment – because the problem is almost always posed as the anti-racist movement itself, not the sexists who dominate sections of it. Finally I found the answer to my question tucked away near the end of the main section: 'We have not left the anti-racist struggle. We did not undermine it. Instead we brought an anti-racist perspective to the women's movement and a feminist perspective to the black struggle.'

I was left wondering why the booklet was written in this particular style, spontaneous and informal but unstructured and almost deliberately lacking a consciousness of history even of the black women's movement. Perhaps it was intended to be in the feminist tradition of women expressing themselves through oral testimonies. Unfortunately, while this works in some articles (like those by Hannana Siddiqui) which are essentially personal accounts, in others it simply creates the impression of confusion. Not only are ambiguous terms left undefined, but even events (like the murder of Balwant Kaur, for example) are sometimes referred to but not described even in outline; there is an impression of close friends talking to and for each other, justifying and celebrating their actions, and preparing for attacks from unseen critics.

This suggests exclusiveness and élitism, but SBS apparently do not want to be either. As *Against the Grain* puts it: 'Strong alliances are absolutely crucial to the success of our various campaigns but so much energy has been put into problematic alliances which have very often ended in splits that we have to ask ourselves where we have gone wrong. Where should we have compromised our political principles in order to prevent splits which are so damaging to the movement?'

It is the phrase 'compromising our political principles' which reveals most about the approach put across in *Against the Grain*. If compromising or not compromising our principles becomes such a central issue, an aim in itself, then transforming our lives and those of other women (including women who may not necessarily agree with us), can become secondary. What happens then, in practice, is what I observed at an Asian women's meeting last summer, where a speaker from SBS discussed religion. She presented her position and, when questioned and challenged, simply restated it. There was no attempt to explain this position, to discuss strategy or to learn from other Asian women who disagreed.

The result of this attitude is alienation from many struggling Asian women who, while aware of the sexist nature of religious institutions, still see their religion as an essential element in their defences against Britain's racist society; women whose everyday experience

tells them that in Britain now, thanks to the Rushdie Affair, all Asians are seen as Muslims and therefore as fundamentalists and that, in view of this, new strategies are needed to combat Asian women's oppression.

What you will find in *Against the Grain* is a reflection of both the positive and negative aspects of SBS's attitude. It is a feminism full of dynamism and courage, but laced with intolerance and arrogance – a politics which is about crusading, not convincing.

Amrit Wilson

Note

This review was written in November 1990, before the Gulf War, and was held over to this issue so that it could appear together with the contrasting review by Julia Bard.

Against the Grain

Orthodoxies are, by their nature, both coercive and exclusive since they claim not only the privilege of unique understanding, but also an institutional right to speak on behalf of others. Although many orthodox groups, whether political, religious, cultural or social, on the left or the right, appear to recruit or even to proselytize, their power rests on their ability to limit the boundaries of debate, thereby defining dissenters as outsiders.

Southall Black Sisters are not just a thorn in the side of the establishments of the Asian communities from which most of them come, but are an important challenge to conventional wisdom on the left and in the women's movement. They have insisted on the right to break ranks with leaders of the Asian community, secular and religious, over issues like arranged marriage and calls to extend the blasphemy laws.

But they have also insisted on the right to break ranks with orthodox antiracism when it creates new myths to avoid extending its analysis to incorporate uncomfortable realities.

Against the Grain is a collection of accounts of the life and work of Southall Black Sisters – a history 'fractured' by conflicts, both within and outside the group, but a history also of resolving those conflicts, of creating alliances and pushing forward the boundaries of political debate.

Since its formation in 1979 the central tension in SBS has been between whether to concentrate on casework or on political campaigning. They have managed to do both and, uncomfortable though that tension has been, it is precisely the impact of their own and other black women's real and immediate concerns on their general analysis which has enabled them to look and move outwards, to develop politically and face the challenge of power and oppression within their community as well as the racism outside it.

Gita Sahgal says in her chapter, 'Fundamentalism and the multi-culturalist fallacy': 'Very early on, women in SBS protested at the death of Mrs Dhillon and her children who had been killed by her husband who set their house alight. They broke the silence of the community on the issue of domestic violence. They challenged also, perhaps inadvertently, the "heroic tradition" of anti-racism . . . Black women were to be celebrated when they came out in their thousands to oppose the presence of fascists in their streets, but not when they tried to create a new movement and consciousness and challenged the notion of a unified community.' (p. 17)

By taking up the issue of domestic violence in the Asian community, SBS were accused of provoking a racist backlash and encouraging the press to pathologize the Asian family. In my view Gita Sahgal treads too gently when she replies that a racist backlash is unlikely in a huge black community like Southall and that domestic violence is a universal problem which needs to be challenged by all women. An old Jewish socialist friend of mine who has fought anti-Semitism since his youth in pre-War Poland says: 'If you want to beat a dog, you can always find a stick.' Racism is not caused by the activities of its victims so it is, at best, pointless to keep your criticisms of institutions such as arranged marriage, confined within the community; at worst it means sacrificing women's lives, in some cases literally, to what turns out to be spurious unity against racism from outside the community.

This collection of essays and interviews reflecting on the experiences and development of SBS, whose first ten years coincided with Thatcher's regime, describes the bleak political landscape in which they were operating and the destructive sectarian battles fought out across the Left. The Parliamentary Labour Party spent those years elbowing its way on to Conservative territory, while municipal anti-racism co-opted activists and blunted dissent. Radical feminists split into increasingly minute groups with increasingly long lists of credentials, and 'networked' with other minute groups, while many socialist feminists despairingly moved into increasingly narrow campaigns or created a breathing space by writing books about the history of the women's movement. But ironically, or rather, dialectically, this period has also revealed a resilience, sophistication and profundity in a few groups whose integrity, authenticity and commitment to developing an analysis grew stronger in response to difficulties while all around them were retreating into old familiar orthodoxies or bowing down to the proliferation of false gods of the eighties such as new wave, new times and born-again religion.

Southall Black Sisters is an example to the Left of how to open debate; of how respect for people's humanity and intelligence encourages them to act politically on their own behalf. Above all, SBS are an example of how necessary it is to reject other people's ready-made theories even if they seem much more comfortable than the truth as you know it to be. If one chapter in *Against the Grain* illustrates how hard this is, it is Pragna Patel's essay on the gangs of boys on the streets of Southall. She breaks with feminist tradition in writing about the problems and dilemmas facing young, poor men, but she also contradicts socialist received wisdoms in insisting that, their oppression notwithstanding, they must be stopped from terrorizing other people, usually women, in the community. None of this prevents Pragna Patel from addressing the issue of police harassment of young black men which has the approval of the community leaders.

She will not allow the gang

phenomenon to pass as 'media hype' as some of the Left would like, nor as the cutting edge of the antiracist movement as others would prefer. But nor will she allow it to be portrayed as a kind of a vicious mafia, indigenous to the Asian community, a picture which would suit the racist police response. Her understanding of the gang phenomenon is based on many, often conflicting, elements, and on a respect for the boys themselves who she sees neither as helpless victims of 'the system', nor as romantic defenders of their community.

Unlike most other analysts, Pragna Patel looks at how the established leadership of the Asian community views the gangs and at the relationship between the police and that leadership. 'The police,' she says, 'are too busy "liaising" with the power brokers within our communities who are more interested in playing off some sections of the community against others.

'There are no easy solutions. When we raise the demands of women, we are only too aware of the implications both for women and other sections of our society. If we raise difficult and complex issues it is not because we regard the interests of women as a sectional interest to set against everyone else. We believe that by illuminating the problems women face we will shed light on all of society in general. We have no easy answers, but only with absolute honesty and compassion can we begin to grope towards a solution.' (p. 54)

Southall Black Sisters have discovered over ten hard years that 'absolute honesty and compassion', as well as being the prerequisite for a genuine understanding of the political world, is also the only workable basis for making alliances. This has been most obvious in the wake of the controversy over *The Satanic Verses* when SBS's clear position in defence of Rushdie led to the formation of Women Against Fundamentalism. This group is a broad and fruitful alliance of women from a wide range of communities – Jewish, Muslim, Hindu, Catholic, Protestant – many with a long history of dissent within those communities, but they have been characterized by a number of well-known, more 'orthodox' anti-racists as 'anti-Muslim'. They are accused of pandering to the wave of anti-Muslim racism which erupted in the wake of the *fatwa* against Salman Rushdie. Socialists and feminists with excellent credentials emerged on this issue as preferring to stay silent on the subject of death threats made by patriarchal tyrants than to find themselves, as they saw it, on the side of the racists. Which takes me back to the dog and the stick.

Hannana Siddiqui's short essay, 'A woman's banner for doubt and dissent', describing the picket against the Muslim Fundamentalist march against Rushdie in May 1989 encapsulates the need to extrapolate our politics from our own experience and the need to make authentic alliances on that basis. It also addresses the crucial question of how the state relates to religious leaders. By accepting fundamentalist leaders as spokespeople for the whole community, the state is able to work on the assumption that either the community is homogeneous or that rebels will be kept under control. This takes its most pervasive form as multiculturalism. Hannana Siddiqui says: 'The fundamentalists are supported by the state, the multiculturalist and the liberal anti-racist lobby. The multi-culturalists see the community as a unified whole. The only demands they listen to are those defined by conservative, religious, male leaders. They refuse to recognise the demands of women within our communities. At SBS Asian women come in on a daily basis experiencing violence, rape and sexual abuse. Women are being forced into arranged marriages, homelessness and denial of education. The multi-culturalists fail to intervene and support these women.

For them it is all part of a culture and religion which must be tolerated. And the anti-racists allow this to continue because they see the fight against racism as the central struggle.' (p. 62)

The courage of Hannana and the other fifty or so women on that picket came partly from their long practice at being dissenters within their community. It also came from the solid basis for their mutual support: an alliance was being forged between the women on that demonstration that is alive and flourishing two years later in the form of Women Against Fundamentalism.

Hannana Siddiqui concludes: 'I do not want men and mullahs to build my future. I want to create my own future in a world where women can choose to live as they please. I want a secular state without blasphemy laws which impose religious censorship. I support Salman Rushdie's right to write *The Satanic Verses* because his right to doubt and dissent is also my right to doubt and dissent.' (p. 62)

The leaders of the Southall Asian communities probably wouldn't mind that doubt and dissent if Southall Black Sisters had done what many other feminists and socialists have done: taken it outside the community. But as Pragna Patel writes: 'We needed to grasp the layered, multi-faceted nature of our existence in which racism plays only a part. If we need to be proud and confident of our histories and cultures, we also need to be critical and honest about its content and development. We cannot keep silent about the daily experiences of degradation and humiliation suffered by women in order to perpetuate a fantasy. Instead we have to challenge the self-appointed community leaders and question their legitimacy to speak on our behalf.' (p. 44)

The challenge posed by Southall Black Sisters is that they insist on working as Asian women, with Asian women *within* the Asian community, and as socialists, feminists and anti-racists *within* the Left. They do not claim to have a perfect analysis on every issue, but they strive for an understanding derived from honest communication and open debate and for strategies derived from alliances which recognize difference as well as joint interests. These are far more dangerous to the powerful than the most well-honed theory whose coherence depends on its excluding uncomfortable and contradictory facts.

Julia Bard

Promissory Notes: Women in the Transition to Socialism

Edited by Sonia Kruks, Rayna Rapp and Marilyn B. Young

New York: Monthly Review Press 1989, £12.95 Pbk, ISBN 0 85345 771 9

Promissory Notes is an 'American production' in the grand style, bringing together discrete, dispersed writings on the connexions and contradictions between the position of women in socialist thought, their role in the transition to socialism and the reality of women's lives in various 'socialist' regimes.[1]

Although the authors propose that the book is essentially a number of case studies it seems that precisely the cohabitation of practical historical analysis of women's situation in certain socialist states *and* the more explicitly theoretical debates by Eisenstein, White, Aguilar, Beneria and others gives an active, critical impetus to the whole.

Essentially this book is sectioned into 'The European heritage' where Joan Landes assesses how the theoretical agenda was set in Europe by Marx and Marxists, ending with the key to the whole in that there was no perceived need within this theory for 'men to wage a conscious struggle to transform interpersonal relations, nor of the political requirements of such a task' (p. 26). The codification of this thought in the Second and Third International is outlined by Elizabeth Waters, who proposes that, 'The metamorphosis of the women's movement remains incomprehensible unless it is seen in the context of the history of the Comintern itself' as the Comintern's aim by the end of the 1920s was the *mobilization* rather than the advancement of women. This is a recurrent key aspect of women's situation in the transition to socialism.

In her work on the new revolutionary order in the Soviet Union, Wendy Zeva Goldman explains how the attempts by the Zhenotdel (women's department) to socialize domestic work were limited by a ruined economy and lack of state resources. When by 1930, the Party abolished the Zhenotdel we realize that the roots of this reversal lay in this early period of terrible scarcity and underdevelopment. For many women 'freedom' was experienced in the context of total social chaos, with women and abandoned children bearing the brunt of many of the unintended outcomes of socialist policy. The sad irony Goldman points out is that by the 1930s the conditions were much more propitious for the realization of some of these visions, but by this time the orientation of the Party had changed.

In the Chinese situation of 1920–27 Christina Gilmartin gives us a picture of active Chinese feminists struggling 'womanfully' against the odds, yet not within the framework of the conventional scholarly debate, which rests on the assumption that the Chinese case 'represented yet one more example of proletarian ideology meeting and overcoming bourgeois feminism'

(p. 82). As Gilmartin shows, women were regarded as an important group to be mobilized and they assumed visible political roles as leaders and grass-roots organizers. Their organization, within the Party and projects like the women's journal, *The Women's Voice*, and a school for 'common women', gave these Chinese feminists an active chance to oversee a massive mobilization of women from different classes. Yet we see that most of the active women were able to attend high party meetings because of the position with the Party of their husbands/partners. Conflict over the 'politicization of gender' became a focus for discontent between the Guomindang and Communist parties, and by 1928 it was apparent that a women's policy which challenged male power-holders was too threatening to this revolutionary coalition of forces.

In the third section, debate centres on the situation of women in 'Third World' revolutions with work on Cuba, Nicaragua, Mozambique, Yemen, Vietnam, West Bengal and post-Maoist China. These studies cover regimes in which the codified statement of the 'woman question' established by the Third International is a principal point of reference. Whilst Muriel Nazzari points out that the solutions posed to the 'woman question' by the Cuban Family Code caused no drain on the national budget, they did require a change in men's lives, which they resisted. Other factors, under a system of distribution according to work, meant that women's unmet needs were dependent upon their husbands' labour, and children were dependent on parents, rather than societal support. As Maxine Molyneux shows in the Nicaraguan context, the relationship that was created and developed between women and the Sandanista Front was compounded by the Front's own conception of how women's emancipation could be achieved within the Nicaraguan context. Molyneux notes the surprise of the AMNLAE leadership at the women's criticisms of their failure to address vital issues such as domestic violence, machismo, abortion, rape and contraception. Again the tensions between working through a mass organization for women, or incorporation of women's issues into existing power structures, arises in the Nicaraguan context. Sonia Kruks and Ben Wisner point out that the 'industrial vanguardism' of FRELIMO politics confounds problems over women and land, and different relations of production. When it can be recognized that 'Polygamy is not simply a "social problem of women": it is also a relation of production' (p. 159), and laws on land, such as the 1979 Land Law recognize the need to establish, clarify and reinforce women's rights to land, then the 'woman question' will be faced, rather than assumed to be overcome in the revolutionary transition. As Kruks and Wisner point out, any analysis that focuses on 'women *as producers*, as well as reproducers, and on family relations and the political and planning process as they affect women *as producers*' (p. 165) will go some way towards clarifying thinking on women's roles and policies to ensure greater egalitarianism. On Vietnam, Christine Pelzer White pinpoints an oft-forgotten aspect of socialism *as a process*. Given the problems concerning external power and hostility which many revolutionary regimes face, the transition towards socialism becomes distorted and thereby should not be confused with what *might* have been if 'social alternatives had been allowed to develop in peace' (p. 172).[2]

Each situation differs, and in Vietnam a particular concern of the Women's Union was the possible cutback of state and co-operative-supported welfare measures which would leave the burden of caring for war-injured relatives on their working wives, mothers and daughters.

Yet as women form the mainstay of marketplace-sellers, the liberalization of the recent reform policy gives Vietnam's peasant women more freedom to trade without bureaucratic obstacles. Important points are stressed, not only concerning the differential impact of social policies upon different groups of women but also as to how needs vary over time in different situations.

Both Maxine Molyneux and Amrita Basu bring into their work the important aspects of religious influence. The People's Democratic Republic of Yemen (PDRY) stands apart from other states under consideration because of its retention of pre-revolutionary legal codes derived from Islam. Women were given the vote ten years after independence in an attempt to draw them into political participation and challenge kin-control and seclusion. The cultural disincentives for women entering paid employment also had to be tackled. Given that Islam has remained the state religion, questions of reform have been posited in terms of Islamic canons and in association with prominent religious jurists. Whilst the Family Law attempted to work towards families as 'basic cells of society' one effect was dramatically to increase divorce rates, leading to later curbs on divorce laws. Although the state, rather than orthodox Islam, can now effect more policy, it is difficult within this legalistic framework to gain a sense of the changing material conditions of Yemeni women's lives and understand how they are actually affected in terms of socialist transition.

From Amrita Basu we learn that the solidaristic values of the Bengali Hindu family and those of the Communist Party of India (Marxist) show that: 'Democratic centralist principles in the home fortify the CPI(M) in the world, at the cost of perpetuating sexual inequality' (p. 215). Basu argues that the Party's conservative approach to women's issues since 1977, when the Left

Front government was elected, is 'closely linked to its reformist approach to class and caste'. In appropriating and reproducing aspects of Bengali Hindu culture, in terms of women being holders of tradition, the CPI(M) limited the extent and forms of political change. In Communist women's dependence on the Party, Basu sees a major factor inhibiting 'recognition of the transcendent nature of women's oppression across class, caste and party lines' (p. 218). Again women's 'propertylessness' is instanced, as is their continuing dependence due to lack of title to land. In all, Basu rejects any 'culturally relativist perspectives' on women's continuing inequality in that the fact that 'Bengali women eat less nutritious and smaller quantities of food than their husbands may be customary but it is also unjust' (p. 225). In terms of the Left in South East Asia, Kumari Jayawardena remarks that 'the question of *women's* liberation – as opposed to *national* or *workers'* liberation – has been merely subsumed under "class struggle" '. Jayawardena notes that on the many issues affecting women's rights in South Asia including extreme cases of stoning women, *sati*, and dowry killing, that have been taken up by feminists, the Left has failed to give any *leadership*. In terms of critiques of 'Western feminism' the point is made that, 'In colonial times diatribes against the British often took the form of vilification of foreign women, and this tradition persists, the current target being "Western feminists" ' (p. 365). Yet there are indications of change and the relationship between the Left and some women's organizations is now more balanced, with a certain mutual respect.

In her work on China, Marilyn Young stresses that 'women *embody* social contradictions' (p. 234) so that no single line of analysis will assess their situation. 'Workers' generally refers to men, while 'women' as a

category are assumed to be classless. Elements of the 'superwomen' complex are apparent in terms of unrealistic expectations of women as workers/mothers/wives, etc. Young points out that with regard to choices of childcare, 'Neither in China nor the West do women fully possess the power of self-definition.' Delia Davin points out that with much of the means of production in private hands 'the failure to implicate women's property rights will reinforce the dependency of peasant women' (p. 356) who are mostly dependent for access to state provision through relationships with men. Although Davin sees a real need for a women's movement in China to work on women's issues, she recognizes the difficulties for its development at present. After the fall of the Gang of Four in 1978, Young proposes that women were freed from an 'imposed asceticism' and in self-expression often turned to hair-perming and interests in fashion, cosmetics and beauty hints. A solution to the problem faced by the regime in being unable to hold out the offer to women of 'liberation through work with socialized childcare', is to proffer a gender ideology stressing 'natural' differences. As a nuclear family underpinned by women has proved an efficient model, it is not to be 'problematized', and limits can be placed upon it in terms of 'one child per family' rules. We gain a picture of the state's need for energy, in terms of mobilization for modernization, yet equally a need to retain centralized control. Whereas class struggle may have been abolished 'by fiat', Young rightly argues that 'class and gender divisions that mark reality in China no less than in the United States cannot be defined out of existence'.

In the Soviet Union, Mary Buckley proposes, the 'woman question' 'ceased to be debated after the 1920s and is only now being tentatively taken up under Gorbachev.' The main focus centres on how women can contribute to reform processes, rather than realize their self-determination. Unlike in Nicaragua and Cuba, the male role in home-work has rarely been debated. Topics such as male violence and homosexuality remain 'taboo' and so far as the dual burden on women is concerned, proposed solutions do not include analysis of gender roles. Buckley analyzes the variety of uses of Soviet ideology from 1930 to 1987. Despite the 'woman question' remaining 'solved' during Krushchev's years, the efforts to broaden political participation meant that the *zhensovety* (women's councils) were encouraged to mobilize women. By the 1960s and 1970s when the economic productivity was seen to suffer from the problems associated with women's participation in the 'double shift', women's issues again became recognized as important, especially with failing birth-rates in the Russian republic. While the debate under Gorbachev is now more lively, certain rigid definitions of masculinity and femininity exist and these have widespread social effects. Buckley points out that this is a complex issue, 'shaped not just by attitudes, but by cultural diversity across fifteen Soviet republics and by the way in which cumbersome bureaucratic structures operate' (p. 255). There are some similarities between the situation of women in the Soviet Union, German Democratic Republic and Hungary. These industrialized countries compare very favourably with those of Western Europe in important areas such as general earning capacities, childcare, maternity benefits and access to middle-level political power. Yet it remains the case that in the Soviet-type countries the division of labour within the home has not been debated. Childcare allowance (GYES) in Hungary was introduced at a time of anticipated unemployment, with women paid a much less than average wage to remain at home for up to three years. Martha Lampland

points out that the narrowness of women's demands may have wider significance in terms of consciousness. The male right-wing backlash against feminism in Hungary in the early 1980s has a role in this but essentially the arguments against 'bourgeois feminism' still have a strong hold in Hungary.[3]

In the German Democratic Republic though, Barbara Einhorn proposes that the state's commitment to women was 'in terms of involvement in the production process and economic independence from men, but also in terms of the full development of individual potential' (p. 287). While by 1986 the GDR legislation on the surface appears some of the most progressive legislation for women in Central and Eastern Europe, it is apparent from the work of women in the GDR that 'the social "achievements" of state socialism must be examined critically.'[4] The transition away from so-called 'state socialism' is something which now must be addressed.

Lourdes Beneria stresses the importance of asking what socialist feminism might mean, in the context of progressive social change. The sexual division of labour is a major obstacle to women's equality and evidence 'cuts across countries and economic systems' (p. 328). It is equally evident that no matter what debate makes up Family Codes such '"spirit" cannot be imposed solely from the top down . . . also needed is a vigorous questioning at the bottom, fed by women's concerns and channelled through women's own networks and organizations' (p. 328).

Zillah Eisenstein proposes the notion of radical pluralism to counter the oppositional stance of Marxist theory which stunts the promise of socialism and feminism – 'The individualist concern with diversity must be incorporated into the socialist vision of equality' (p. 335). Issues of food and sex, hunger and equality would thereby be recognized as integrally related within a feminist vision promising socialism 'a radical egalitarianism that recognizes individuality' (p. 337).

Delia Aguilar suggests that linking racial inequalities and women's inequality by formulating a theory to account for racial inequality 'is a project that could prove illuminating for gender oppression' (p. 344). White argues that socialist feminists 'do need a less ethnocentric definition of "feminism" which appreciates the realities of the third world.' Here too the importance of international solidarity is central given the apparent contradictions in the dynamics of international solidarity among women. Access to the means of violence is also proposed by White as having major implications for gender politics with possibilities for transforming the cultural norms of manhood.

At the outset the authors of *Promissory Notes* state that their subject is contentious and the title 'can be read as implying a contract, in which socialism promised to bring forth women's liberation in exchange for women's support in revolutionary struggle' (p. 7).[5] The sticking points in this mutual support tend to remain in the realms of power and perception. Men's monopoly of power and privilege within the revolutionary and post-revolutionary situation has rarely been adequately challenged because the discrepancies have not been problematized. By this I mean that issues of work and sex are vital to the monopoly of power. It is apparent that in cases where the state has tried to direct policy concerning equalization of domestic work and care, notably in Cuba and Nicaragua, this has not been straightforward and questions remain as to whether mobilization can come from the state or whether social relations have to be tackled within politically active community debates. Problems remain too in definitions of 'duties' which are generally gendered, in that man's duties are often in the financial realm whereas, although women's duties also include financial responsibility, other expectations concern very emotive, emotional ties which can result in the 'guilt-tripping' of women. In terms of looking at sex and sexuality it has to be recognized that sex is power and that there is a strong need to explore the ways in which perceptions regarding sex/sexuality shape certain images which build into pre-set patterns of hierarchical behaviour. Sexuality has long been a taboo in so-called 'state socialist' societies and this is one area in which feminism can give critical impetus. Eisenstein rightly asserts that socialism cannot be feminist until individuality (*not individualism*) and the female body transform the meaning of sex equality – 'it must be specified in more than economic and legal terms' (p. 335).

For me though, the basic weakness of *Promissory Notes* remains that there is no overall teasing out of the basic tenets of feminisms, including socialist feminism. As has been noted by Beall, Hassim and Todes (1989: 34): 'Socialist feminism, while not having the rich intellectual and political history of Marxism, is the hybrid product of growing experience in women's struggles and research, *both in the west and in the Third World*. It represents a consensus that women's struggles against both capitalism and sexism cannot be separated from issues of class, race and imperialism. The class reductionist or economistic analysis of orthodox Marxism is unacceptable.'

My question here concerns those feminists emerging within the Central and Eastern European countries who have been struggling against a form of so-called 'state socialism', not outright capitalism. Feminists have redefined aspects of Marxist thought, as Eisenstein points out: 'The oppositional stance of Marxist theory, which assumes the clear division between nature/culture, real/ideal, true/false, stunts the promise of socialism and feminism. It is a way of thinking about the relations of power that construct women's lives while limiting the capacity for addressing their inequality.' (p. 335)

Perhaps now is the time for critical feminists to rethink the 'socialist feminist' stance and to further problematize the ways in which women lose out in mutual support work towards revolutionary change.

It remains the case that women and men need the conditions in which to discuss such issues in the public arena, not having to 'personalize' them, which is at women's cost. Feminist debates based on revolutionary practice can then continue to feed into fresh considerations of the strategies for achieving equality in societies.

Chris Corrin

Notes

1 These regimes have been labelled in a variety of ways including 'state socialist'. It is pertinent for future discussion on feminisms, including the feminist voices from Central and Eastern Europe.

2 When we consider that three times the amount of bombs were dropped on revolutionary Vietnam than in World War Two and that Vietnam has now lost as many men in Kampuchea attempting to secure a 'friendly neighbour' as the US lost in the Vietnam War, we again see the immensity of the struggle.

3 That 'bourgeois feminists' were depicted in the Hungarian media as failed women who hated men instances the depth of problems associated with the imagery of feminism in Hungary.

4 See also Dölling (1990).

5 Here lies a central connexion/contradiction of the whole, as Marxist thought on the 'woman question' is debated, modified and in several senses revised, when states enter a revolutionary transition to socialism.

References

BEALL, J., HASSIM, S. and TODES, A. (1989) '"A bit on the side?": gender struggles in the politics of transformation in South Africa' *Feminist Review* No. 33, pp. 30–56.

DÖLLING, I. (1990) 'Between hope and helplessness: women in the GDR after the "turning point"' *IVth World Congress of Soviet and East European Studies*, Harrogate.

Mad Forest
Caryl Churchill

A lonely vampire, recently come down to the city from his Transylvanian castle, encounters a starving mongrel in an empty church. The dog is desperate for a master and they strike up a pact: although the fastidious ghoul finds canine slavishness distasteful, it will at least be company, so he agrees to vampirize the dog. They go off to feed together on the human *mêlée* of easy victims in Romania's post-Ceaușescu chaos.

This gruesome coupling, played as dark comedy, was one of the most forceful and surprising moments in *Mad Forest*, a play by the British dramatist Caryl Churchill, which was written during the trip that she and a company of student-actors made to Romania, and in discussion with students of the Caragiale Institute of Theatre and Cinema and other citizens of Bucharest, in the spring of 1990. It was performed in London at the Royal Court Theatre (home of much innovative and radical theatre) later that same year, and so clearly was produced at white heat while political events were themselves rushing forward. Yet despite the speed of its production and its focus upon the events of December 1989, the overriding concerns of *Mad Forest* went far beyond the topical and are not likely to date: like the image of the vampire and the dog which has stayed with me over the months, as an allegory for some of the darker forces of social revolutions, the play as a whole went beyond the occasion of its writing: it asked us to consider the nature of political change itself and the different kind of theatres in which it takes place, the dramas which are enacted in the theatres of the mind and of the emotions, as well as on a more public stage.

Churchill's achievement in *Mad Forest* was to represent the collapse of communism as in part a kind of derepression: political transformation seen not just as the overthrow of oppressive regimes and tyrannical hierarchies, but as turning the psychic world upside down, launching a landslide of emotional securities, opening up the internal floodgates. This state of flux and fragmentation produced a volatility both potentially emancipating and undermining. Churchill's characters were dislocated people experiencing a kind of inner meltdown, finding that the taken-for-granted truths of their lives had come away from their moorings; the goal posts, as we might say, had been moved. Rather than the crude Cold War image of a regime run by cynical functionaries who had long since stopped believing in the system, Churchill gave us the much more disturbing portraits of those 'ordinary people' who had, despite all the odds, really wanted to believe, who had tried to make their lives work in this belief, however threadbare, and who now felt a kind of bereavement: the schoolteacher who is about to be dismissed for having been a propagandist and whose professional and home life is now breaking up, 'Twenty years marching in the wrong direction . . . Twenty year's experience and I'm a beginner.' As her son turns against her and her husband, sneering at their use of Party jargon and furious at their having toed the correct line, we see her left with a vacuum where once was self-affirmation and a sense of pride in her work, hollowed out by change and paralyzed by it.

Exhilaration but also puzzlement, relief but also apathy and fear, all these were represented as the different and simultaneous re-sponses to violent changes, changes which, even when they improve upon the quality of life, involve a sense of loss. At one point a young woman expresses her increasing sense of anger at what she sees as the bloodthirsty heroic posturing of her male friends and their fomenting of hatred and division, by saying that she feels oddly bereft: 'I miss him', she says of the dictator whose downfall she also welcomed. And in a scene where the newly liberated young Romanians visit their elders in the country, utopian fantasies and the vicious pathologizing of others go hand in hand. As they lie on the ground in the sun, they let their wishes spiral, imagining for themselves a new life in which they can have everything from Toblerone to immortality. Meanwhile, their peasant grandmother abuses the local gypsies and warns them off Hungarians as murderous people.

Both the emergence of suppressed racial prejudices and of impossible and romantic desires appear in the play as a kind of speaking out of what had formerly been silenced. Atavistic demons, like the vampire and the dog, and unbounded appetites, in excess of the socially possible or acceptable, seem to have been loosed upon the world by the crumbling of the old structures of repression and control. It is as though the events of December had set in motion an unstoppable train of psychic as well as social and economic demands, and throughout Churchill's play we hear the insistent clamour of these unmet needs, which, like masterless dogs, wander in the ruins of the state, threatening to feed upon their fellows.

But such desires and fears, however wildly individualist they seem and however uniquely they are experienced, are always within an historical context, a time and a place; they are part of a common history and a shared life. This relationship between different levels of change – psychic, cultural, economic – is what

Mad Forest asked us to contemplate, and indeed it is what has long made Caryl Churchill's work of especial interest to feminists. Instead of giving us a history written from 'the top down', as it were, charting the effects of state policies, the machinations of military-economic complexes, or the doings and failures of great men, *Mad Forest* began from inside the different responses of two very different families – the one professional and university-educated; the other 'blue collar' – resisting any easy division between what is usually called 'the private and the public', and suggesting just how much that division obscures. Further than this, we were asked to acknowledge too the dreams and nightmares of those living through such changes. Not in order to see them as simple reflections of political events but in order to recognize how often they are out of kilter with them: a psychic life not simply determined by public activities but also shaping and limiting, and often contradicting them. Churchill's point seemed to me to be that we have to make this kind of imaginative leap into these other interiors if we are to make sense of political change. A historical record which can offer no account of subjectivity, and which makes no attempt to understand the cultural shaping and containment of unconscious as well as conscious needs is no history at all.

Churchill's play also worked hard to remind its London audience that there are limits to how far those who were trying to understand another people's struggle in translation, as it were, could 'identify' with the action they were watching. Flagging each scene with Romanian phrases and putting us in the position of pupils learning a language, our authority, as observers who could pass judgement on what we saw, was called in question. As the programme notes told us, where Bucharest now stands there used to be a large forest, especially impene-

trable to foreigners who did not know the paths through it and had always to go round: to them it was 'Teleorman' or 'Mad Forest'. In this sense Churchill's play was taking us round the events and the aftermath of December 1989 and not aiming to cut a clear swath of meaning through them. Those who wanted the surety of arriving at a definitive or authorized version of historical or political truth would have been disappointed.

Churchill's technique, which was increasingly to destabilize our assumptions and ready formulations as the play progressed, gained force as it took us further inside the unfinished material from which, in fact, we make history and make sense of events. This impulse to go beyond the apparent meaning of what was being said on the stage was reflected very simply in the form of the play which divided into three very different and yet closely connected acts, each of which effectively commented upon the others and upon the different kinds of knowledge they produced. This was why the play moved between apparently realist or documentary scenes of family life or public events, to hallucinatory and bizarre moments of the fantastic and the folkloric like that in which the vampire and the dog made their entrance.

The first act of the play was a kind of prologue to the events of December. It gave us a sequence of almost silent tableaux in which we saw not the dramatic or sensational horrors of state torture and police brutality but the routine pressures upon expression and language in everyday life which had become the common culture and history of Romanians. It stressed the actual mental and physical effort involved in living even in the most humdrum ways in an atmosphere of constant anxiety and suspicion: friends turning up the radio to blaring pitch in order to speak in whispers to one another; a father asked to report on the activities of his daughter's friends in order that the other members of the family keep their jobs; a doctor going through the motions of preaching on the crime of abortion as he accepts money to perform the operation. Where the only loud speeches are the official ones, private communication is at its most expressive when it says least: the moment when, for example, a woman as a matter of course scrapes up a broken egg from the floor in order to save it. And this despite it having come as a gift from a sister's American boyfriend whose impending marriage is making the family the object of official displeasure and leaving them shunned by neighbours and friends. Throughout these scenes we caught glimpses too of the contradictory buried thoughts and feelings beneath the quiet surface of their lives, the frustration and anger which made its way into jokes, the sad internal monologue of a woman who talks to her dead grandmother in order to hold on to a lost past; the confused and agonized priest who communes with an angel in the hopes of quieting his conscience.

Where the first act hushed its audience into listening hard to what was not being said, the second was entirely a polyphony of voices, eager to speak and tell us what happened during the last weeks of December, from the reverberations of the shootings and demonstrations in Timisoara to the execution of the Ceausescus and the setting up of the National Salvation Front. After the cramped sentences of the first act the audience was overpowered by a medley of different eyewitnesses all offering their accounts from a variety of viewpoints: the student, the doctor, the soldier, the housewife, the painter, the bulldozer driver, reliving again what the rest of us saw on our TV screens during those Christmas holidays. As an oral history it was at once very moving and engrossing. One immediately assumed these testimonies were based upon interviews with 'real' people and that this was the kind of reportage that could form a reliable history of shared public events. It was only in the final act that we heard how many questions remained unanswered about the events themselves ('How many people were killed at Timisoara? Where are the bodies? Who was shooting whom on the 22nd? Why did no one turn off the power at the TV station?'), and how fractured and dissonant this apparently collective experience was.

There is no easy fit between the languages of public activity and events and the people who make them and are made by them. Even that most material and determinate of events – the execution of the Ceausescus – was understood in the play as producing a backwash of panic and guilt even in those who supported their shooting. That event took on terrifying proportions not by being realistically staged but in the recurring nightmare of violence taking place in one woman's head: we saw her dreaming of herself as Elena, trying desperately to escape, being seized and captured, giving up her money and few remaining favours, and then, appallingly, her hands and feet, until only her torso was left. A soldier opens and shuts her mouth: it blurts out like a ventriloquist's dummy the sound of the jubilant crowds. Ceausescu and his wife appeared in the play, not as 'real people' but indeed, as they were to the majority of their subjects, as representations: the figures that other people had painted on posters and walls, and carried in their minds as symbols of belief and of authority. Later a group of highspirited students out on a binge make street theatre of the execution as a drunken charade; its horror is a kind of personal and national trauma which needs to be acted out over and over again in order to be exorcized. We are impressed by a sense of the enduring violence done to human sensibility by this act, whatever its justice: the idea that the Ceaușescus were not removed by their execution; on the contrary, their power as disturbers of psychic peace, as internalized objects of hatred and fear, envy and ambition, may have expanded.

Churchill's play was clearly deconstructive in tendency; itself a remarkable piece of ensemble playing and collective work, it tried to capture the moment in which territories shift, the moment of the dissolution of collective beliefs and systems. As such it was under no obligation to offer grand strategems or to cast political horoscopes and predict the future; in any case the assurance with which we might rely on older forms of political narrative has itself been undermined by the crisis of socialism, making older vocabularies, at the very least, inadequate. Rather, *Mad Forest* concentrated upon the mess of actuality and the improvised nature of human activity which our interpretations then harden into consistency or fact. Whilst what we call history may have now moved on, the psychic terrain remains in uproar and turmoil.

It seems to me that the politics of the play lay in its capacity to bring those who were outside it to ask questions with respect; to hold off from pronouncements and assumptions, to hang fire and to listen, and where we can, and as far as we are able, to understand the complexities of a cultural history which is a history of human emotion as well as one of legislation or economic organization. There seems to be more than a strong case for this kind of listening and watching. As we recognize with dismay the rearing up of violent nationalisms in the wake of collapsing authoritarian orders, the pathologizing and hounding of other racial groups, the attacks upon alternative sexualities (to name but a few of the unleashed Furies of the last year or so), we are obliged to ask questions not only about the economic and social structures of those countries, but also about what it means to lose one's national identity, the scaffold of collective belonging which, although it may have been rigid and even punitive, was nevertheless a firm framework of support. The play brought us to the point where we could begin to understand the shocking reversal of feeling and expectation which might bring a Romanian to say of the last twenty years, 'I felt free then. I don't now.'

Mad Forest ended with a wedding between the two families in which carnival exuberance teetered on the edge of violence – a common feature of family life – but also a correlative for the state of the country as a whole. Throughout the play the creative energies released, the coming together of different groups and the possibility of new alliances always remained hedged about by fear of others and of oneself; was always likely to be capsized. Churchill's play, beginning with the singing of a Romanian socialist anthem, necessarily attached more emotional force to the travesties of communism than to its earlier idealism, and this was one of its inevitable historical and dramatic limitations. For those of us of a younger generation than Churchill, who grew up on the Cold War, on Orwell, Koestler and Solzhenitsyn, but also James Bond and le Carré, and who may have relatively little experience of any kind of political organization, there is so much one also needs to hear, not about corruption and the bankruptcy of beliefs, but about belief itself. It is perhaps relatively easy, especially for us in the West, to understand that what were once communism's shared ideals became structures of repression; less easy to reverse the process and free up what is now frozen into rigidity, seeing how it might once have been the much-desired way of giving form to the contingencies of social existence. It is relatively easy to descry aggressive nationalisms; much harder to understand the ways in which they have also been progressive forces; it is relatively easy to attack the role of religion, much harder to see the moments when it provided a platform for rebellion against other authorities.

Mad Forest left me wanting to see more of those other prologues to the drama that we watched on stage – some tapping of those other well-springs of the action which took place in the 1920s and 1930s, or even earlier. These accounts can perhaps only be written by insiders but they would give those of us who have been neither believers nor belongers more ways of understanding the appeal and the excitement, the collective drive and commitment that had created and sustained those now crumbling regimes. Without a sense of the achievements and the pleasures of those idealisms how else can we fathom their present-day perver-

sions or seek to channel those incorrigible desires and fears anew?

For even the vampire and the dog were lovable once. They are distortions of humane possibility: the dog's mindless obedience to his master is the twisted image of the need to devote oneself to something bigger than the individual, to find something to love that is beyond oneself, something to make larger sense of one's own small life. And seen through another lens, the vampire feeding on his fellows is a metaphor, though a sinister one, for how much we all must take our nourishment from other people if we are to be a truly social species. Both are tokens of human interdependency, refusals of the increasingly privatized and defended world-of-one which might sometimes seem to be capitalism's ultimate goal.

Alison Light

LETTER

Dear *Feminist Review*

Clara Connolly's thesis in *Feminist Review* 36 on the disservice that the politics of Pratibha Parmar did feminism is tenable only if we assume that without the antiracist perspective, all sexism in the ethnic minority and Black communities would have been effectively combated. Considering that even in the dominant society, where her theory would seem to imply that there would be no conflict for 'right-on' feminists, we have not even adequately dealt with equal pay and access to abortion, I cannot see any grounds for her assertion.

Many of the young Black and Asian women currently on the lesbian scene are there because the likes of Pratibha Parmar have made them feel that they do not have to erase their Black identity and fit into some rigid social stereotype as the price of expressing their sexuality.

Of course, I can understand that Clara Connolly might feel sheepish being asked to take part in dances in which she has no interest, but I don't see why she should seek to deprive those of us who do wish to do so of that opportunity nor to imply that because she has no interest in them that they are not part of the cultural baggage of other Irish women.

Two years ago, the Irish Lesbian Network held a very successful ceilidh as part of Lesbian/Gay Pride. Despite a public transport strike, the place was packed. The dance floor was packed and no one seemed any more uncomfortable than at regular discos. I bumped into some English friends there who were thoroughly enjoying themselves as were women of many nationalities!

Why can't we take traditional cultural forms and re-make them? Many of us relate more to these forms than we do to certain aspects of 'modern' culture such as disco-dancing and pop music. Why shouldn't it be a valid project for those of us who are familiar with traditional art forms to remake them as we please? I don't know many modern feminist lyrics which have created the kind of pandemonium that arose when the words of the old anti-dowry song 'Maids when you're young, never wed an old man' were altered to run 'Never wed any man, Cause We've got our fingddurums fol diddle-i-uri-mi . . .' – clearly indicating fingers as an alternative sexual organ to the penis – at another Irish women's event.

If I have to live within the confines of what Clara Connolly regards as 'feminist', I think I would rather not be a feminist. It seems to me that she would rather blame the antiracists for challenging some of the inherently exclusive presumptions of feminism than rise to the challenge of dealing with those aspects of feminism, itself forged as part of our history within this colonizing power, which still carries notions of an 'us' who are right and a 'them' who have to be brought around to 'our' way of seeing things.

Perhaps, it might be that Clara Connolly was not equipped to be a useful youth worker in such a multiracial environment as she describes. Perhaps facing this possibility might be a more appropriate response to its failures than to target those who have experienced racism within the feminist movement and who have attempted to educate us on how to combat it.

Marian Larragy

NOTICEBOARD

Social Justice: Issues on Women and the Social Control of Gender
Two issues of *Social Justice* analyze the status of women in the 1990s.
Authors show how the social control of gender and the reinforcing of
traditional gender roles have increased. Topics include reproductive
rights, women of colour, human rights, imprisonment, criminality and
feminism.

Available from *Social Justice*, PO Box 40601, Dept. W, San
Francisco, CA 94140

Women in Israel Speak: Learn the complex history of the situation
through grass-roots women's voices. $15. YPS 151 Main Street, North-
ampton, Ma 01060. $3 postage and handling.

An Office Guide to Repetitive Strain Injury £3.00 from City Centre,
32/35 Featherstone Street, London EC1Y 8QX.

Sister George Productions
Sister George Productions in Sheffield are currently researching a
television documentary about lesbian culture of the 1950s and 1960s.
We are eager to contact women who have already done research in this
area and/or women who want to share their memories from this era.
Please contact Helen or Alison at: Iris Productions Ltd, AVEC Brown St,
Sheffield S1 2BS, Tel. 0742 725946

The Hen House
The women's holiday and study centre is offering courses on Me and
Myself; Creative Writing; Assertiveness; Me and My Body: Growing Old
Disgracefully. For details of the full diary of events contact The Hen
House, Hawerby Hall, North Thoresby, Lincs DN36 5QL, 0472 840278.

Women's History Review
A new feminist international journal will appear in 1992 with the aim of
providing a forum for the publication of new scholarly articles in the
rapidly expanding field of women's history. The journal will be published three times a year (March, June and October).

The time-span covered by the journal includes the nineteenth and twentieth centuries as well as earlier times. The journal seeks to publish contributions from a range of disciplines (for example, women's studies, history, sociology, cultural studies, literature, political science, anthropology and philosophy) that further feminist knowledge and debate about women and/or gender relations in history.

The editors welcome a variety of approaches from people from different countries and different backgrounds. In addition to main articles, usually between 3,000 and 10,000 words, the journal also publishes shorter viewpoints (about 3,000 words) that are possibly based on the life experiences, ideas and views of the writer and may be more polemic in tone.

Articles for submission to the journal are now being actively sought. Each article should be accompanied by a summary of 100–150 words on a separate sheet of paper. All submissions will be seen anonymously by two referees.

Manuscripts (four copies) should be sent to June Purvis, *Women's History Review*, School of Social and Historical Studies, Portsmouth Polytechnic, Burnaby Road, Portsmouth PO1 3AS, United Kingdom. Authors in North America should send their manuscripts to Philippa Levine, Department of History, University of Southern California, Los Angeles, CA 90089, USA.

Booklists
New annotated booklists available:
Gender and Women's Studies: 60p plus s.a.e.
Lesbian Fiction: £1.00 plus s.a.e.
Forthcoming list on Lesbian Politics and Lives from Compendium, 234 Camden High Street, London NW1 8QS.

Since its founding in 1979 **Feminist Review** has been the major Women's Studies journal in Britain. **Feminist Review** is committed to presenting the best of contemporary feminist analysis, always informed by an awareness of changing political issues. The journal is edited by a collective of women based in London, with the help of women and groups from all over the United Kingdom.

● WHY NOT SUBSCRIBE? MAKE SURE OF YOUR COPY

All subscriptions run in calendar years. The issues for 1991 are Nos. 37, 38 and 39. You will save over £6 pa on the single copy price.

● SUBSCRIPTION RATES, 1991 (3 issues)

Individual Subscriptions
UK	£19.50
Overseas	£26
North America	$42

A number of reduced cost (£15.50 per year: UK only) subscriptions are available for readers experiencing financial hardship, e.g. unemployed, student, low-paid. If you'd like to be considered for a reduced subscription, please write to the Collective, c/o the Feminist Review office

Institutional Subscriptions		**Back Issues**	
UK	£45	UK	£8.50
Overseas	£50	North America	$16.50
North America	$86		

☐ Please send me one year's subscription to **Feminist Review**

☐ Please send me_____copies of back issue no._____

METHOD OF PAYMENT

☐ I enclose a cheque/international money order to the value of_____ made payable to Routledge Journals

☐ Please charge my Access/Visa/American Express/Diners Club account

Account no. ☐☐☐☐☐☐☐☐☐☐☐☐☐☐☐

Expiry date_____ Signature_____

If the address below is different from the registered address of your credit card, please give your registered address separately.

PLEASE USE BLOCK CAPITALS

Name_____

Address_____

_____Postcode_____

☐ Please send me a Routledge Journals Catalogue

☐ Please send me a Routledge Gender and Women's Studies Catalogue

Please return this form with payment to:
Sharon McDuell, Routledge, 11 New Fetter Lane, London EC4P 4EE

BACK ISSUES

23 SOCIALIST-FEMINISM: OUT OF THE BLUE
Feminism and Class Politics: A Round-Table Discussion, **Barrett, Campbell, Philips, Weir & Wilson**. Upsetting an Applecart: Difference, Desire and Lesbian Sadomasochism, **Ardill & O'Sullivan**. Armagh and Feminist Strategy, **Loughran**. Transforming Socialist-Feminism: The Challenge of Racism, **Bhavnani & Coulson**. Socialist-Feminists and Greenham, **Finch & Hackney Greenham Groups**. Socialist-Feminism and the Labour Party: Some Experiences from Leeds, **Perrigo**. Some Political Implications of Women's Involvement in the Miners' Strike, 1984–85, **Rowbotham & McCrindle**. Sisterhood: Political Solidarity Between Women, **Hooks**. European Forum of Socialist-Feminists, **Lees & McIntosh**. Report from Nairobi, **Hendessi**.

24 Women Workers in New Industries in Britain, **Glucksmann**. The Relationship of Women to Pornography, **Bower**. The Sex Discrimination Act 1975, **Atkins**. The Star Persona of Katharine Hepburn, **Thumim**.

25 Difference: A Special Third World Women Issue, **Minh-ha**. Melanie Klein, Psychoanalysis and Feminism, **Sayers**. Rethinking Feminist Attitudes Towards Mothering, **Gieve**. EEOC v. Sears, Roebuck and Company: A Personal Account, **Kessler-Harris**. Poems, **Wood**. Academic Feminism and the Process of De-radicalization, **Currie & Kazi**. A Lover's Distance: A Photoessay, **Boffin**.

26 Resisting Amnesia: Feminism, Painting and Post-Modernism, **Lee**. The Concept of Difference, **Barrett**. The Weary Sons of Freud, **Clément**. Short Story, **Cole**. Taking the Lid Off: Socialist Feminism in Oxford, **Collette**. For and Against the European Left: Socialist Feminists Get Organized, **Benn**. Women and the State: A Conference of Feminist Activists, **Weir**.

27 WOMEN, FEMINISM AND THE THIRD TERM: Women and Income Maintenance, **Lister**. Women in the Public Sector, **Phillips**. Can Feminism Survive a Third Term?, **Loach**. Sex in Schools, **Wolpe**. Carers and the Careless, **Doyal**. Interview with Diane Abbott, **Segal**. 'The Problem With No Name: Re-reading Friedan, **Bowlby**. Second Thoughts on the Second Wave, **Rosenfelt and Stacey**. Nazi Feminists?, **Gordon**.

28 **FAMILY SECRETS: CHILD SEXUAL ABUSE:** Introduction to an Issue: Family Secrets as Public Drama, **McIntosh**. Challenging the Orthodoxy: Towards a Feminist Theory and Practice, **MacLeod & Saraga**. The Politics of Child Sexual Abuse: Notes from American History, **Gordon**. What's in a Name?: Defining Child Sexual Abuse, **Kelly**. A Case, **Anon**. Defending Innocence: Ideologies of Childhood, **Kitzinger**. Feminism and the Seductiveness of the 'Real Event', **Scott**. Cleveland and the Press: Outrage and Anxiety in the Reporting of Child Sexual Abuse, **Nava**. Child Sexual Abuse and the Law, **Woodcraft**. Poem, **Betcher**. Brixton Black Women's Centre: Organizing on Child Sexual Abuse, **Bogle**. Bridging the Gap: Glasgow Women's Support Project, **Bell & Macleod**. Claiming Our Status as Experts: Community Organizing, **Norwich Consultants on Sexual Violence**. Islington Social Services: Developing a Policy on Child Sexual Abuse, **Boushel & Noakes**. Developing a Feminist School Policy on Child Sexual Abuse, **O'Hara**. 'Putting Ideas into their Heads': Advising the Young, **Mills**. Child Sexual Abuse Crisis Lines: Advice for Our British Readers.

29 **ABORTION: THE INTERNATIONAL AGENDA:** Whatever Happened to 'A Woman's Right to Choose'?, **Berer**. More than 'A Woman's Right to Choose'?, **Himmelweit**. Abortion in the Republic of Ireland, **Barry**. Across the Water, **Irish Women's Abortion Support Group**. Spanish Women and the Alton Bill, **Spanish Women's Abortion Support Group**. The Politics of Abortion in Australia: Freedom, Church and State, **Coleman**. Abortion in Hungary, **Szalai**. Women and Population Control in China: Issues of Sexuality, Power and Control, **Hillier**. The Politics of Abortion in Nicaragua: Revolutionary Pragmatism – or Feminism in the realm of necessity?, **Molyneux**. Who Will Sing for Theresa?, **Bernstein**. She's Gotta Have It: The Representation of Black Female Sexuality on Film, **Simmonds**. Poems, **Gallagher**. Dyketactics for Difficult Times: A Review of the 'Homosexuality, Which Homosexuality?' Conference, **Franklin & Stacey**

30 Capital, Gender and Skill: Women Homeworkers in Rural Spain, **Lever**. Fact and Fiction: George Egerton and Nellie Shaw, **Butler**. Feminist Political Organization in Iceland: Some Reflections on the Experience of Kwenna Frambothid, **Dominelli & Jonsdottir**. Under Western Eyes: Feminist Scholarship and Colonial Discourses, **Talpade Mohanty**. Bedroom Horror: The Fatal Attraction of *Intercourse*, **Merck**. AIDS: Lessons from the Gay Community, **Patton**. Poems, **Agbabi**.

31 **THE PAST BEFORE US: 20 YEARS OF FEMINISM:** Slow Change or No Change?: Feminism, Socialism and the Problem of Men, **Segal**. There's No Place Like Home: On the Place of Identity in Feminist Politics, **Adams**. New Alliances: Socialist-Feminism in the Eighties, **Harriss**. Other Kinds of Dreams, **Parmar**. Complexity, Activism, Optimism: Interview with **Angela Y. Davis**. To Be or Not To Be: The Dilemmas of Mothering, **Rowbotham**. Seizing Time and Making New: Feminist Criticism, Politics and Contemporary Feminist Fiction, **Lauret**. Lessons from the Women's Movement in Europe, **Haug**. Women in Management, **Coyle**. Sex in the Summer of '88, **Ardill & O'Sullivan**. Younger Women and Feminism, **Hobsbawm & Macpherson**. Older Women and Feminism, **Stacey; Curtis; Summerskill**.

32 'Those Who Die for Life Cannot Be Called Dead': Women and Human Rights Protest in Latin America, **Schirmer**. Violence Against Black Women: Gender, Race and State Responses, **Mama**. Sex and Race in the Labour Market, **Breugel**. The Dark Continent: Africa as Female Body in Haggard's Adventure Fiction, **Stott**. Gender, Class and the Welfare State: The Case of Income Security in Australia, **Shaver**. Ethnic Feminism: Beyond the Pseudo-Pluralists, **Gorelick**.

33 Restructuring the Woman Question: *Perestroika* and Prostitution, **Waters**. Contemporary Indian Feminism, **Kumar**. 'A Bit On the Side'?: Gender Struggles in South Africa, **Beall, Hassim and Todes**. 'Young Bess': Historical Novels and Growing Up, **Light**. Madeline Pelletier (1874–1939): The Politics of Sexual Oppression, **Mitchell**.

34 PERVERSE POLITICS: LESBIAN ISSUES
Pat Parker: A tribute, **Brimstone**. International Lesbianism: Letter from São Paulo, **Rodrigues**; Israel, **Pittsburgh**, Italy, **Fiocchetto**. The De-eroticization of Women's Liberation: Social Purity Movements and the Revolutionary Feminism of Sheila Jeffreys, **Hunt**. Talking About It: Homophobia in the Black Community, **Gomez & Smith**. Lesbianism and the Labour Party, **Tobin**. Skirting the Issue: Lesbian fashion for the 1990s, **Blackman & Perry**. Butch/Femme Obsessions, **Ardill & O'Sullivan**. Archives: The Will to Remember, **Nestle**; International Archives, **Read**. Audre Lorde: Vignettes and Mental Conversations, **Lewis**. Lesbian Tradition, **Field**. Mapping: Lesbians, AIDS and Sexuality An interview with Cindy Patton, **O'Sullivan**. Significant Others: Lesbians and Psychoanalytic Theory, **Hamer**. The Pleasure Threshold: Looking at Lesbian Pornography on Film, **Smyth**. Cartoon, **Charlesworth**. Voyages of the Valkyries: Recent Lesbian Pornographic Writing, **Dunn**.

35 Campaign Against Pornography, **Norden**. The Mothers' Manifesto and Disputes over 'Mutterlichkeit', **Chamberlayne**. Multiple Mediations: Feminist Scholarship in the Age of Multi-National Reception, **Mani**. Cagney and Lacey Revisited, **Alcock & Robson**. Cutting a Dash: The Dress of Radclyffe Hall and Una Troubridge, **Rolley**. Deviant Dress, **Wilson**. The House that Jill Built: Lesbian Feminist Organizing in Toronto, 1976–1980, **Ross**. Women in Professional Engineering: the Interaction of Gendered Structures and Values, **Carter & Kirkup**. Identity Politics and the Hierarchy of Oppression, **Briskin**. Poetry: **Bufkin, Zumwalt**.

36 'The Trouble Is It's Ahistorical': The Problem of the Unconscious in Modern Feminist Theory, **Minsky**. Feminism and Pornography, **Ellis, O'Dair Tallmer**. Who Watches the Watchwomen? Feminists Against Censorship, **Rodgerson & Semple**. Pornography and Violence: What the 'Experts' Really Say, **Segal**. The Woman In My Life: Photography of Women, **Nava**. Splintered Sisterhood: Antiracism in a Young Women's Project, **Connolly**. Woman, Native, Other, **Parmar** interviews **Trinh T. Minh-ha**. Out But Not Down: Lesbians' Experience of Housing, **Edgerton**. Poems: **Evans Davies, Toth, Weinbaum**. Oxford Twenty Years On: Where Are We Now?, **Gamman & O'Neill**. The Embodiment of Ugliness and the Logic of Love: The Danish Redstockings Movement, **Walter**.

37 SPECIAL FEATURE: WOMEN, RELIGION AND DISSENT
Black Women, Sexism and Racism: Black or Antiracist Feminism?, **Tang Nain**. Nursing Histories: Reviving Life in Abandoned Selves, **McMahon**. The Quest for National Identity: Women, Islam and the State in Bangladesh, **Kabeer**. Born Again Moon: Fundamentalism in Christianity and the Feminist Spirituality Movement, **McCrickard**. Washing our Linen: One Year of Women Against Fundamentalism, **Connolly. Siddiqui** on *Letter to Christendom*, **Bard** on *Generations of Memories*, **Patel** on *Women Living Under Muslim Laws Dossiers 1–6*, Poem, **Kay**. More Cagney and Lacey, **Gamman**..

38 The Modernist Style of Susan Sontag, **McRobbie**. Tantalizing Glimpses of Stolen Glances: Lesbians Take Photographs, **Fraser and Boffin**. Reflections on the Women's Movement in Trinidad, **Mohammed**. Fashion, Representation and Femininity, **Evans and Thornton**. The European Women's Lobby, **Hoskyns**. **Hendessi** on *Law of Desire: Temporary Marriage in Iran*, **Kaveney** on *Mercy*.

NEW *from* ROUTLEDGE

Professions and Patriarchy
Anne Witz

This impressive and original study combines mainstream sociology with feminism in exploring the subject of the professions and power.

International Library of Sociology
January 1992: 224pp
Hb: 0-415-05008-1: £35.00
Pb: 0-415-07044-9: £10.99

Women Organising
Helen Brown

Helen Brown analyses and explains what is special about the way women organise. In so doing she brings together organisation theory and the real life experiences of groups of women.

December 1991: 224pp
Hb: 0-415-04851-6: £35.00

Reflecting On Miss Marple
Marion Shaw and Sabine Vanacker

Violence, murder, and a sweet, white-haird old lady are an unlikely combination. Why is this apparent contradiction so potent a formula?

Heroines?
August 1991: 144pp
Pb: 0-415-01794-7: £6.99

Reflecting on Nana
Bernice Chitnis

Radically challenging the view of *Nana* as the story of an old-fashioned 'femme fatale', Bernice Chitnis offers a feminist reading which claims Nana as a heroine who manages to overturn patriarchy.

Heroines?
August 1991: 112pp
Pb: 0-415-04134-1: £6.99

Reflecting on The Bell Jar
Pat Macpherson

As challenging and provocative as Sylvia Plath's novel itself, *Reflecting on The Bell Jar* provides a new approach to one of feminism's most difficult heroines – Esther Greenwood.

Heroines?
August 1991: 112pp
Pb: 0-415-04393-X: £6.99

Romantic Longings
Love in America 1830-1980
Steven Seidman

Romantic Longings charts the change from a Victorian spiritual ideal of love to efforts by modern reformers to sexualize love.

October 1991: 256pp
Hb: 0-415-90404: £35.00

For further information, or a FREE Gender and Women's Studies Catalogue, please contact: The Promotion Department, ROUTLEDGE, 11 New Fetter Lane, London EC4P 4EE. Telephone: 071 583 9855.

ROUTLEDGE

The Youngest Doll

Written and translated by Rosario Ferré

"Graceful and compelling. The collection is distinguished for its mastery of style, its often grotesque humor, and for its feminist positions with respect to the situation of women in the Caribbean." – Francine Masiello, University of California, Berkeley. £7.95 pa, £19.95 cl

The Tongue Snatchers

Claudine Herrmann Translated by Nancy Kline

"Don't miss or mistake the pun in the title of this book . . . Herrmann means to draw our attention to the way women must twist new meanings out of male language." – *Booklist*. £6.95 pa, £18.95 cl

The Book of Promethea

Hélène Cixous Translated by Betsy Wing

"Destined to be a classic. It is one of Cixous's most widely recognized and celebrated fictional texts, and Betsy Wing's translation is masterful." – Alice A. Jardine, Harvard University. £7.95 pa, £19.95 cl

Feminist Utopias

Frances Bartkowski

"[Bartkowski] holds that 'utopian thinking is crucial to feminism,' and through her perceptive analysis convinces us that this is so." – *Feminist Collections*. £6.95 pa, £20.45 cl

Now available in paper

Hélène Cixous
Writing the Feminine Expanded Edition

Verena Andermatt Conley

This first full-length study of Cixous in English looks at Cixous as writer, teacher, and theoretician. Conley takes up Cixous's ongoing search for a terminology less freighted with emotion and prejudgment. £6.95

The University of Nebraska Press
c/o AUPG · 1 Gower Street
London WC1E 6HA

"*Nebraska*"

publishers since 1941

Women's Studies *Highlights*

Disciplining Foucault
Feminism, Power and the Body
Jana Sawicki, *University of Maine*
Sawicki looks at Foucault's analyses on power and knowledge and rejects
that his theories are thoroughly masculinist and of no use to feminism.
November 1991: 160pp 234x156
Hb: 0-415-90187-1: £30.00 Pb: 0-415-90188-X: £8.99

Feminism Without Women
Culture and Criticism in a 'Postfeminist Age'
Tania Modleski, *University of Southern California*
Examines 'postfeminism' in popular culture, especially popular film, and in
cultural studies. Films covered range from *Three Men and a Baby* to *Lethal
Weapon* and social isssues from surrogate motherhood to lesbian S&M.
September 1991: 160pp: 234x156
Hb: 0-415-90416-1: £30.00 Pb: 0-415-90417-X: £8.99

The Woman Reader
Learning and Teaching Women's Writing
Jean Milloy, *Co-ordinator, Adult Numeracy Project, London* and
Rebecca O'Rourke, *Writer and lecturer in Adult Education, London*
A practical guide for students and teachers of women's writing looking at key
issues such as equal opportunities policies, race, autobiography and sexuality.
November 1991: 256pp: 216x138: Illus. 32 b+w photographs
Hb: 0-415-00983-9: £35.00 Pb: 0-415-00984-7: £10.99

Partial Visions
Feminism and Utopianism in the 1970s
Angelika Bammer, *Emory University*
Traces the radical utopianism of feminist politics in Euro-American, French
and German women writers of the 1970s, arguing that feminist utopianism is
visionary but also time and culture-bound.
November 1991: 256pp: 234x156
Hb: 0-415-01518-9: £35.00 Pb: 0-415-01519-7: £10.99

Sharing the Difference
Feminist Debates in Holland
Edited by **Alkeline van Lenning**, *Katholieke Universiteit Brabant*
and **Joke Hermsen**, *University of Utrecht*
Brings together the best of current women's studies debates in Holland
focusing on the themes of equality versus difference, theory and history, the
body, French feminist thought and psychoanalysis.
September 1991: 256pp: 216x138
Hb: 0-415-06138-5: £35.00 Pb: 0-415-06139-3: £9.99

**These books are available from all good bookshops. In
case of difficulty, for more information or to order your
copy of the Gender and Women's Studies Catalogue
1991/2, please contact: Liz Reynolds, Promotions
Department, 11, New Fetter Lane, London EC4P 4EE.**

ROUTLEDGE